And Then

A Novel

by
Anita Sumariwalla

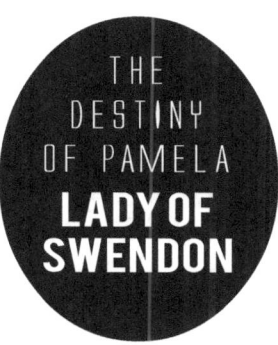

THE
DESTINY
OF PAMELA
**LADY OF
SWENDON**

EXPLORA BOOKS
700 – 838 West Hastings St. Vancouver, BC V6C 0A6
www.explorabooks.com
Phone: (604) 330 6795

ISBN: 978-1-998394-60-9 (Paperback)
978-1-998394-62-3 (Hardback)
978-1-998394-69-2 (eBook)

AND THEN?

THE DESTINY OF PAMELA, LADY OF SWENDOWN

A NOVEL BY
ANITA SUMARIWALLA

Dedication

To my beloved husband, Russy Sumariwalla, who, sometimes, could not understand why it took so long to tell a story but has read this twice!

Thank you, darling!

Acknowledgement

I wish to express my deep appreciation to my three special lady friends: Bunny Barinaga, Barbara Guichard, and Lillian Maksymowicz, who read my manuscript for this story more than once!
Thank You!

Table of Contents

List of Characters

Pamela Desirée Payne	Heroine, teacher (Farmington, UK)
Andrew Edward Michael Prescott, Esq.	Barrister and mayor (Farmington)
Mrs. Henrietta Spencer Hood	Deceased; widow of
Henry George Hood	Opera singer; deceased
Alexander Henry George Hood	Son of Mr. and Mrs. Hood; deceased
Ms. Marion Thrifoot	Headmistress, Maria Montessori Academy for Teachers (Farmington)
Winston Henry James Payne	Uncle of Pamela Payne
Hillary Margaret Payne	Aunt of Pamela
Bambi	Nanny of Pamela
Timothy Carter Wentworth Jones	Former sea captain (1799-1877); deceased builder of Mrs. Hood's cottage
Caroline Emily Jones	Wife of T. Jones (1799-1867); deceased
Inspector Healy	Police chief (Farmington)
Constable Rogers	Assistant to Inspector Healy
Neil Brown	Foreman, fire department (Farmington)
Betty, Harry, and George	Pamela's neighbors (Farmington)
Colonel Adrian Christopher Nigel Payne	Pamela's father; deceased (Chislehurst)
Lady Elizabeth Mary Rose Payne	Pamela's mother; deceased
Lord William Henry Scott	Grandfather of Pamela, Earl of Swendown; deceased
Lord Edward Crighton	Friend of Pamela's late father
Mannon	Butler at the Payne Manor (Chislehurst)
Maddy	Lady's maid at the Payne Manor
Lord Michael Anthony Donald Prescott	Father of Andrew, Earl of Tarrington
Lady Priscilla Mary Prescott	Mother of Andrew, Countess of Tarrington

Lady Lucille (Lilly) Mary	Younger sister of Andrew
Lord Anthony (Tony) Henry	Younger brother of Andrew
Lady Eleanore (Elly) Prescott	Wife of Lord Anthony
Lord Gordon Scott (Scotti)	Youngest brother of Andrew
Lady Aimee Louise (Lis) Prescott	Wife of Lord Gordon
Eric Thompson	Hobby-Archaeologist; deceased
Mr. Gather	Manager, My Fair Lady (Newhurst)
Vicar	St. Paul's Church (Farmington)
Mr. Ravi Gupta	Head/owner of travel agency (London)
Mr. Kumar Patel	Travel agent / guide within India
Dalal, Soli, Khan, Shar-ma	Car drivers in Indian cities
Ms. Bannerji	Headmistress, The Lady Elizabeth Mary Rose School (LEMRS) in Dhalarnabad, India
Mrs. Chowdry	Teacher and board member, LEMRS
Mr. Chowdry, Mr. Murthi, & Mr. Pano	Former board members, LEMR; deceased
Lord Anthony Wood	Baron of Tremston—??? of Pamela
Lord Edward Sommers	Friend of Lord Anthony (Lonavla, India)
Dr. Vinod Sharma	Physician, friend of Lord Edward
Lady Grace	Dean of a college; friend of Lord Edward (Lonavla, India)
Adrian Woolsley	Teacher at LEMRS
Sanjid Ray	Teacher at LEMRS
Kumar Singh	Music teacher at LEMRS
Mr. Goodriji	Bank manager (Lonavla, India)
Inspector Murthi	Chief of police (Lonavla, India)
Nami Ferez	Houseboat manager (Cochin, Kerala, India)
Ali Achmed	Cook of houseboat (Cochin, Kerala, India)
Esquire Abbott	Barrister of Prescott family (Tarrington)
Vicar	Church in Tarrington
Mr. Gather	Owner/manager, My Fair Lady

CHAPTER 1

Two Unexpected Letters

*A*nd then … when Pamela Desirée Payne arrived back at the boarding house in Shrewsbury from the graduation celebration luncheon for herself and one other Montessori teacher, a letter was waiting for her on the small hope chest in the foyer next to the only telephone. The three-story Victorian building that was a residence-pension for single ladies. She studied the envelope to find the name of the sender. There was a stamped name and address indicating the sender: Andrew Prescott, Esq., Mayor, City of Farmington, Kent.

Pamela thought, *I don't know anyone by that name… the mayor in Farmington? She* frowned. *A letter from the mayor?* She hung up her winter coat on one of the seven-hooks rack and removed her boots. She inserted her feet into her warm slippers that she kept under the old wooden hope chest before climbing the steep stairs to the third floor. At the end of the narrow hall was the smallest room; it used to be a storage room that had been converted for her at a reduced rate. Even then she could hardly afford to rent. The room was barely large enough to accommodate a bed, a dresser, and a desk with a chair. But Pamela did not mind because it offered a pretty view beyond a low stone fence into a lovely park in which birds nested and sang their songs from before sunrise until the increasing darkness of each oncoming night.

From the dresser she withdrew a letter opener and slit the envelope carefully open before going to the window to sit down to read the letter. Her heartbeat had increased as she wondered what the mayor of Farmington had to inform her about. There was one plain sheet of paper with the same stamped name and address at the top. She began to read:

31 March 1980

Dear Ms. Pamela Desirée Payne,

I have the sad duty to inform you that Mrs. Henrietta Wood died of a heart attack on her eightieth birthday at her cottage here in Farmington on 28 March 1980.

I personally met Mrs. Hood for the first time on January 2, 1980, when she came to my office to give me an envelope to be given to you in person at the time of her demise. She explained that she had no heirs. Mrs. Hood also told me that she had observed you on various occasions while you were a teacher-trainee working with students at the Maria Montessori Academy for Teachers here in Farmington. She had been impressed by you. She had discreetly inquired about you. Ms. Marion Thrifoot, the headmistress of the academy, had informed her that you have no family and that you stayed during holidays at the academy as you had nowhere else to go.

During her visit here at my office, Mrs. Hood expressed her wish that you inherit her entire estate, which comes with a cottage. Since it is within easy walking distance to the new Montessori kindergarten and elementary school, she thought you would find it convenient to live nearby.

I would appreciate if you could come to my office at the town hall in Farmington at your earliest convenience in order to give you the abovementioned envelope and to finalize some details regarding your inheritance, should you wish to accept Mrs.

Hood's gift.

Looking forward to meeting you, Ms. Payne.

Sincerely Yours,

Andrew Prescott, Esq., Mayor

Farmington, Kent

Pamela had to read the letter of the mayor again. Who is this Mrs. Hood? I don't think I ever met her. Ms. Thrifoot never mentioned her to me, and yet this Mrs. Hood had talked to her about me. Today is Thursday, and I have no special plans. I better go to Farmington to meet the mayor. This Mr. Andrew Prescott, Esq.

Pamela combed her shoulder- ength auburn hair into a chignon at the nape of her neck to look older and changed into a navy-colored skirt and pale-pink blouse. She descended the two flights of stairs, put on her navy-colored winter coat and black boots, and set off to the bus stop to catch the next bus to Farmington. Even though she looked through the bus window as the still half-frozen landscape slipped by, she was unaware of the scenery as her thoughts were still puzzled by the letter from the mayor and this Mrs. Hood.

The bus stopped right in front of the town hall. Because Farmington was a small town of only twelve thousand inhabitants, the building was modest. A small plaque read "Andrew E. M. Prescott, Esq., Mayor of Farmington" on the second door to the right. Pamela knocked, then entered when she heard a man's voice call "Come in."

Andrew Prescott stood up and came around his desk when he saw her enter. "Good afternoon, Ms. Payne? I am Andrew Prescott at your service."

"Yes, I am Pamela Payne. Good afternoon, Mr. Prescott."

They shook hands before he invited her with a courteous gesture to the chair opposite his desk. "Please, take a seat, Ms. Payne." He smiled. "I was expecting you." He pulled out the top drawer in his desk, withdrew an envelope, and offered it to Pamela. "This is for you from the late Mrs. Hood. Did you know the lady?"

"No, I don't think I ever really met her ... or at least, I didn't know her personally." Pamela looked puzzled.

"I am not surprised." Mr. Prescott nodded. "I understand that Mrs. Hood was a person completely content with her own company. She told me that she had been a musician, a cellist. Until last December Mrs. Hood had volunteered at our modest town library but was not involved in any other community activities."

Pamela shook her head, still in awe. "I must admit that I feel overwhelmed."

He smiled. "I can well understand."

"Was Mrs. Hood ill? You mentioned in your letter that she had no heirs. She must have been a widow. But how did she notice me?"

"Please allow me to explain. When Mrs. Hood came to me on January 2 with the letter I just gave you, she said that she had observed you for quite some time and took a liking to you. She also mentioned that her late husband, George Henry Hood, had been a celebrated opera singer. They had traveled all over the world. The lady told me that at her advanced age, she was very content and happy with all the exciting memories of interesting people and places they had seen."

"Was she ill when she came to you?"

"No, Mrs. Hood looked to be in good health. But perhaps she felt that her future on earth was short. She engaged me as her barrister. She gave me several legal documents and several keys to her cottage. I can take you there, if you wish. Mrs. Hood emphasized that she hoped that you would accept her gift of her estate."

Pamela needed a moment to absorb the news, and then she shook her head with embarrassment. "Yes, of course! How could I not accept?"

"Good." Mr. Prescott smiled. "I could take you there by car, or we could walk. It isn't very far from here."

"I would like to walk."

During their walk, Pamela marveled. "You see, Mr. Prescott, it is still unbelievable to me that a complete stranger would gift me with a cottage! When I came here to Farmington three years ago to inquire about the possibility for my teacher's training at the Maria Montessori Academy for Teachers, I thought that this town was at a very beautiful spot, surrounded by farms, some forests, and the gentle hills. It would be lovely to live here."

Mr. Prescott stopped in front of a low sky-blue-painted wooden gate. "Here we are!"

A low stone fence surrounded the neatly kept garden, and a slate path led toward the cottage. In spite of the cold spring weather, several brave little crocuses in purple, white, and pink peeked at the soft sunlight between tiny green tips of tulip and daffodil leaves hesitatingly pushing through the hard earth. The two-story cottage was an old timber-and-brick structure with a carefully trimmed thatched roof protecting the whitewashed walls contrasting the dark wooden beams. The window frames were painted sky blue, matching the front door. Delicate lace curtains offered privacy from within the cottage. He unlocked and opened the front door then stepped aside to allow Pamela to enter first.

About four feet inside the door was an enclosure with dark-red velvet curtains reaching from floor to ceiling to buffer the cold during winters. Opening them, Pamela and Mr. Prescott found themselves in a cozy living room with an open fireplace opposite the entrance. The walls were chalk white. On each side of the fireplace were built-in seats with bright-red velvet pillows and a small window above each seat to provide light for anyone sitting there. On a well-worn persian carpet, facing the fireplace, were a comfortable light-brown leather sofa and two matching chairs, creating an inviting place to socialize. Three small elephants in rosewood with tiny ivory tusks were arranged on the dark wooden rectangular coffee table in the center.

To the left side of the living room was a one-step-up elevated section where a dining room table with six chairs awaited diners. A dark-stained wooden credenza with open shelves offered neatly arranged blue-and-white delft china. A large window overlooked the still-slumbering flower and vegetable garden at the back of the cottage.

In an additional wing to the left of the cottage was the music room. It housed two large built-in bookcases on either side of an inviting fireplace. Two royal-blue Queen Anne chairs were set on a plush blue-and-beige Audubon carpet that covered the slate floor. There was a tall narrow window with a view toward the side of the house. Next to a large mahogany desk with a comfortable-looking swivel chair was a special stand that braced Mrs. Hood's precious antique cello, which she had inherited from her late father, who had also been a cellist. A black concert piano was partially covered with a paisley-designed cashmere throw. On the wall were framed photos that appeared to be of Mrs. Hood's husband, Henry George Hood, taken during various performances at famous opera houses. Opposite that wall, below large windows, were built-in, glass-enclosed cabinets with carefully arranged record disks and a small table with a record player.

Retracing their steps through the living room, they found the kitchen with a pantry, a large water heater, and a laundry and washroom with a door leading into the back of the cottage. In the kitchen was an ancient built-in woodstove next to a newer gas stove and built-in cabinets. A large square stone sink was set in a corner with a small boiler above the water faucets. Next to it was a window overlooking the front garden. A white refrigerator was next to a rectangular well-used work table. A smaller table covered with a bright-yellow tablecloth with blue butterflies and two wooden chairs with matching pillow covers were arranged in front of a large picture window inviting the sun to warm the place in winter.

Between the kitchen and living room were a small powder room and narrow stairs leading up to the second floor.

There were two bedrooms and a bathroom in between. The larger bedroom had an additional alcove with a large window framing the view over the garden behind the cottage and the landscape beyond. The bed appeared to be extrawide and looked comfortable. It was covered with a warm mustard-colored spread and pillows matching the heavy velvet drapes. A small vanity table with a seat were next to the window facing the front of the house. A handsome antique dresser stood beside it. One wall had floor-to-ceiling closets. Over the bed hung an oil painting of a Tuscan landscape that reflected the honey-mustard colors of the bedspread and drapes. An afghan rug covered almost the entire wooden-plank floor.

The other bedroom was smaller with a queen-size bed, a dresser, and a vanity with a stool in front. The curtains, bedspread, and vanity set were pale blue. The window offered the same view into the garden and landscape. Over the bed was a beautiful print of an early Picasso from his blue period.

After they returned to the living room, Mr. Prescott asked, "So what do you think, Ms. Payne?"

She pressed her palms together and shook her head. "I feel stunned and overwhelmed. I don't know what to say. It is a very charming and beautiful cottage. It is still unbelievable for me that this lovely cottage should be mine! Are you absolutely certain about this, Mr. Prescott?"

"Yes, I am quite certain. Mrs. Hood's letter I gave you, which you have not yet read, will reassure you. Unfortunately, I had no time to see the house after Mrs. Hood's funeral yesterday and had no idea how it was inside. It looks ready to move in, doesn't it?" Andrew Prescott checked his watch. "I am afraid I have to go back to my office. Perhaps you may wish to stay here and read the letter?"

"Yes, of course. But before you leave, can I offer you some tea or coffee ..." She paused and chuckled. "I have no idea if there is any in the kitchen."

"Thank you, Ms. Payne. I would like to take you up on your kind offer, but I really must get back to my office. Perhaps another time? Should you decide to accept the inheritance, there are several documents that need your signatures. Could you stop by a little later?"

"Yes, thank you, Mr. Prescott. I will see you later."

While walking back to his office, Andrew Prescott thought about this young teacher, Pamela Payne. She is quite delightful. Her hazel eyes light up her face and turn radiant when she smiles . . . but there seems to be a certain sadness about her. I wonder what happened. She has no family! She is tall ... almost as tall as I am. But her beautiful auburn hair styled into a chignon makes her look older than she is. He smiled. It was charming to observe her reaction while she was discovering the lovely cottage! I hope she will be very happy in it.

After Mr. Prescott left, Pamela walked once more through each room, studying the books and the paintings and photographs on the walls. In the library/music room, she admired an original oil painting portraying a female musician playing a cello. *This must be of Mrs. Hood!* she thought. Pamela studied it more closely, but the face was not very visible because her head was slightly bent over the cello. *I wonder if there are any photographs ... ah, but I must first read Mrs. Hood's letter!* After carefully slicing open the envelope, Pamela settled down on the sofa in the living room and began to read:

1 January 1980

Dear Miss Pamela Desirée Payne,

I begin this beautiful New Year's Day with this—my letter to you! I do not know when the time will come when I will follow my dearest George Henry and my dearest Alexander.

I imagine that you are somewhat surprised to receive this letter from an elderly lady whom, you think, you do not know. Perhaps even more so when you will read the content of this letter from me to you!

Please allow me to introduce myself. I am (or will have been by the time you will receive this letter) Henrietta Spencer Hood. I married George Henry Hood when I was nineteen years old, after a whirlwind three weeks of knowing him. He was then thirty-nine years old and quite famous! We met when his opera company traveled within Asia. George Henry had been gifted with a most glorious, vibrant, and deep bass voice that mesmerized audiences all over the world! Can you imagine a young, impressionable girl of nineteen years having been asked to marry this wonderfully gifted man? Please allow me to tell you how this all came about.

I was asked by my mentor/sponsor and music teacher to fly to Tokyo, with only four hours until departure time, to replace the principal cellist of the orchestra, who had been taken ill. According to the conductor and my teacher, there was no other cellist to be found who was free to join the orchestra at such short notice. Amazingly, I had just finished my contract as principal cellist playing Boris Godunov in London. My teacher judged me skilled enough and knew me to be familiar with the music scores to replace the most unfortunate cellist.

Perhaps you can imagine how excited yet scared to death I was when the plane carried me closer and closer to Tokyo. I arrived just in time for the final rehearsal before the premiere of Boris Godunov. I remember vividly how frightened I was when I was dropped off at the opera house before I was even allowed to go to my hotel room to freshen up!

And I remember how exhausted I felt when I was finally introduced to the conductor. He was standing in the corridor near the dressing room for VIPs with a gentleman who was fleetingly introduced to me as George Henry Hood. Of course, I had heard of him and had read rave reviews from many places around the world, but I was too exhausted to recognize him. When George Henry was told by the conductor of my having been flown in to the rescue, he laughed and laughed while looking at my wilted appearance.

He was, however, alert enough to recognize my needs—to freshen up and, most importantly, to be revitalized and to change from my wrinkled traveling clothes to a black gown. He invited me to his dressing room while ordering the attendant to bring a noodle dish, lots of strong coffee, and to find a black gown for a tall lady. By some miracle, both food and a gown were produced.

So while I was freshening up behind a screen in George Henry's dressing room, he was scaling the octaves to warm up and tune his marvelous voice. He was very discreet and never glanced in my direction while I was changing into the black concert gown, which was a bit too long. To my surprise, he found pins in the vanity and knelt down to adjust the length of my gown. Soon I was reasonably respectable to meet with the cellists and orchestra to go over the most challenging scores of the opera. At first I felt terribly intimidated because most cellists were men and much older than me. After I realized how relieved they were to have me, I began to relax.

Well, to make a long story short, everything turned out well! We had three more cities in Japan to present the opera. We found the Japanese charmingly curious and most appreciative and sophisticated.

Somehow, during the whole Asia tour, it was George Henry who kept making certain that I had what I needed, especially after I had told him that there had been no time for me to pack enough clothes for the three-week tour. At first I thought he considered me as a needy little girl until I realized that he was seriously concerned and, to my greatest surprise, even interested in me as a person.

While on tour through Japan, we had very little free time for personal talk. George Henry was amazing because he always managed to reserve a seat for me next to his on the company buses, to the chagrin of the two other VIP ladies who sent daggers and hostile glances at me! It was during this Asia tour that we got to know one another. Luckily, after a hectic three weeks with travel and performances, the opera company embarked on an ocean liner that promised us most welcome relaxation.

It was just before we embarked that George Henry offered me a lifetime present with his declaration of his love for me and marriage with the protection of his name! We were married that very first day on the ship by the captain!

Dear Pamela, you see, like you, I was orphaned at age six and had been taken in by the brother of my father, who became my guardian. He and his wife did not have children. There was little affection between them, and none for me. At the beginning they showed me off like some kind of a prize, but soon their enchantment in me faded. Perhaps because I was dreadfully untalented in all sport activities they participated in and excelled at. Sport was most important in their lives. With the money I had inherited from my parents, I was soon shipped off to a boarding school for girls.

It turned out to be a blessing because the headmistress recognized that I needed additional musical instructions. I had inherited my late father's precious old cello, which I loved as it was able to rejoice as well as weep! Whenever I played it, I felt very close to him. At age fifteen I had been most fortunate to be accepted as a protégée by a famous cellist to whom I owe my career! He was very demanding. He arranged for me to play with an orchestra in London. My mentor was eager for me to play as soloist. I performed a good number of times as soloist with various orchestras and received praise from professionals reviewers in the press.

Shortly before my nineteenth birthday, after having performed for almost four years, my teacher/mentor was trying to arrange a contract for me to be appointed principal cellist with a famous orchestra when he received the call from Tokyo. The contract had not yet been agreed upon, therefore, I was free to fly to Tokyo immediately to join the traveling opera company, where I met George Henry Hood … my future husband!

It was the first time since my parents had passed away that I felt loved and cherished. For me it was like a miracle! And yet I was so afraid that George Henry and I were too happy and that, at any time, our happiness would shatter. Even though he tried to protect me from anyone who would hurt me, there were two divas, one soprano and one alto, who claimed that George Henry had promised to each that he would marry her. They were mean and did all sorts of things to harass me. However, when one of them hid my precious cello shortly before a performance that forced me to play on a cello I was not familiar with and when, finally, after the performance, it was suddenly found—hidden behind some discarded sceneries—George Henry was spitting fire at the culprit and threatened to sue her if she did not leave me alone!

I stayed with George Henry and with whatever opera company he would be engaged with. On our first wedding anniversary we were in Bombay, India. While George Henry sang the role of Radamnes in Verdi's glorious Aida, I gave birth to our baby son who was named after George Henry's grandfather—Alexander Henry George. Such beautiful names for a tiny baby!

Over the next twenty years, he grew into a fine singer, having inherited his father's rich bass voice. Alexander traveled with us wherever we went. He resembled his father so much that I could see my husband the way he had looked when he had been young. Having grown up surrounded by music, it was not surprising when Alexander decided to study musical scores in the hopes of becoming not only a conductor but, perhaps, also a composer. Alas it was not to be. Alexander drowned during his twentieth birthday party at Oxford along with some of his friends. George Henry and I were devastated and mourned him deeply. I believe we never stopped mourning him. With him so much hope, joy, and pride died within us!

George Henry sang until his sixtieth birthday. By then he was tired and felt he should leave the many challenging roles to a younger generation of talented men. It was at that time we looked for a place to call home and found this lovely cottage! We both fell in love with it and bought it right away. It had belonged to a sea captain who had researched and found out that the cottage had been constructed with old ship beams during the eighteenth century by another sea captain. We added the indoor plumbing, heating, and bathrooms for our convenience.

During our stay here, it had been a very happy home filled with music … until George Henry's demise and, with him, the painful loss of his gorgeous bass voice! Sadly, he followed our dearest son, Alexander, on the first day in January 1971.

Dear Pamela, I am afraid this turned out to be a far longer letter than I had intended. I just want you to know who I was—as well as who my husband, George Henry Hood, and our son, Alexander, were.

There is one more thing I wish to let you know—how I selected you! I had always been interested in the teaching methods of Maria Montessori. As the library is adjacent to the academy and school, I visited often by sitting in the back of the rooms while you were teaching and working with individual students. You have a gentle, sensitive, and reassuring but firm way with children.

I have observed repeatedly how well they respond to you! I liked you immediately and wished I had a daughter like you! I hope you will forgive me in learning that I did make some inquiries about you. When I learned that you have no family, I sort of adopted you!

There were times when I was tempted to introduce myself. I did not because I did not want to disturb your routine. If you are curious and interested in my husband, son, and me, you will find photo albums in the bottom drawer of the desk in our music room. Perhaps you may even realize that you have seen me at various events regarding the academy and school as I am—was—one of the founding members of the Maria Montessori Academy for Teachers here in Farmington.

I do hope you will accept your inheritance as I would feel very pleased for you to have my home!

Dear Pamela, I wish you a fulfilling and rewarding life, blessed with joy and happiness!

Yours truly,

Henrietta Spencer Hood

Pamela was stunned. She remained seated for a while until she remembered that she had promised the mayor to return to his office. It was already 4:30 p.m. when she locked up the cottage and walked back to the town hall. The mayor's office door was open.

Andrew Prescott waved her in. "So how do you feel, Ms. Payne?"

"I am still utterly amazed! Especially after reading Mrs. Hood's letter," Pamela admitted. "She must have been a very interesting and wonderful lady! I am so very sorry for never having met her properly."

"Do you remember ever having seen her?"

"Yes, I think I can guess who she is ... was. She mentioned photo albums in the music room."

"Perhaps when you live in the cottage you will get a better understanding for her."

"Yes, that would be nice. Did you know that she was married to the world-famous opera singer George Henry Hood? They had a son who drowned on his twentieth birthday at Oxford. He was hoping to become a conductor and composer."

"How very sad. Did Mrs. Hood explain why she made you her heiress?"

"It is a very long story, but she mentions that she, too, was orphaned at age six, like myself. She had observed me working with my children. Mrs. Hood said she wished she had a daughter like me."

"I assume that you have decided to accept the inheritance?"

"Yes. It is an astonishing and overwhelming gift. How could I refuse?"

Andrew nodded his approval. "Very good! You have plenty of time to explore and discover your new home. But before you do, I need your signature on several documents."

"Ah, yes, I almost forgot."

"As you know, I am a barrister and must offer you to read through the documents carefully before signing them to see if everything is to your satisfaction. There is the title deed, and here is Mrs. Hood's last will and testament naming you as the sole heiress to her entire estate. The will is very solid and cannot be successfully contested by anyone. There are other documents like bank accounts and car registration."

"Have you read them? Do they seem in order?" Pamela asked.

"Yes to both your questions."

"In that case, I will sign all the necessary documents. Thank you, Andrew for advising me." Pamela started to sign the documents.

"It is my pleasure." Andrew watched her writing her name carefully on each document. "You need to register the title deed and some of the other documents with Mr. Farlow, our town registrar. It is too late to do so today. Can you stop by tomorrow?"

"No, I am afraid not. I have to teach from nine o'clock until four-thirty." She looked at her watch. "Oh, it is past five o'clock! I am sorry to keep you."

"Please don't worry. I don't keep regular office hours. Can you come by on Monday to register the documents? Would you like me to keep your documents until next week in my locked desk to keep them safe?"

"You wouldn't mind? I do appreciate your offer. You see, I have no safe place to keep important documents at my boarding house."

"Let me see if Mr. Farlow is still here. His office is next to mine."

The mayor returned a minute later. "Mr. Farlow has already left for the day. Please remember you must come in next week to fulfill all the required procedures."

"Yes, I will. On Monday my teaching schedule begins at ten o'clock. I can come before then."

"In that case, I see no reason why you cannot move into Mrs. Hood's cottage over the weekend." For an instant Andrew was tempted to offer to help her with moving, then decided against it.

Pamela shook her head, smiling. "This is still such a miracle for me!"

"I am very pleased for you." Andrew opened a drawer and withdrew a key chain. "Mrs. Hood gave me not only the keys to her—now your—cottage. She also trusted me with the keys to her safe box at the bank, her car, as well as her statements of her bank checking and savings accounts. All you will have to do is go the bank manager on Monday to sign the transfers to your name."

Pamela hesitated a moment. "I wanted to ask you about Mrs. Hood's funeral costs."

"You need not worry, Ms. Payne, Mrs. Hood thought of everything. She told me that she had already made arrangements and paid to be cremated."

Pamela digested this information, then asked, "Where are her ashes now? Do you know?"

"I can find out for you from the funeral home, if you wish."

She smiled at the mayor. "Thank you. I think I would like to find out myself. I feel somehow that Mrs. Hood belongs to me. Perhaps I can bury the urn in the garden?"

"There may also be the urns of her husband and son."

"Ah, yes! Perhaps I can bury them together?"

"May I offer my assistance with the urns? They will be heavy."

"You are very thoughtful, Andrew. Thank you. I would like to accept because I cannot use Mrs. Hood's car. I must first learn how to drive and obtain a license."

"Very good." Andrew paused an instant. "May I suggest something?"

"Yes?"

"I think you should celebrate receiving your unexpected inheritance!"

Pamela reflected for an instant, then retrieved her wallet from her purse to check how much money she had. She looked up at him and smiled. "Perhaps you wish to join me? Because it would be sad to celebrate alone. I think I have enough money to buy us a dinner somewhere, if you like?" Pamela offered.

"Oh, no!" Andrew laughed. "I want to invite you! After all, Mrs. Hood trusted me with all her keys and documents. So you see, it would be my pleasure to offer you a modest dinner celebration since I intend to drive you home later."

She hesitated an instant. "But we only just met …"

Andrew nodded. "That is true. It is completely up to you—whatever you prefer."

After a moment of contemplation, Pamela explained, "I would invite you to my place, but I live in a pension for women in Shrewsbury. We are not allowed to entertain gentlemen other than for sherry in the lounge."

"How about my place, which is not far from here? My landlady always cooks generous portions of food for me. I am confident that there will be enough food."

"That is very kind of you, thank you."

CHAPTER 2

Sharing Some Memories

On their way was a grocery store. Pamela asked. "Could we stop in? I would like to buy a bottle of bubbly for the celebration."

"That would be very nice indeed!"

The landlady had prepared spaghetti and a hearty bolognese sauce with a salad. Andrew Prescott was right. There was more than enough for both.

While Andrew was warming the dishes, Pamela looked around the living room. She was impressed by how neat and tidy everything was arranged in order for it to be efficient yet comfortable. Facing the fireplace was a sofa with a small coffee table. The dining table with two chairs was in one section of the room with a small chandelier over it. Two tall bookcases were on the opposite wall. In front of them stood an old mahogany desk with stacks of neat piles of files. The kitchen was very small but adequate for a bachelor.

"How do you like my place?" Andrew held two large and two smaller plates with cutlery in his hands.

"It is very nice. It is at least four times as large as my bedroom. What do you see from the windows?"

"They overlook the garden. In another month, we'll have pretty spring flowers."

"That will be lovely." Pamela smiled while extending her hands. "May I set the table?"

Andrew chuckled. "Yes, if you wish. Thank you."

She noticed that the china was attractive Wedgwood and the cutleries were of sterling silver. "These are very nice."

"Thank you. My mother gave them to me to remind me of home. I use them only on special occasions, which are very rare indeed. Come to think of it, there has been none since I came here to Farmington."

"You are so kind to make this a special occasion! As soon as I will be settled, I will be happy to reciprocate your hospitality."

"I am looking forward to it. Thank you, Ms. Payne."

They went to the kitchen.

While Andrew stirred the sauce, he said, "It will be fun for you to discover more about your benefactor in your new home."

Pamela's face lit up with a radiant smile. "Home! It sounds so lovely! I have not felt at home since I was six years old. The meaning sounds wonderfully reassuring and secure. I must say that I am very much looking forward to living without constant, watchful eyes of other people."

"I can only imagine how it must feel. Enjoy your new freedom!"

"Oh, I will!" Pamela assured him.

"I think the food is hot and we are ready to eat. Please take a seat. I hope you are very hungry."

"Yes, I am. It smells very tempting."

After placing the dishes on the table, Andrew went to open the bubbly. "Spaghetti with bolognese sauce is hardly a meal to go with champagne."

"Oh, it doesn't matter! This is such a lovely treat for me."

Andrew offered her one of two crystal champagne glasses and sat down opposite her. "Ms. Payne, I wish you a very rewarding and very happy new chapter in your life and in your new home!"

Pamela had to blink away tears and swallow before she could respond. "Thank you so very much for everything!"

They sipped the refreshing cool bubbly.

"How and when did you decide to study the Montessori teaching method?"

"Oh ... this may be a long answer."

Andrew smiled. "I don't mind. We have the whole evening."

"Until my parents' death in India—I was six at that time—I had my beloved nanny whom I called Bambi. She was as dear to me as my mother. Perhaps even more so. You see, my parents had founded a school in rural India for village children who lived too far away to go to school. My mother had selected a village for the school that was about in the center between several other villages so that the students were able to walk to and from school each day." Pamela paused.

"If you don't mind my asking, why did your parents not allow you to live with them in India?"

"Because they explained that the climate and facilities were not suitable for me. Bambi and I lived in my parents' large house in Chislehurst. We mostly used the nursery wing. There were Bambi's and my bedrooms, a playroom, and a small sitting room where we would read near the fireplace. We dined year-round downstairs in the small dining room. In the evenings we used the music room because Bambi had been a pianist. Unable to earn an adequate income to meet her expenses, she accepted the position as nanny.

There were only one chambermaid, the cook, and a gardener while my parents lived in India. I cannot remember ever having gone out with Bambi. The rest of the house was closed up with the furniture covered and all the drapes and shutters closed. Except when my parents were home. Then the house was bright with lights and sparkled. It was filled with lots of noisy guests, music, and laughter. Mama would sometimes come up to say hello, but Papa never came to the nursery."

"Did you have any playmates?"

"No. I didn't know of any other children. We, that is Bambi and I, never visited or received visitors."

"Did you ever feel lonely?"

"No, not as long as I was with Bambi. She would read to me and taught me to read and write. She even taught me to read music and play the piano. I enjoyed our little world. At bedtimes she would read fairy tales, which I loved."

Andrew Prescott noticed that Pamela's smile had disappeared. "What happened?"

"One day, a severe-looking man, a stranger, came and talked first to Bambi alone. By the time she called me to meet the man, I could see that she had been crying. She then introduced the stranger as my uncle and guardian. He told me that my parents had died in India and that it was high time for me to be weaned from my nanny and learned useful things. Bambi was given two days to pack up her belongings and leave. When she explained this to me after this uncle and guardian left, I cried as I couldn't imagine life without Bambi. She tried to reassure me that a new governess my uncle had engaged would be very nice and interesting for me ..." Pamela's voice choked, and she stopped talking.

Andrew waited for Pamela to control her emotions. "You don't have to tell me if it is too painful for you to remember."

"No, it is all right. I am sorry. You see, I still miss Bambi."

"Was the governess at least nice to you?" Andrew Prescott asked.

"No, not at all! She was mean and punished me for things I had not done." Pamela shook her head, remembering. "I prayed each night that she would die. She told me that my parents had died when their car was hit by a big truck. It was overloaded, and the driver had lost control, barreling left and right on the narrow country road. She also told me that my parents had no business living in India while leaving me here. Even though I understood that my parents had died and would never return, I naively wrote a letter to my mother, telling her how mean the governess was to me. I begged Mama to come home! Little did I know that my letter was discovered and, of course, never sent. It only increased the anger of the governess and my uncle. Soon after that incident, I was sent to a boarding school for girls."

Pamela continued. "My uncle told me that he put the house up on the market for sale. I never saw one penny from the sale, nor did I ever hear from my uncle as my guardian or his wife again. At the boarding school, it was the first time I lived with girls of my own age. I soon realized how protected I had been by Bambi and how odd I must have seemed to them. I became an object of ridicule for the girls, employees, and some teachers."

Andrew Prescott nodded with sympathy. "I can imagine how terrible and helpless you must have felt. Children and grown-ups can be very cruel. I am so sorry."

Pamela smiled, reminding him, "You asked me why I decided to become a Montessori teacher. I think it was mostly due to my governess and life at the boarding school. I felt instinctively that one can teach children without hurting them. By the time I left public school, I knew I wanted to become a teacher."

"You have triumphed over the hardship of your youth. You should be very proud of yourself!" Andrew Prescott praised.

Pamela smiled at him. "Thank you. You are very kind. However, I do have some regrets—that my parents nor Bambi ever knew how I turned out. I know Bambi would have been very pleased."

"Did you stay in touch with Bambi?"

"I had one address for her, but all my letters were returned unopened. I don't know what happened to her."

Andrew refilled the glasses. "I think we should drink a toast to your emancipation and triumph! I know that your future students will be lucky to have you as their teacher. May they always remember you with appreciation and affection!"

It was quite late when Andrew Prescott drove Pamela to her pension in Shrewsbury. Before getting out of the car, she promised to reciprocate his hospitality as soon as she felt settled in her new home.

Later that evening, while she packed her modest possessions into two suitcases, her thoughts were about her impression of the young barrister and mayor of Farmington, Andrew Prescott. *He seems very nice. It is amazing that he appears to be even happy for me to have inherited Mrs. Hood's cottage! He is quite handsome. He is only a couple of inches taller than I am. How come he is not yet married? I am certain he must be very popular with a good number of ladies! His unruly almost-black hair, which is longer than fashionable, looks good on him and renders character to his finely chiseled face. I like his eyes. They are of a most unusual deep blue. But what I like most about him is his sensitivity. He really looks too young to be an accomplished barrister and mayor!'*

Pamela slept very little during the next two nights in her tiny room at her pension.

After the first week in her new home, Pamela invited Andrew Prescott over. She told him on the phone that she had found the photo albums and did recognize Mrs. Hood having visited her classrooms on several occasions. Sadly, the lady had never introduced herself, and Pamela had been too shy to ask.

Pamela's guest arrived at her cottage with a bouquet of white tulips.

"Oh, how lovely they are! How very kind of you, Mr. Prescott. Thank you! I have the perfect vase for them."

He watched her arrange the flowers in a crystal vase and set it on the coffee table.

She noticed that he was wearing a soft cashmere sweater of deep burgundy with a white shirt collar peeking out at his neck and sleeves. "Please select the most inviting seat since you are the very first and only guest tonight."

Sitting down, Andrew Prescott observed that Pamela wore a floor-length skirt of rich purple with a pale-pink silk blouse that had laces gently embracing her neck and wrists. She had parted her hair in the center and allowed it to fall freely around her shoulders. She looked very attractive. Looking around the living room, he didn't see much change. The dining table was set with Limoges china, Waterford glasses, and sterling silverware. Two red candles in silver stands were already lit. On the coffee table near the gently burning logs in the fireplace was a platter of homemade appetizers.

"Mr. Prescott, what would you like to drink? I discovered a liquor cabinet with scotch, gin, vodka, brandy, and sherry. There are additional after-dinner liquors. So what would you like? Perhaps you wish to prepare your own drink?"

Andrew got up and followed her to the kitchen. "Do you have soda water and ice?"

"Yes, there are small bottles of each in the refrigerator. An ice tray with fresh ice is in the freezer section. Please help yourself."

"What would you like to drink, Ms. Payne? I could fix your drink."

"I would like a gin and tonic, please."

They settled down on the sofa. Pamela offered the appetizers.

"With the fireplace lit, the room looks very cozy," her guest remarked.

"It is the first time I lit it in here. I usually retire to the music room to listen to the stereo. It is also very charming and comfortable. We can go there after dinner."

"May I propose a toast to the beautiful new mistress of this cottage?"

Pamela blushed. "Thank you! May I add 'Good health and happiness to my first visitor, Mr. Andrew Prescott'?"

"Thank you." Andrew paused for an instant. "Ah, yes! This brings me to another proposal." He stopped and looked at Pamela. "I would like to simplify our names to Pamela and Andrew. What do you think?"

She laughed while admitting, 'I am so very glad because I can easily remember your first name, Andrew, but I always have to search my mind for your last name."

"In that case, I am delighted to be Andrew to you. Thank you, Pamela!"

The appetizers disappeared quickly while they enjoyed the drinks.

"Andrew, I hope you are more experienced in opening bottles of wine. The cork got stuck somehow," Pamela admitted with embarrassment.

"Let's see. Ah, a nice Bordeaux!" Andrew took the bottle, released the cork and inserted the corkscrew again slowly. This time it worked. He poured the wine.

"I tried to make a casserole from a cookbook I found in the bookcase. I have no idea how it s supposed to taste. The recipe calls it Shepherd's Pie Fit for a King." She brought the casserole to the table and served Andrew first.

Andrew waited for her to start, then tasted it. "Even though I am not a king, it could easily please royalty. It is very nice!"

Pamela sounded relieved. "I am so glad! You see, I cheated a bit. I substituted some ingredients, like kidney and liver. They don't appeal to me, so I replaced them with lean bacon and lamb, of course."

"In that case I think the dish should be named Shepherd's Pie Fit for a Queen."

"For the dessert, I didn't want to take a chance. To be sure, I bought a chocolate tart from the bakery. I hope you will like it. Would you like tea or coffee?"

"Just the chocolate tarte alone sounds irresistible."

Andrew offered to light the fire in the music room while Pamela rinsed the dishes.

"Before we settle down, would you like to select an after-dinner drink? I saw an old port, some French liquors, and schnapps. I am not familiar with them. Please select whatever you wish."

After inspecting the supply, he said, "Since the old port bottle is open, we could both enjoy some of it."

"I seldom have after-dinner drinks. Yes, I would like to taste it."

"Pamela, were you never invited to parties by friends or colleagues?"

She blushed with embarrassment. "No. Out of boarding school, I attended St. Mary's College. I was never part of groups of girls socializing. I guess I am a loner. After graduation, I enrolled right away here at the Maria Montessori Academy for Teachers. I told you already that I had no home to go to during holidays. There were never parties at the academy."

Andrew looked shocked. "You mean even on Christmas and Easter you didn't go anywhere to celebrate?"

"No. I always stayed alone at the boarding school. However, while at St. Mary's, I received an allowance. It made it possible for me to spend days at museums and libraries. I saved as much as possible to attend concerts, plays, and operas. But all this ended after I graduated from St. Mary's because my monthly allowance was cut off. I never heard from my uncle. It was during the last vacations at college, I came here to Farmington to apply for a scholarship at the academy. Luckily, I also received a modest loan for my living expenses. Even at the pension in Shrewsbury, while everybody went home to be with family, I stayed here."

Andrew shook his head. "Nobody ever invited you to join?"

"I guess it never occurred to them." Seeing Andrew's upset face, Pamela quickly added, "I never expected to be invited, so I never felt hurt or disappointed."

"I am so dreadfully sorry, Pamela."

She suddenly felt awkward and decided to change the subject. "Would you like to hear some music? Mrs. Hood has an amazing selection of recordings of her husband's operas and lots of beautiful baroque music."

"Perhaps some other time. I am afraid I have imposed on you with so many questions. I hope you didn't mind," Andrew apologized.

Pamela shook her head. "No, not at all. I am surprised at myself as I find out it is good to talk about my unusual upbringing. In spite of everything, I hope I turned out reasonably acceptable."

Andrew laughed. "More than reasonably acceptable, I would say."

"It is amazing when I think back. I remember now that Mrs. Hood had once joined me over a cup of coffee in the teachers' lounge. She had not introduced herself. I only knew that she was a board member. She particularly praised the painting session with my kindergarten children. The school had been given a large roll of heavy white paper. It was three feet wide, the same size as the low tables. I joined several tables together into one long row with chairs on either side and stretched the paper from one end of the tables to the other end. Then I put watercolor paint jars in the center at intervals so that each child could reach the paints. The purpose was that they had to negotiate with one another about sharing space. Mrs. Hood was amused and thought it very good training. Of course, no matter how you looked at the finished work, one side was always upside down. Luckily, the children didn't seem to mind. I draped the long painting along our classroom wall and promised to turn it over each week."

Pamela chuckled and continued. "On the following day, a father of one of my students came and challenged my way of teaching. He said, 'What rubbish are you teaching? My Emilie came home and told us that there are people who walk upside down in upside-down houses under the earth.' For a moment I had to think. Then I remembered and went to show him the globe I used to demonstrate what I had been saying about people on the other side of the earth … that it would appear, looking from outside the globe, that there will always be some countries in which it would seem people lived upside down."

Andrew laughed while shaking his head. "Was the father convinced of your explanation?"

"He felt embarrassed and apologized."

"How long are you committed to teach here in Farmington?"

"My contract with the academy is for three more years to reimburse the cost of my tuition and the modest loan I received for living expenses. My new teaching job and salary, which will begin in March, would have been very modest. But after receiving Mrs. Hood's inheritance, I decided to reimburse the academy for the entire tuition fee and loan. You see, I feel very uncomfortable to owe money to anyone. As a result, I'll be paid a full salary."

"Does that mean that you may leave Farmington sooner?"

"Oh, no! I will continue teaching here as I feel most grateful for having been given the opportunity to train and become a teacher. I love the job and the children!"

Andrew nodded. "Yes, I agree it was a good idea to free yourself financially. I am glad you plan to remain here."

Suddenly Pamela's face lit up. "Oh, Andrew, I must show you what I found in the dresser in the bedroom! I have to ask you to come upstairs." She led the way and opened a drawer for him to see the wonderful materials for making clothes. "I made this skirt yesterday. The blouse I found in another drawer. There are beautiful dresses, jackets, coats, even a couple of mink coats, and lots of long gowns that fit me perfectly!" She opened a closet to show him. "I remember my mother during her visits back home in Chislehurst. She wore such formal gowns to attend performances at Covent Garden or Royal Albert Hall. They often attended balls and were invited to the Queen's garden party, receptions, and other diplomatic events. I don't think I'll ever have an opportunity to wear such magnificent gowns."

"I was admiring your look today. The skirt and blouse are perfect! You seem happy and adjusted to your new life."

"Just imagine"—Pamela felt almost embarrassed—"two weeks ago I was a modest teacher living in a pension with little joy and today ..." She turned somber. "I wish there were a way to thank Mrs. Hood for this miracle!"

"I think she knew and wanted you to have this gift of her estate so that you don't need to worry about money and concentrate on being the best possible Montessori teacher."

"You may think I am mad ... but I feel sometimes as if Mrs. Hood is here, and I find myself talking to her."

"This is not at all surprising. Her spirit, if you will, is preparing and molding you to grow in new ways. Who knows where your future life will lead you?"

"This reminds me. I talked to the owner of the funeral home about Mrs. Hood's ashes as well as the urns of her husband and son. He said he would prepare the necessary documents for release and turn them over to me. The transfer of the urns will have to be recorded at the Farmington county office."

"I have already selected a place in the garden near an apple tree. I want to bury them together."

"If you like, I'll be happy to help. It may be hard for you to dig a deep enough hole."

"Are you sure, Andrew?"

"Absolutely." He laughed. "I need some exercise!"

"Thank you! I selected the apple tree because it is close enough to the house. In spring and summer, I can keep the windows open and play the magnificent opera-recordings of *Boris Godunov, Aida,* and others sung by George Henry Hood himself!"

It was again late when Andrew wished good night to Pamela and walked home.

The spring sun lured Pamela into the garden. She enjoyed discovering more and more leaves pushing out of the earth. Among pink, red, and white tulips and several varieties of daffodils grew deep-purple and dark-blue irises. forsythias, hazel, and fire-blossom bushes grew along the old stone wall under the dogwood and birch trees.

On Friday afternoon she composed a bouquet of spring flowers and wrapped the stems in a wet washcloth and a small waterproof bag to surprise Andrew. She had intended to leave the flowers on the small bench next to his office. When she approached his office, the door was open.

"Oh, what a welcome visitor! Pamela, please come in."

"I really didn't mean to disturb your work. I just wanted you to enjoy these flowers over the weekend."

He was surprised to notice that she felt almost shy. "Thank you so much. They are very beautiful indeed! I am delighted that you came, Pamela. This gives me a wonderful excuse to leave here in a couple of minutes. Would you mind waiting?"

She was about to leave to wait outside when he stopped her. "Please wait here. I have only a few papers to sort out and file this before I can join you." He concentrated on his work, filed the papers carefully, and then smiled. "Voilà! I am all yours." After locking up the file cabinet and desk drawers, Andrew came around the desk. "Do you have any plans for this evening?"

"Not really. I usually read while listening to music, or I write. I made a hearty vegetable soup with Italian sausages and was on my way to the bakery to get some bread. Come to think of it, there is more than enough if you care for soup."

Andrew chuckled. "Vegetable soup with sausages."

Pamela laughed, realizing her mistaken description of the soup. "Well, it started out as a vegetable soup, but then I added the sausages to enhance the flavor."

"And you are inviting me to taste it?"

"Yes! It would be very nice to have company!"

They bought the last loaf of bread.

During dinner Pamela told Andrew that the urns were ready for pickup at any time. The burial place—Mrs. Hood's garden—had been approved and already recorded with the county clerk.

"Do you still want to bury them near the apple tree? Remember, I promised to help."

"Thank you, Andrew. I really appreciate your offer. At the funeral home I lifted one urn. It was surprisingly heavy. I already told Mrs. H—" She stopped herself.

"Yes, I know." He smiled. "It is very nice that you talk to her."

"I am so glad you understand!"

"I happen to have my car here. We could stop to pick up the urns. We can bury them tomorrow morning if you like."

"Oh, that would be great. I have taken a couple of driving lessons but don't have a driver's license yet. I cannot use Mrs. Hood's car."

"Are there garden tools—shovel and rake?"

"Yes. There is a shed at the end of the garden that is filled with all sorts of tools. I think I have enough for my project."

"Pamela it is 'we have' and 'our project'!" he reminded her teasingly.

"Yes. I am sorry."

When they brought the three urns home, Andrew asked, "Where do you want to put them for overnight?"

"Is it disrespectful to put them in the laundry room?"

Andrew chuckled. "I don't think they will mind."

After Pamela lit a couple of candles, they sat down to enjoy the vegetable soup with sausages.

Andrew reached for her hand. "Pamela, sometimes it takes people ages to become friends, and other times it kind of happens instantaneously. I have the feeling we both are the instantaneous types. What do you think?"

While gazing into Andrew's eyes, Pamela turned very serious, realizing a new awareness. "Oh, Andrew, I am so glad you feel that way." Her voice almost choked. "It is heartwarming to have you as a … very special friend. Thank you."

It was the moment their kindred spirit connected.

Andrew kissed her hand. "Yes, Pamela, you, too, are my very special friend."

She smiled at him. There was no need to say anything more.

CHAPTER 3

An Amazing Surprise

On the following morning, Andrew showed up at eight o'clock. Pamela had already had her bath and was just preparing breakfast for both.

"Good morning, Pamela. I am ready to go to work!"

"Good morning, Andrew. You must have a hearty breakfast first."

While they ate, she said, "It is awfully kind of you to help me bury the urns."

He smiled. "I feel partly connected because it was Mrs. Hood who came to me and trusted me with not only her will and other documents but even her house, car, and safety box keys!"

Pamela turned pensive. "Do you think she wanted us to get to know one another?"

"I wouldn't be surprised." Andrew had brought his wellies and put them on outside the kitchen. "Where is the spot you selected for the urns?"

She walked toward the apple tree. Before she reached it, she discovered one lonely violet flower between the grass. She stopped and reconsidered. "I think here, next to the violet."

Pamela had already assembled two shovels, rakes, and a large plastic sheet. "I watered this area last night to soften the soil."

Andrew started carefully digging to remove the top layer of grass so that it could be replaced after the urns were buried. He piled the soil on the plastic sheet.

"How deep do you think we have to dig?" Pamela asked.

"The urns are about one foot tall. If you want to plant anything on top, you will need a good amount of soil over them. I would say at least three feet deep."

"Can I take over and dig?"

"No, thank you." He smiled, "I rarely get good exercise!"

"It doesn't seem fair. After all, it was my idea."

"A very nice idea. I think Mrs. Hood would be very pleased." Andrew continued digging until his shovel hit something hard. A stone perhaps. He dug around it. It wasn't a stone but a tin box! It was covered with rust. "It looks very old."

"Who would bury a tin box so deep in the ground?" Pamela wondered aloud.

"Someone who didn't want it to be found for quite a while."

Even though rusty, the lid resisted stubbornly to yield. It required Andrew's pocket knife and a hammer to force it open. The content was wrapped in an oilcloth. Whatever was in it was very heavy. "Stones!" Andrew joked. He gave the parcel to Pamela. "You open it."

A heavy leather sack tied with two leather strings, a square green partially decomposed velvet jewelry case, and an envelope that had been wrapped additionally with oilcloth to resist humidity were revealed.

They both stared at the items for a moment.

Andrew, being a barrister, suggested, "You must first see what is written in the letter. Perhaps there are instructions as to whom this belonged and to whom this needs to be returned or forwarded to."

"Let us go inside to open the wrapping with a knife," Pamela suggested.

They sat at the kitchen table. A letter written with somewhat faded black ink on parchment came to light. It was extremely brittle! The script was very elegant.

"Andrew, please read it. It is in old English. You will understand it better."

He read aloud:

It is the Year of Our Lord 1867. The ninth day in December.

To Whom It May Concern!

I, Timothy Carter Wentworth Jones, am the author of this document. It is my Last Will and Testament.

I begin this document while we are on my proud clipper, Lady Silhouette, on high sea near Cape Horn. We are enduring a most savage storm! As her captain and master, I am determined to ride out the storm as my Lady Silhouette is very capable and brave!

However, I am heartsick to report that my beloved lady wife for forty-nine years—Caroline Emilie Jones—had succumbed to a severe "mal-de-mer" lasting thirty-seven cruel days! Before departing this earth—and sea—she begged me to give all her jewelry and clothes to charity, except the pearl necklace I had presented to her on the most joyous occasion on our wedding day! It is in the original green velvet case, herewith enclosed.

Meanwhile, according to my late lady wife's wishes, I have given to family members and Caroline Emily's favorite charities all her earthly possessions.

This document—my Last Will and Testament—was continued on this day of Our Lord 1876 on the thirtieth December.

The coins in the leather purse are to be given and must belong, as my gift and endowment, to the destined person(s) who will find this humble tin box to do with what he, she (or they) deem(s) best! The applicable taxes and fees to Her Majesty's government have been paid faithfully by myself. The coins are the honest proceeds of the sale of my proud clipper, Lady Silhouette. I sold her upon my return to England. I will never see my beautiful lady wife, Caroline Emilie, stand at the railing while gazing at the restless waves and hear her giggle each time a mischievous spray baptizes her!

I built this cottage with the wood beams from another clipper to still feel connected with my beloved sea! It has been my refuge! On some occasions, I have been visited by the spirit of my beloved Caroline Emily! She usually sits at her favorite place, the left niche next to the fireplace in the living room, and embroiders.

I most fervently hope that all persons who will live in this cottage after I am gone will love it as dearly as I do!

Last night, my beloved Caroline Emily came to visit me. I know she was telling me that it was time for me to join her!

Therefore, I am burying this precious tin box in my garden. Who knows how long it will take for someone to find it, if ever? I only hope that the contents will bring joy!

I am, respectfully yours,

Timothy Carter Wentworth Jones.

1. *This document has been read and witnessed by my first mate, Mr. Kasper Markson.*

2. *A signed copy of this document, my Last Will and Testament, was duly filed at the court house in Farmington, Kent.*

Today is the Year of Our Lord 1877, the eighth June.

Pamela looked at Andrew. "What shall we do? Let us see if the pearls survived." She flipped the small gold clasp and opened the lid. The pearls were covered with a thin layer of mildew. She removed the necklace gingerly and rubbed one pearl closest to the clasp to see if it could be wiped off with her soft handkerchief. "Yes, look, Andrew." She beamed. "The pearls are still beautiful underneath!" After gently rubbing the necklace with a flannel cloth, the pearls regained some of their luster. "Oh, Andrew, this is amazing! Do you think I can keep it?"

"Yes." He agreed. "You found the spot where it had been buried. The captain said that it will belong to whomever found the box."

"But you found the box, Andrew! The necklace should be yours!"

He laughed. "Should I wear it to my office on Monday?"

"Please be serious. Perhaps you want to keep it to give to your wife someday? But it needs to be restrung with new silk thread."

"Pamela, listen carefully. This is your garden, your property. Therefore, the tin box and its content are yours. Since the captain mentioned explicitly that the taxes for the coins—"

"The coins!" Pamela interrupted. "We haven't even opened the leather satchel yet. The coins must be in there!"

Andrew had brought in the leather sack with him and held it out to her. "It's your turn to open."

Accepting the sack, she was surprised. "It's heavy!" With patient fingers, she untied the two leather strings and tilted the sack to spill the contents on the kitchen table. They both stared in disbelief.

Andrew picked up one of the coins and studied it. "These are exquisite English sovereigns! They look brand-new, having never been traded."

"How much are they worth, do you think?"

"I have no idea—a pretty penny, I am sure!"

Pamela started counting the coins. "Andrew, there are one-hundred-forty-eight! They must be worth a fortune! Do you think we can keep them?"

"Yes. According to the document, the appropriate taxes have been paid. The letter states that the person who finds the tin box can keep the content!"

"But you, Andrew, found the tin box by hitting it with the shovel."

"That doesn't count. I already told you that you decided on the spot!"

"It was the violet!" Pamela smiled. "I don't think even Mrs. Hood knew of the hidden tin box."

Andrew reminded her, "We have a job to finish."

"Oh, yes, of course."

"While we work in the garden, you may want to put the coins and the pearls in a safe place, perhaps upstairs, until you can deposit them in a bank safe next Monday."

They returned to the garden and finished digging the hole down to three feet deep. Then they arranged the three urns carefully so that they leaned against each other.

They gently packed some soil around the urns and filled the hole. Andrew replaced the patches of grass and patted them back into the soil. One could hardly tell that the place had been disturbed.

"I am going to plant roses here as soon as the weather gets warmer. We are the only ones who know that they will mark the graves."

"The law requires that you mark the grave, a family grave."

"With a tombstone?"

"It could be just a small stone with the names and dates of births and deaths. They must be recorded at the county office."

"I will do that." Pamela agreed. "Perhaps I can go next week to London to have the pearls restrung by my mother's jeweler. I am amazed that I remember where the shop is. I hope it is still there! The owner, an Indian, used to create jewelry for my mother with the gems she brought home from India. She took me to his shop a couple of times. I cannot remember the name, but I'll recognize the place. It's on Regent Street. " She turned pensive. "I wonder what happened with all the jewelry my mother had?"

"Would you like to join me? I have a client in London who wants me to review his will," Andrew asked. "Perhaps you may want to take one of the coins with you to visit a reputable coin dealer to find out how much it is worth?"

"Since I am now released temporarily from teaching, I am flexible."

"Great. I'll let you know which day. By the way, does your uncle know that you have graduated from the academy?"

"No, I don't think so, unless he keeps track of me without my knowing it. I have not heard from him since he sent me to my first boarding school when I was six years old. He had arranged for me to go to St. Mary's College and graduate. I know because my parents' trust fund paid the fees and my monthly allowances. After my graduation, the monthly pocket money was cut off. I don't know if he knows that I received a scholarship to study at the Montessori academy here. I also don't know if he knows that I recently graduated. To be very honest, Andrew, I am glad if he leaves me alone. I don't think he is interested or eager to contact me, and nor do I wish to contact him." Pamela smiled. "I turned twenty-one and am of age now!"

"In any case, Pamela," Andrew cautioned, "the reason for you coming of age may lead your uncle to trace and contact you. If he succeeds, may I suggest you do not tell him of your inheritance nor of what we found today?"

Pamela laughed. "If he and his wife knew, they would become very good friends! Luckily, his tyrannical guardianship has expired on my last birthday, thank God!"

"Do you know if there has been a trust established for you by your parents to inherit their estate?"

"No, I don't know. But I really don't care anymore. I have this beautiful cottage now!" she exclaimed. "Just imagine, I am free!"

"If there is a trust, it is most likely handled by a solicitor who will trace you independently and inform you."

During the following week Pamela finished her driving lessons and received her license. She enjoyed the freedom the car provided her to do errands effortlessly. The first thing she did was buy dark-red, white, and pink roses and other plants at a nursery. She set the rose bushes as close as possible to each other so that they would intertwine their branches and flowers. She also selected a square granite stone and commissioned a stone mason to engrave the names and dates of the Hood family to be placed on their grave.

On the following Thursday, Andrew drove Pamela in his car to London. He dropped her off in front of the jeweler's store. She recognized it when she saw the inscription on the display window, Gems to Treasure.

"Can we meet for lunch?" Andrew asked. "There is a nice Indian restaurant a couple of blocks from here. It is called the Mumtaz Palace. How about in an hour?"

"Lovely!" She smiled. "If for any reason you are delayed, I'll just wait at the restaurant for you."

"It shouldn't take me longer than one hour. May I advise you? Count the pearls before you leave the necklace with the jeweler. Ask for a detailed receipt with the count and sizes of the pearls and an estimated value."

"I already counted them! There are forty. Each pearl is almost one centimeter in size!"

"Very good! I'll see you at Mumtaz Palace in about one hour. Good luck!"

After Andrew drove off, Pamela realized that she was, for the first time, alone in London. It was thrilling! She entered the store.

A head with white hair was bent over a magnifying glass set on a corner table next to a display case. When the doorbell jingled, the man looked up and greeted Pamela politely. "Good morning, miss."

"Good morning, sir."

"How may I help you?" the jeweler asked.

Pamela withdrew the green case from her purse and opened it. "Could you please restring these pearls?"

The jeweler first frowned at the condition of the case. He picked up the necklace with careful hands and inspected it closely. He reached for a soft wool cloth and wiped one pearl gingerly. "These pearls are of exceptional quality … but in dreadfully neglected condition! May I ask, how did you get them, miss?"

For an instant, Pamela had to think of an explanation. "I inherited them."

The man studied the gold clasp and nodded. "I recognize the seal on the clasp. This necklace is at least one-hundred years old! It must have been purchased from the famous pearl merchant and jeweler in Kobe, Japan. The pearls are very old and precious."

"Yes, I know." Pamela agreed. "I came to you because my mother used to have her jewelry made by you."

The old man looked at her and studied her face. "May I inquire your name, miss?"

"Pamela Payne from Chislehurst."

A smile of recognition spread over the jeweler's face. "Yes, yes! I remember well a Lady Elizabeth Payne from Chislehurst and India."

"She was my mother."

The smile disappeared on the old man's face. "You said – *was!*"

"Yes. She and my father were killed in India in a truck accident."

"Oh, how very sad indeed. I am so very sorry to learn of it. My condolences, miss."

"Thank you, sir." Pamela felt awkward. "I was here at your store only a couple of times with my mother when I was about six years old. I am afraid I have forgotten your name."

"I am Jehangir Dalal from Bombay. I remember your dear mother very well. She would arrive here with a handful of gems and some sketches as to how she wanted me to create brooches, necklaces, rings, and bracelets." He shook his head. "She was far too young to die, and your father too, of course!"

"Thank you, Mr. Dalal. It happened fifteen years ago." Pamela was eager to change the subject. "I remembered you. This is why I am bringing you this special pearl necklace. What can you do for it?"

"I will have to take it apart and clean each pearl—make certain that all moisture and mildew is removed from inside the string holes before restringing them. It will take some time."

"I am not in a hurry. Is it going to be very expensive?"

He counted the pearls. "There are forty. After cleaning them, I may want to put them for a short while under a warm lamp to dry them completely. Restringing is no problem. I will secure each pearl with a knot of silk thread."

"Yes, that sounds fine." Pamela hesitated to repeat her question.

"I am going to give you a special price, a friendship price! It will cost you forty pounds."

She almost gasped, thinking, *So much?* Luckily, she remembered just in time that she was now able to afford the money. "Yes, thank you. How long will you need to keep the pearls?"

"You mentioned that you were in no hurry. I estimate, with the drying process after cleaning the pearls, I would like to keep them at least twenty days."

"That is fine."

"I am going to write you a receipt with a copy of it in my safe. Also, with your permission, I am going to take a couple of photographs of the pearl necklace and give you one copy. I will give you a ring when the necklace is ready, if that is acceptable."

"Yes. Here is my telephone number. I live in Farmington now."

Andrew was already at the Mumtaz Palace when Pamela arrived.

"How did it go?" he asked.

"The jeweler, Mr. Dalal, remembered my mother. He thinks he can restore the necklace. He seems knowledgeable. It will cost forty pounds."

"That sounds very reasonable! Did you leave the necklace with him?"

"Yes. He said it would take about twenty days. He will call me."

"Did he give you a receipt?"

"Yes, and a photocopy. He seemed very professional. He immediately recognized the quality of the pearls. He even recognized the old signature clasp of the Japanese jeweler in Kobe!" She withdrew a paper from her purse. "It's a receipt for a pearl necklace of forty one-centimeter-size pearls in the value of … thirty-five-thousand pounds!"

Andrew was surprised at the estimated value. "He sounds honest."

"Yes, I think he is trustworthy."

"Good! I hope you are hungry?"

"What are we going to eat?"

"May I suggest we share a dish of lamb curry, an okra with onions and tomatoes dish, basmati rice, dahl, and naan. Do you like beer?"

"I am not sure. Can I have a sip from your glass before you order one for me?"

The meal was delicious! It was the first time Pamela had tasted authentic Indian cuisine, and she loved each dish.

"How did your mission go?" Pamela asked Andrew.

"The gentleman gave me his draft to study. I am afraid I'll have to go back after lunch to discuss details as I have some questions."

"That is no problem! I'll go to the National Gallery to see the originals of paintings I have seen in books. How long will it take you?"

"At the most two hours."

"Where can we meet?" Pamela asked.

"My car is parked at the home of my client. I could come and pick you up at"—he glanced at his watch—"around 3:30 in front of the church St. Martins-in-the-Fields. It is across from the National Gallery."

"Wonderful! I'll have time to see many paintings!"

During the drive back to Farmington, Andrew told Pamela that he would have to go to France and possibly Greece to interview clients.

"How long will you be gone?"

"At least two weeks if all goes well."

"Ohh ... who will replace you as mayor?"

"The job of a mayor is mostly ceremonial. Farmington has had mayors on and off for years. It is honorary, not a paid position."

"I see." Pamela's voice betrayed her disappointment.

Andrew noticed and smiled at her. "Only two weeks! Just think what you can do in the meantime!"

"I will have to keep myself busy."

Andrew was gone for over three weeks. He called Pamela often to inform her that the case turned out to be very complex because there were high stakes involved.

CHAPTER 4

Unwelcome Visitors

*O*ne morning Pamela was working in the garden when a car stopped in front of the gate. At first she didn't pay attention until she heard her name being called. When she looked up, she immediately recognized her uncle and aunt. Her mind froze instantly before she was able to control her emotions. *Do they know that the cottage is mine? Is this why they came?* she thought in panic. She pulled herself together and greeted them politely. "Good morning, Uncle Winston and Aunt Hillary."

"You look as if you own this place the way you are working in the garden," her uncle remarked.

"I love gardening."

"Won't you invite us in for a cup of tea?" her aunt asked.

While removing her garden gloves, Pamela forced a smile. "Yes, of course." She welcomed the suggestion, thinking that it would give her a moment to collect herself alone in the kitchen. She exchanged her boots with her shoes. "Please make yourselves comfortable on the sofa while I wash my hands and prepare tea."

Sitting on the sofa, her relatives looked around the living room. But after a few moments, they joined Pamela in the kitchen.

"This is a nice place," Aunt Hillary said. "By the way, we prefer coffee to tea."

"So you have moved without informing me, your guardian," Pamela's Uncle Winston said.

"Well, yes. This happened quite unexpectedly."

"Where is your landlady?" Uncle Winston asked.

It took only an instant for Pamela to answer. "She is gone. I have the place to myself."

"How lucky you are!" her aunt remarked enviously.

After arranging the coffee tray, Pamela suggested, "Let's go to the living room. I hope you like the cake I made yesterday." She chuckled. "It's my first attempt in baking."

Aunt Hillary took a tiny bite. "It is not bad for a first attempt."

"Thank you. Do you like cream and sugar?" She prepared each cup according to their wishes. Eager to find out the purpose of their unexpected visit, Pamela asked, "What brings you here?"

"You might well ask!" her uncle responded. "I am told that you graduated from the Maria Montessori Academy for Teachers, am I correct?"

"Yes. I am now a licensed Montessori teacher," Pamela admitted happily.

"You did not have the decency to inform me, your guardian. I have the right to know what you are doing."

Pamela felt nervous. For an instant, anger filled her, but she knew she must control her temper. "Yes, as long as you were my guardian, you were supposed to stay in touch with me. But I never heard from you after you put me in the boarding school and then at St. Mary's College."

"Don't be rude, Pamela!" Aunt Hillary warned.

"How did you manage to enroll at the academy? I found out that it is quite expensive!" Uncle Winston asked.

"I never heard from you, so it was up to me to decide what to do next. I love teaching."

"How could you afford the tuition and board?"

"I was fortunate enough to receive a full scholarship and a modest loan for living expenses.'

"And now that you have graduated, what are your plans?" Her uncle wanted to know.

"When I was accepted at the academy, it was with the understanding that I would have to teach here for the next three years to pay off my scholarship and loan with a reduced salary."

"You shouldn't stay here alone in this place while your landlady is gone," Aunt Hillary remarked.

"Oh, it is quite safe here. Farmington is a small town. People know each other and are very friendly and helpful."

There was an awkward silence until Uncle Winston proposed, "I think you should come to live with us for a while."

His wife stared at him. She seemed taken by surprise at his suggestion.

Pamela had to force herself to smile. "Thank you, Uncle. But as I just told you, I am committed for the next three years to remain here to teach." She was very glad to have this excuse.

"As your guardian, I can insist that you come with us."

Pamela looked at him. "You may have forgotten, uncle. I am twenty-one! Your guardianship has expired."

While she reminded him, his eyes grew into narrow slits. She could tell that he was very angry.

"You, Pamela, are impertinent and ungrateful for all I—we—have done for you!"

She matched his anger. "I thank you for whatever you have done for me. I truly cannot remember what it might have been."

"Well!" Uncle Winston's face turned dark red while his voice deepened. "I selected the best boarding school for girls after you were rude to the governess I had hired." Suddenly, without warning, his mood changed. He continued, chuckling, "You were dumb enough to write to your mother, who was already dead, to come and get rid of the governess! Oh, yes, your governess found your letter and forwarded it to me. We had a good laugh!"

Trying to remain calm, Pamela asked, "Please tell me what else you did for me?"

"How dare you?" Aunt Hillary challenged but was ignored by her husband.

"I made arrangements to pay for your tuitions and kept track of your grades. Don't forget, I got you into St. Mary's College!" He nodded. "I must admit you were an excellent student."

"Thank you." Finally, Pamela could not wait to ask and said, "What happened to my parents' house? Mama had always assured me that it will be mine forever, even while they were in India."

Uncle Winston's lips disappeared into a thin line. "You dare ask!"

It was very hard to remain polite. "Yes, Uncle Winston. This is the first time we are talking face-to-face as adults. You managed my youth, but your duties and responsibilities for me are over."

"By asking about your parents' house, do you mean to imply that your uncle robbed you?" Aunt Hillary sounded outraged.

Pamela turned to her. "I am only trying to find out what happened to my home after I was sent away."

There was a moment of suspense until her uncle started to explain. "Well, let me tell you. The house was almost in ruins and needed extensive repairs before it could be put on the market for sale. Again, I made all the necessary arrangements to pay for those repairs. I justly reimbursed myself for all the trouble I endured regarding the house."

"I see." Pamela nodded but silently did not believe him. "When was the house sold?"

"Two weeks after you left. Why?"

"Two weeks?" she repeated with disbelief. She shook her head. "So in two weeks, all the extensive repair work had been done?" she challenged.

"Young woman, you are impertinent! If you were younger, I would take you over my knee to teach you a lesson you wouldn't forget so easily!"

Pamela realized that there was nothing to gain from any further discussion. "It appears that we have nothing else to discuss. You are angry with me, and I am not enchanted by your unexpected visit. I am sorry." She stood up in a clear signal that she wanted them to leave.

"And now you throw us out?" Aunt Hillary complained.

"No, but I would like to finish my work in the garden before it starts to rain."

"Well, Whinny, I can see that we are not wanted here. Let us leave."

To Pamela's great relief, her unwelcome visitors stood up.

However, at the front door, Uncle Winston fired the last salvo. "As far as I am concerned, I consider this relationship with you terminated! Let me tell you one last thing. In my opinion, you are not worthy of the proud Payne family name!" He took his wife by the elbow and left.

Pamela was so shocked at her uncle's last words that she barely managed to say goodbye.

Her relatives didn't respond.

From the front door, she watched them get into their car and drive off. Pamela then closed the door and leaned against it to catch her breath. She was trembling with shock and felt weak with mental exhaustion. *He said I was not worthy of the proud Payne family name. What have I done to dishonor it?* She wiped her tears and thought, *I hope I will never see them again!*

On the following day, Sunday, Pamela heard the phone ring. After an initial hesitation, fearing that it was her uncle calling, she picked up the receiver. "Good morning."

"It's me, Andrew. How are you Pamela?"

She smiled, relieved. "Oh, it is so good to hear your voice, Andrew! Welcome back!"

"Thank you. It's good to be back! How are you?"

"I am recovering."

"Recovering?" Andrew sounded alarmed. "From what? Were you ill?"

"Not physically but emotionally. I am so very grateful Andrew that you called. It will take my mind off the mess I am afraid I created with my relatives."

"Your relatives? You mean your aunt and uncle? Is it that serious? I hope it isn't irreconcilable!"

"I really don't know."

"Would you like me to come over?"

"Oh, Andrew, would you mind? But you must be tired. When did you get back?"

"Before midnight last night."

"Did you have breakfast?"

"Not yet. I was very eager to let you know that I am back."

"Come over for breakfast, and we can talk if you like."

"This is the best invitation I have received so far today!" Pamela could hear laughter in his voice. "I'll be over in ... exactly ... five minutes and twenty-three seconds!"

When Andrew entered the living room, Pamela went straight to him and hugged him spontaneously. "Thank you so much for coming."

"If I had known that I would receive such a heartwarming welcome, I would have come over last night!" he teased. He noticed that she wore the same skirt and blouse she had worn when she had come the first time to his office. But when he studied her face, he could see that she had not slept and looked very tired. "What happened?"

"Would you mind sitting in the kitchen? I have a quiche in the oven. It will take another ten minutes until it will be ready. How about some orange juice and coffee while we wait?"

"Whatever you will serve me will be most welcome. I never had supper last night."

"There are already bacon, onions, and cheese in the pie. Perhaps you would like to start with muffins? Please help yourself to everything."

"Thank you. Yes, I am starving." While buttering a muffin, Andrew asked, "Now please tell me what happened."

"I fear I made bitter enemies ..." Pamela began as she described her relatives' visit.

"Do you think your uncle has found out about your inheritance?"

"I am not certain. They asked where my landlady was. I told them that she was gone."

Andrew chuckled. "A good neutral answer."

"Do you think they can find out that the cottage is mine?"

"Yes. The change of title deed has been recorded at the county. The information is available to the public."

"Oh, dear! What should I do if or when they come back?"

"You mentioned that your uncle said that the relationship between you and him is terminated. It is not likely that he will return." Andrew thought for an instant before continuing. "But when money is involved, people can be very persistent! I found that out relating to my client and his ex-wives in Greece and France."

"Were you able to resolve the problems?" Pamela asked with concern.

"There is hope for a mutually agreeable compromise."

The quiche was ready. It smelled great and was enthusiastically eaten by Andrew. "Going back to your problem, Pamela, what worries you most?"

"I got the distinct feeling that Uncle Winston lied about the sale of my parents' house. He said that it was almost in ruins and required extensive repairs. According to him, all repairs were done within the following two weeks before the house was put up for sale."

"You do know that the sale of your parent's house, if it was sold, and the names of the new owners and title deed have been recorded at the courthouse in Chislehurst, right? Like your title deed was registered here. You can find out all the details. Even how much it was sold for."

"I don't want to do that. All I want is to be left alone."

"Yes. Perhaps it would be best to leave it at that. Luckily, your uncle has no claim over you nor over what you own. You are twenty-one years old. You are totally independent from him and his wife or other relatives."

Pamela sighed deeply. "What a relief! You see, during all my childhood, since my uncle became my guardian, he has been like a sinister cloud or dark shadow over me. I was always very scared of him and his wife. To tell you the truth. I was actually grateful that they never invited me to stay with them during holidays."

"How sad …"

Pamela stood up. "I have to show you something. I will bring it down."

A few moments later, she offered Andrew a small carton. "Open it and look what was in the safe at the bank."

He opened the carton. "Goodness! If they are real, they are quite expensive."

Pamela removed one item after another. There were four rings, one two-strand pearl necklace, one gold-link necklace with amethysts, and one diamond necklace with matching earrings. "What am I going to do with all these?"

Andrew laughed. "Wear them! Enjoy these treasures!"

"How can I? People know that I am not rich. I cannot suddenly walk around wearing expensive jewelry."

"For now you may want to keep them safely at the bank. Who knows what will happen in your future?"

Andrew left after breakfast. "I have two law cases pending. Each will require quite a bit of research and concentration on my part. I plan to spend the coming week preparing for them. But it was a treat to have such a delicious breakfast with you. Thank you, Pamela."

"You are most welcome, Andrew. Anytime you feel like calling or"—she chuckled—"are hungry, you are most welcome to come over! I promise I won't detain you, but you must eat!"

"It is a tempting thought, but for now I must concentrate on my work. I intend to win both cases!"

"I promise not to call or distract you. I wish you every success!"

CHAPTER 5

Unpleasant Consequences

A couple of weeks later, Pamela was awakened from her sleep by some noise downstairs. She sat up in bed and listened, but there was no additional sound. Still she opened the bedroom door to see if there was light downstairs. Everything was dark. *It sounded like glass shattering. What could it have been?* For an instant, Pamela wondered if she should go downstairs to investigate but decided against it. For the first time, she locked her bedroom door. It was hard to go back to sleep as she was still half listening. There was no further sound.

She must have fallen asleep again because when she woke up, she saw an unusual light reflected on the ceiling in her bedroom from the front-facing window of the cottage. The alarm clock showed 3:23 a.m. She jumped out of bed, wrapped a large shawl around her shoulders, and hurried downstairs. To her horror she discovered the music room wing was on fire. *Oh my god!* For an instant, Pamela panicked but quickly recovered. She reached for the phone in the hall. It was dead! *I must get help … the fire department!* She ran upstairs, put on a dress, and rushed downstairs. The fireplace between the two floor-to-ceiling bookcases was feeding the fire.

Luckily, a neighbor had also noticed the fire and came running over to use the water hose in an insufficient attempt to extinguish the fire.

"Have you called the fire department?" he yelled to Pamela.

"No, my phone is dead!"

"Here, hold the hose. I'll call them." While he was still speaking, the fire truck with blasting sirens came racing down the street.

The firemen were amazingly well coordinated and soon had full control over the fire. The foreman introduced himself as Neil Brown. He asked Pamela, "Ma'am, did you forget to dampen the fire last evening?"

"No. I didn't use the fireplace at all during the last three days."

While talking, they approached the still-smoldering fire. Foreman Brown noticed something. "Look at all this wood and cartons piled up even outside the fireplace! Do you always store so much wood here?"

"No," Pamela responded. "I have no idea where all this wood and cartons came from."

One of the firemen called out, "Look over here! It seems that someone broke the side window and got busy! The glass was broken from the outside to gain entrance."

At that moment Police Inspector Healey and Constable Rogers arrived to survey the scene. They introduced themselves. "I'll have my men look for finger and shoe prints in the morning. Don't touch anything, miss." He went over to the side window. "The culprit or they came through the broken window. Look at the dirt with the broken glass." He turned to Pamela. "I am sorry, miss, but I don't know your name."

"I am Pamela Payne. Good morning, Inspector, Constable."

"Good morning, Ms. Payne. Is Mrs. Hood's cottage yours now?"

Foreman Neil Brown joined them.

"Yes, the cottage is mine. Thank you all for coming so promptly!" They shook hands.

Inspector Healey said, "You probably aren't used to fireplaces. One must always let the fire go out before retiring."

Fireman Brown said, "Ms. Payne says that she had not lit the fire during the last three days. The way I see it, the fire must have been set by whoever forced entry through the window here."

"What about all this wood and these cartons?" Inspector Healey asked.

"They are not mine," Pamela explained. "I don't know how they got here."

"Hmm … I see. It was forced entry with intent to do harm. We are looking at a crime scene," Inspector Healey stated.

Both Fire Foreman Brown and Constable Rogers agreed. The constable started taking pictures of the scene.

"You were very lucky, Ms. Payne," Inspector Healey said. "The bookcases fed the fire for some time. It could have been a lot worse had it spread across the carpet and the main cottage. As I said earlier, Ms., don't touch anything! We need to study the place carefully during daylight. Can I use your phone?"

"I am sorry, the phone is dead."

By that time, several of Pamela's neighbors had come to look. One of them offered theirs, saying, "You can use ours, Inspector. We live next door.

Foreman Brown asked Pamela, "Will you be all right, Ms.? I'll leave one of my men here to keep an eye on the fire scene so that no further damage can be done."

Pamela addressed all the men, "Before you leave, can I offer you some coffee or tea?"

"No, thank you, Ms. Payne. We all need to go back to our stations. First thing in the morning, you must inform your insurance agency," Inspector Healey reminded her.

"Ah, yes, thank you for telling me. I will."

"Ms. Payne," the Inspector asked, "do you know of anyone who would do such a thing?"

Pamela thought for an instant. *My uncle? Would he do such a mean thing?* She dismissed the thought. "No, I am new here. I don't know many people in Farmington."

"Do you know of anyone who could be jealous for your having inherited Mrs. Hood's cottage? A relative of Mrs. Hood perhaps?"

"No, I was given the impression that Mrs. Hood had no relatives."

"Who told you this?" the Inspector asked.

"The mayor, Mr. Prescott."

"How was he involved?"

"Mrs. Hood had visited him and asked him to handle the transfer of all legal documents and other related issues regarding her last will and testament. She had also given him a letter for me in which she had designated me as her sole heiress."

"And you cannot think of anyone who would want to hurt you?"

Pamela hesitated a moment. "Well, I am not certain if I should even mention it to you. I have an uncle and aunt in Chislehurst. They aren't very happy with me. I cannot imagine them doing such a horrible thing!"

"Anyone else?"

"No."

"Thank you, Ms. Payne. I'll arrange that your telephone will be reconnected as soon as we have taken more photos of the crime scene."

Inspector Healey and Fireman Brown left to write their separate reports.

Several neighbors approached Pamela.

"What a way to meet, miss. We are Betty and Harry Bloomsbury from next door. Would you like to sleep at our place?"

Pamela was surprised. "Thank you, you are very kind! I don't think I could go back to sleep. Luckily, the fire was only at the fireplace wall. The rest of the music room and cottage are fine."

Another neighbor approached. "I overheard that your phone is dead. If you need to call anyone, just come over. We live across the street. The kitchen door is always open."

"My name is George Benton. I live on your right side. I have to ask you. Did you have anyone deliver wood yesterday evening around eleven o'clock pm? There was no light in your cottage, and someone was dumping wood and cartons at the side of your house in the dark."

"No." Pamela was surprised. "I had enough wood in the vault to last for several more fires. You said you actually saw someone around eleven o'clock am?"

"Yes. Mind you, I am not a nosy neighbor. I was walking Grumpy, my cocker spaniel, and saw a small delivery truck parked a bit to the side of your cottage. I thought it strange that there was no light anywhere. But it never occurred to me to inquire. I am sorry."

Pamela was shocked. "You actually saw a man carrying wood and cartons from a truck to the side of the cottage? What did he look like?"

"I didn't see clearly. I guess he was about middle-aged. He had dark hair. Mind you, it was dark. He didn't seem to be in any hurry. I don't think he saw me. Were you out last night?"

"No, I was at home reading in the living room with only a small floor lamp on. I doubt that one could see the light from the outside unless one would walk up to the window. Please tell Inspector Healey about the man you saw. It may be important."

Harry Bloomsbury said, "Last night, my Betty thought that she heard glass shattering. But we didn't think it was anything serious, like a break-in."

"What time was it when you heard, Betty?" George Benton asked his wife.

"It was … I think it was around three o'clock, very soon after three o'clock."

Pamela nodded. "Yes, I woke up at 3:11 to the sound of a crash. I should have gone downstairs to investigate. But I felt scared and, like a coward, locked myself in the bedroom until the light from the fire woke me up at 3:24."

Harry shook his head. "No, miss, it was fortunate that you didn't go down to confront the criminal! He might have been armed."

They all stood huddled with combined sympathy for Pamela in their woolen wraps, bed robes, and slippers, wondering what to do.

Pamela was feeling cold. "Thank you all very much for your help! I am very pleased to meet you. Even if it is a rather odd time."

George added, "And we are all wearing our most elegant and formal attires!"

After brewing some coffee for the remaining fireman, Pamela went upstairs to take a quick bath and get ready for a busy day ahead.

It was shortly after eight thirty that morning when Andrew stopped by. He found Pamela and the fireman in the music room. He hugged her. "Pamela, are you all right? You didn't get hurt, did you?"

It was only then that she broke down in tears. "Mrs. Hood's books burned down last night!"

He looked closely at the blackened books. "Not all are damaged. Since they were tightly arranged, it looks like many have only their spines burned. Toward the ceiling they seem not too badly damaged. I think we'll be able to save many of them!"

She stopped sobbing to look more closely at the blackened books.

"Why didn't you call me?" Andrew asked.

"The phone was cut off."

He put his arm around her shoulder. "Thank god you are not hurt."

She tried to smile at him. "Not physically, at least. Do you really think we can save most of the books?"

Andrew recognized Fireman Tom and shook hands with him. "Good morning, Tom. How bad is it?"

"Good morning, mayor. It looks pretty bad as far as the books on the bottom shelves are concerned. But as you say, some have only the spines ruined."

"Did you forget to dampen the fire last night?" Andrew asked.

"No, I didn't even enter the room for the last three days."

Fireman Tom approached them. "If I may say so, mayor, it looks like a forced entry and perhaps burglary. Look at the broken window. All that wood and cartons piled in front of the fireplace were brought in through it!"

Andrew asked Pamela, "Do you have any idea who could have done this?"

She shook her head. "No. I hardly know anyone in Farmington. Why would anyone want to burn down this beautiful cottage? I am glad Mrs. Hood is no longer alive to see this disaster. Who told you about the fire?"

"I came early to my office when I ran into Inspector Healey. So I came straight here to see if you are all right."

"Thank you, Andrew. Yes, I will be all right."

"Inspector Healey suspects forced entry with intent to do harm."

"Yes." Pamela agreed. "I have to stay here for him to return to inspect the scene and take pictures and finger and shoe prints. As soon as the phone is repaired, I must inform the insurance company."

"One of the documents you signed at my office is from the insurance agency. Do you have the documents here?" Andrew asked.

"Only all the copies. The originals are at my bank safe."

"The copy will have the contact number. Call them as soon as possible. They may want to send someone over to assess the damage."

"We are not to touch anything until Inspector Healey has finished his investigation," Pamela explained.

"Have you had a look around the outside of the cottage to see if there is any other damage?"

"No, not yet. I'll wait for Inspector Healey to do so."

"After the phone is reconnected, will you please call me?"

"Yes, Andrew, I will." She smiled. "You mentioned that you went early to the office. You must have a lot of work to do. Fireman Tom is with me, I'll be fine. Please don't worry."

"I am afraid I won't be able to come back until later this afternoon. I have a court hearing. One never knows how long they can take."

Pamela ushered Andrew toward the door. "Thank you for being so concerned. I will be fine, and I don't mind waiting for you. Perhaps you may wish to join me for supper here after the court adjourns, whenever that may be?"

"May I let you know?"

"Yes. I am not planning to go out today."

A short time later, Inspector Healey returned with Constable Rogers. They combed very thoroughly the approach from the street to the side wing to the cottage where the window had been broken and the telephone wire had been cut. There were truck tire imprints. Clear shoe prints proved that it had required several trips back and forth between truck and the broken window. Constable Rogers found discarded rubber gloves and bits of cut telephone wires on the ground. After comparing the wood stored in the vault and the wood brought to the fireplace, it was clear that they were not the same.

Once again Inspector Healey asked Pamela the same questions about people she knew in Farmington. "Earlier you mentioned your uncle and aunt. Can you tell me a bit more about your relatives and your relationship with them?"

Pamela was surprised. "Surely you don't think—"

"Ms. Payne, I do not think." The Inspector interrupted her. "I only ask questions at this time. I have to explore all possibilities and probabilities. You mentioned that they were 'not very happy with you.' Why? What happened?"

"Oh, it's a long story ..."

"I have the time to listen."

While Pamela described briefly her childhood up to the recent surprise visit from her aunt and uncle, the Inspector scribbled notes in a notebook. He seemed interested in her relatives in Chislehurst. Finally, he asked, "What are the names of your uncle and aunt?"

"Winston Henry James Payne and Hillary Margaret Payne. They live at Windsor Road, 30 Horseshoe Crescent in Chislehurst."

"And your parents' names? Their residence was also in Chislehurst?"

"Yes. My father was Colonel Adrian Christopher Nigel Payne, and my mother's name was Elizabeth Mary Rose Payne. We lived at 1 Stonehenge Crest. Our house was the only one at Stonehenge Crest in Chislehurst."

"I am afraid I have to ask you some personal questions. You mentioned that your parents lived and died in India. During their absence, you were staying at their house in Chislehurst, correct?"

"Yes."

"Who stayed with you?"

"My nanny. I called her Bambi."

"Anyone else?"

"We had a gardener, a chambermaid, and a cook. They were all very nice."

A fleeting smile crossed the Inspector's face before he continued. "Until when did you reside at your parents' house?"

"Until my sixth birthday—fifteen years ago. After my parents had passed away, I was sent to a boarding school. Uncle Winston said that he sold my parents' house."

"Are there any other relatives you know of?"

"No, as far as I know there are none other."

"Were you close to your relatives, this uncle and aunt?"

"No. I met my uncle only when he came to tell me that my parents had passed. Then once more when he and his wife took me to the boarding school. I never heard from them again until their recent surprise visit here I told you about."

"Then why do you think they were very unhappy with you if you hardly knew them?"

Pamela had to think for a moment. "I really cannot say exactly. I was not very hospitable to them. I don't know how they traced me to here. I wondered if they knew that I had inherited the cottage. They asked all sorts of questions."

"What sort of questions?"

"About this cottage, about my landlady. They somehow knew that I had graduated from the academy. At one point my uncle offered me to go and live with them, but I could see my aunt didn't want me. I didn't trust them. Uncle Winston tried to threaten me as my guardian. But I reminded him that I was twenty-one and told him clearly that his guardianship had ended."

"How did he take this information?"

"He must have known it, of course, but hoped that I wasn't aware of it. I told him that I am committed to stay here in Farmington to teach for the next three years. When I asked him questions about my parents' house, both he and my aunt got very angry. It was then that my uncle said just before leaving that our relationship was terminated. I wasn't worthy of the Payne family name."

"They never mentioned if they knew that you owned this cottage?"

"No. Mr. Prescott told me that they can easily find out from the county."

"Where did you live before moving here?"

"In Shrewsbury at a pension for ladies."

"Do you know someone there who might be jealous or wants to harm you?"

"No. We hardly ever met. Sunday afternoons there was sherry served in the lounge. It was the only time some of us got together. I joined very rarely."

The Inspector closed his notebook: "Thank you, Ms. Payne. I will write my report. I must ask you to remain in Farmington for possible further questioning. Good day."

"Thank you, Inspector Healey. Good day."

Andrew called at eight o'clock and asked if he might still be welcome.

"Have you had supper?" Pamela asked.

"Not yet."

"Good! Come over as soon as you can. I made my first Indian curry!"

It was 8:30 p.m. when Andrew rang the doorbell.

"Come in, Andrew. You look exhausted!"

Pamela had set the table in the living room with the Wedgwood china and lit two candles. She served first Andrew, then herself with the curry.

"I have beer, ginger beer, and white wine. Which would you like?"

"Ginger beer sounds tempting, thank you."

After serving the beer, Pamela asked, "How did the case go?"

"Our case came up late and was very intense. I have two surprise witnesses in store for the defense for tomorrow!" He smiled. "There is a very good chance that we'll win the case for my client."

"Oh, I very much hope so! You worked so hard you deserve to win!"

"Thank you." He smiled at her. "This curry is very good! Where did you learn how to cook?"

Pamela laughed. "I found a wonderful Indian cookbook here. Luckily, I discovered all the necessary spices in a kitchen cabinet. I am so glad you like it. Thank you."

Andrew began to relax. "While waiting to present my case it occurred to me that you need a dog—a fierce-looking dog!"

Pamela was surprised. "You were thinking of me while you were in court?" She laughed. "Yes, I would love to have a dog—a labrador!"

Andrew shook his head. "A labrador can never look ferocious! You need a German shepherd or a doberman that can snarl frighteningly."

"Oh, Andrew, when I was little I had a labrador puppy—a white fluffy little thing! He followed me everywhere. He would have slept with me in bed if Bambi had allowed it. His name was Buffy. He was taken away at the same time Bambi was fired."

"That's it! We'll get you another one!" Andrew promised.

Pamela smiled. "Yes, that would be lovely!" She turned serious. "What do you think of Inspector Healey?"

"He is one of the best! Very professional and thorough. I have worked with him on a number of criminal cases, and I was always impressed by his instinct! Why?"

"He asked me so many questions. In particular about my parents, my uncle, and my aunt. I am afraid he is going to investigate my uncle. I am worried if my uncle finds out."

"It is Inspector Healey's job to explore all possibilities."

"Yes, I know. Still, I am worried!" She paused when she saw that Andrew had finished his second helping. "I have vanilla ice cream."

"I'll have only if you have some."

"I am so glad you came! It creates a welcome distance between what happened last night and this evening."

"Will you be able to sleep tonight, or are you still worried?"

"I don't think anyone will dare to return. The police were around all day. I know that my neighbors will be keeping an eye out as well." She smiled at Andrew. "No, I am going to sleep very well tonight!"

Before Andrew left, they inspected the remains of the books. They didn't seem so bad as they had initially thought. "Many can be salvaged!"

Andrew won his court case on the following day. He called Pamela. "Good news, Pamela! We won, and my client is very pleased!"

"Congratulations! I was thinking of you all day." She chuckled. "In my mind, I kept my fingers crossed for you!"

"Thank you! How are you? Did you sleep well last night?"

"Yes, very well, thank you."

"One problem with winning a case is that one receives more urgent requests to take over other cases," Andrew explained.

"That is good for you! It means that you will become famous!"

"What it really means, my dear, is more—much more—work on my part!"

"Yes, I understand and am very happy for you! But you'll have to eat. Do you feel like coming over for a relaxing dinner?"

"I am looking forward to doing so. Thank you, Pamela!"

CHAPTER 6

Inspector Healey's Discoveries

*S*ix months passed without, Pamela thought, a sign of progress made regarding the attempt to burn down her cottage. Whenever she would ask Andrew if he had heard anything from the Inspector's investigation, his responses were negative. But he advised her to be patient.

At the end of October, Inspector Healey asked Pamela to come and see him at his town hall office. She went with little hope of learning anything new and helpful.

The Inspector greeted Pamela before she had a chance to knock on his door. "Ah, good morning, Ms. Payne. Please come in and have a seat."

"Good morning, Inspector Healey."

He went to sit behind his desk. "You may think we have forgotten you." He smiled. "No, we have not! I would like to ask you once more about your late parents' house address in Chislehurst."

"Yes, of course. It is, was, 1 Stonehenge Crest. It was the only house on that road."

"And your parents' full names?"

"Colonel Adrian Christopher Nigel Payne and Elizabeth Mary Rose."

"And your uncle's address to the best of your knowledge, please?'

"It is Windsor Road, 30 Horseshoe Crescent, also in Chislehurst."

"And your uncle's and aunt's full names, please?"

"Winston Henry James Payne and Hillary Margaret."

The Inspector consulted his report, then nodded. "Interesting."

Pamela was not quite certain what he meant and offered, "Perhaps my uncle moved?"

"Yes, he moved indeed."

"In that case, I don't know his new address. I am sorry."

The Inspector appeared to enjoy this conversation. Pamela didn't know why.

"Ms. Payne, you will be surprised to know your relatives' present address is your late parents' house address, 1 Stonehenge Crest!"

She stared at him, then shook her head. "There must be a mistake! Perhaps our family names, being the same, got mixed up somehow?"

"No, Ms. Payne. I am quite certain about this. I sent my constable to Chislehurst to verify the official records at the courthouse. The mailing address is correct. The gate at the house at 1 Stonehenge has a plaque that reads 'Winston Henry James Payne.'"

Pamela frowned. "I cannot believe this! Why would he say he sold my parents' house after all the extensive repairs? And after he had sent me safely to a boarding school and college later on?" She thought for a moment, then realized something. "This is probably why I was never invited to visit them for the holidays during all these years! But why would he do such a thing?"

"Why?" Inspector Healey chuckled. "Think, Ms. Payne! He had everything to gain by not selling your parents' house and taking possession of it. He thought that no one could challenge his claim because you were a minor and his ward. You were the only heiress to your parents' estate. He got safely rid of you, so to speak. At least for some time! Of course, in an acceptable way by sending you to a respectable boarding school and college. Nobody knew of his scheme. He had assumed that there was no last will and testament left by your late parents. But your uncle forgot to inquire at the Home Office!" Inspector Healey paused for a moment. "Your father had left clear instructions and all the necessary documents for your secured inheritance with his friend, Lord Edward Crighton. It took us awhile to trace him. As it turned out, Lord Crighton had tried, unsuccessfully, to trace your whereabouts. He kept all the documents for all entitlements as your parents' only heiress to their estate. To your uncle, Winston Henry James, your father bequeathed the amount of one-thousand pounds sterling."

Pamela sat stunned while staring at the Inspector. "How did you find this Lord Edward Crighton?"

"Our investigation led us to the Home Office where we found Lord Crighton. He said that all his inquiries and attempts to inform you of his having possession of your father's last will and testament and other documents were returned to him in the unopened envelopes with the remark Addressee Unknown!"

"It must have been my uncle. But why would he return the envelopes?"

"He probably hoped that this way the sender would assume that the house had been sold and there was no chance of finding you."

Pamela was puzzled. "But why would he turn up all of a sudden? He even asked me to spend some time with them. I don't understand."

"It was a ruse. He already knew that you had inherited Mrs. Hood's cottage but wanted to test you to find out how committed you are to stay in Farmington. He was afraid that you might appear in Chislehurst one day to claim your parents' inheritance. He wanted to make certain that you hated him and that you would never return to Chislehurst to look for him."

"But what about the fire? Why would he burn the library?"

"He was very clever. The fire was not large enough to burn down the whole cottage. It was just enough to scare you to leave—hopefully, to go somewhere else."

"Did my uncle set the fire? Do you know?"

"No. He hired a jobless man who would do anything for money."

"Amazing." Pamela frowned. "Was my uncle afraid that I might come to Chislehurst in spite of my knowing that he was angry?"

"You would have gone to Windsor Road, 30 Horseshoe Crescent, wouldn't you?" Inspector Healy suggested.

"Yes, of course."

"That house has had several owners over the last fifteen years. It would have been difficult for you to trace your uncle to his present address. He has an unpublished telephone number, and the Royal Mail will not disclose owners of their addresses unless it is Scotland Yard asking."

"What happens now?"

"If you wish for Scotland Yard to arrest him, we have enough material for a criminal case. The decision is entirely up to you, Ms. Payne."

Pamela shook her head in dismay. "I have to think about this."

"If I may suggest, since you already know Andrew Prescott, who is one of the best barristers we have in this county, you may wish to consult him for sound advice."

"Yes, your suggestion is welcome!" She smiled and extended her hand. "I cannot thank you adequately for all you have done! I will let you know of my decision." They shook hands.

"Good. I'll be here. Goodbye, Ms. Payne."

"Again, thank you, Inspector Healey. Goodbye."

Pamela passed by Andrew's office and hesitated for an instant before knocking on his door. On his "Come in" response, she entered. "Hello, Andrew."

"Hello, Pamela, how are you?"

"I come from Inspector Healey's office and couldn't resist the temptation to see if you were in."

Andrew put down his pen and leaned back in his chair. "Any good news?"

"He didn't tell you?"

"No, of course not! I told you he is very professional."

"Well, he called me. What he told me was quite a revelation!"

"Sounds interesting! Care to share?"

Pamela laughed. "Oh, it's a very long, somewhat complicated story. Are you free tonight? Can I entice you to come over for supper?"

"Only if we go out to eat and I am allowed to invite you!" he teased.

"Oh, wonderful, that is a deal! At what time and where?"

"I'll pick you up at seven o'clock."

"Thank you, Andrew. I'll be ready!"

CHAPTER 7

A Commitment

*P*amela's mind somersaulted in her head while she took a bath and selected a long deep-honey-gold velvet skirt with matching jacket and an ivory silk blouse with a high embroidered neck. She decided to wear the gold necklace with the amethysts. She combed her hair high in the back of her head into a soft twist and fastened it with a filigreed horn clasp. When she glanced in the mirror, she worried that she was too elegantly dressed. *What if we go just to Harry's for fish and chips?* She chuckled.

However, when she opened the door for Andrew, she saw a very elegant young gentleman at her doorstep! They both smiled, having guessed each other's mind.

He bowed. "My lady."

She curtsied playfully. "My lord."

It turned out that Andrew had made reservations at the best hotel restaurant called My Fair Lady in Newhurst, not far from Farmington.

Without asking, the waiter brought and poured champagne.

"To a beautiful lady called Pamela Desirée Payne." Andrew toasted.

"Thank you, Andrew." She took a sip before putting the glass down. "Are you in the mood to listen to the latest revelations?"

"Yes, I am most eager to know."

Pamela laughed while picking up her glass. "But before the tale I wish to toast to my smashingly handsome escort for tonight by the name of Andrew Prescott, Esq."

"Thank you, Pamela. How long are you going to keep me in suspense?"

"I need one more sip so that I will feel fortified enough to tell you everything!" She teased smilingly before turning serious. "You will see, in hindsight, how many things fit together!" She admitted that she had practically given up on receiving any further news from Inspector Healey regarding the fire. "I didn't want to pressure him, so I kept quiet. Then today he asked me to come to his office. It was a bombshell what he told me!"

She was about to repeat the whole conversation and Inspector Healey's findings regarding her uncle's scheme when the waiter returned with a platter of various hors d'oeuvres and refilled their champagne glasses.

When they were alone again, Andrew listened attentively. At the end he asked, "How do you feel about this?"

"I am not sure. In a way, I want to be left alone and live my life in peace. But on the other hand, I would like my uncle and aunt to be punished somewhat for their deception and what they did to me. But I wouldn't want them to go to jail or suffer in their advanced age. What do you think Andrew?"

"Perhaps, Pamela, you need more time to think this through," he cautioned. "I am glad that you don't want them to go to jail. It would be too harsh at their age. However, you do have a legitimate claim for your parents' estate. Perhaps you may want them to move out of your parents' home?"

"As you know, I will be staying here in Farmington for the next three years. I would feel mean and vindictive to ask them to move out. I know they have no other home. If you saw the house … it is huge. It has three self-contained wings. They could easily stay in one wing, if ever I were to move back home."

Andrew reached for her hand across the table. "Pamela, you are a very nice and compassionate person. I really like what you said." He smiled. "You know, I expected you to be forgiving and generous."

She gently laid her other hand on his. "I think if you were in a similar situation, you would feel the same!"

"I hope I would feel the same."

When the hors d'oeuvres had disappeared, the waiter brought a large platter with a fantastic looking *filet de boeuf* accompanied with several vegetables, which he served carefully on two plates. Then he offered Andrew a bottle of Pomerol—first for inspection and then to taste. After Andrew nodded his approval, the rich red wine was poured into a decanter and only then poured carefully into the crystal glasses for them.

Pamela watched with amazement, then asked, "Andrew, what are we celebrating?"

He smiled mischievously. "Does one always need to have a reason to celebrate?"

"Yes, absolutely! This is far too grand!"

"Can we postpone the reason for a few minutes?"

Pamela appeared nervous. "You sound mysterious …"

"No, not mysterious, rather somewhat hopeful."

"Oh, Andrew! The suspense is killing me! How much longer do I have to wait? Can't you tell me now?" She appeared very young.

"Ah ... the lady has a weakness. She suffers from impatience," he teased.

Pamela realized her impatience. "I am sorry. You are right about my being impatient."

Andrew smiled at her before turning serious while reaching for both her hands. "Pamela, I need to ask you, how do you feel about me? Our relationship?"

She gazed at their joined hands. She swallowed before responding. "I feel ... I feel that you have become a gift, a most precious gift for me."

Andrew kissed both her hands. "How beautifully you said that, Pamela! Thank you! I feel exactly the same! You came into my life quite unexpectedly. But at that moment, the sun began to shine in my heart! Yes, you, too, are my most precious gift. Thank you, my love!"

They gazed at each other for a long moment.

Pamela was the first to speak. "In that case, we have a most joyful reason to celebrate!"

"Pamela, can you imagine a future with me as my loving wife? A small-town barrister and beyond to whatever the future holds?"

"Oh yes! I feel so very honored, Andrew, that you want to spend your life with me as your wife."

"You have no idea how much happiness you give me! I do love you, Pamela."

A radiant smile lit up her face. "I am so very happy because I love you too, Andrew, my darling!"

"Could we make this our very own engagement celebration?"

"Yes, it would be so wonderful!"

Andrew raised his wine glass. "Here is to my very special and very beautiful brand-new fiancée and my wife-to-be—the only Pamela Desirée Payne I know and shall love all my life!"

"Thank you." Pamela blushed while sipping the wonderful Pomerol. "May I also propose a toast?"

Andrew laughed. "Yes, of course! As many as you wish!"

She paused for a moment before saying solemnly, "To amazingly wonderful and totally unexpected events of the past, the present, and our future together! No matter what will happen, may our lives be filled with profound love and happiness!"

Suddenly she realized that tears were sliding down her cheeks, but she smiled and asked, "Why didn't you ask sooner?"

Andrew gently wiped away her tears with one finger. "I wanted to be absolutely certain that I would receive a yes."

"And now you have it!"

"Yes," he smiled. "We both have it! It is wonderful because from now on, we'll face whatever happens together," he promised.

"How soon do you think we can get married?" Pamela asked.

Andrew laughed with relief. "As soon as you wish, my love!"

"Do we need to send out notices of our engagement?"

"It's too late ... we are already engaged! Unless you feel very strongly, I think we can skip them. However, we need to send out invitations to the wedding!"

Pamela turned thoughtful. "Andrew, do you realize how little I know about your family? Do you have a large family?"

"Not overly large."

"Please tell me about them."

"Well, both my parents are still very much alive and in charge!" He chuckled. "You'll receive two brothers-in-law. They are both younger but are already married to very nice ladies, and then there is my little sister who is still in the dreaming stage of youth. She'll be thrilled with you!"

"Where does your family live?"

"In Tarrington, in a very ancient house, you will see."

They were served chocolate mousse with Cognac but declined coffee or tea.

While tasting the chocolate mousse, Pamela grew thoughtful. "Andrew, I feel I must reach out to Uncle Winston and Aunt Hillary one more time to see if we can reconcile. I think we should at least invite them to our wedding."

"Perhaps we ought to drive up to visit them." Andrew suggested before the wedding.

"You mean to surprise them and see how they react?"

"Yes. It will give us an idea if they are willing for a reconciliation."

When they were about to leave the restaurant, the owner approached Andrew and offered a small package. "We couldn't help overhearing part of your conversation. May I offer you, my lord and lady, my warmest congratulations to your engagement? Perhaps you wish to celebrate your wedding reception here? I would like to give you this package that explains all our facilities and what we can offer for a festive wedding celebration."

At first Andrew wasn't sure whether he was pleased or annoyed. "We will have to think about your offer. Thank you." He accepted the package.

On their drive back to Farmington, Pamela asked, "Could you please give me a list of your family and relatives whom you wish to invite?"

"You are so efficient. I wish I had you as my secretary."

"Thank you. I'd rather be your wife!" she teased.

On the following day, they began to draft their wedding announcement. They decided on December 31, New Year's Eve, for their wedding day!

CHAPTER 8

A Surprise Visit

*W*hen Pamela and Andrew arrived at 1 Stonehenge Crest in Chislehurst, the gate stood open. They walked to the front door and rang the bell.

An elderly butler opened the door. "Yes?" He looked more closely at Pamela, blinked, and then stammered, "Is it you, Ms. Pamela?"

She was so happy to have been recognized that she spontaneously embraced the stunned old butler. "Yes, Mannon, it's me!"

"Beg your pardon, my lady. I am ever so pleased to see you." The butler had to wipe away a tear while mumbling with embarrassment, "Please forgive an old man."

"Dear Mannon, there is nothing to forgive. You are the first to know. Please meet my fiancé, Andrew Prescott," she blurted out.

"Congratulations, my lord! You made a fine choice, if you don't mind my saying so." The butler smiled.

Andrew extended his hand. "Thank you, Mannon. Yes, I consider myself very fortunate indeed." They shook hands.

An annoyed-sounding female voice from upstairs called, "Mannon, who is it? You are getting too old for your duties."

Pamela gestured to Mannon not to announce them. She took Andrew by the hand and went upstairs. She entered the library where her uncle and aunt were enjoying a peaceful evening. "Good evening, Aunt Hillary and Uncle Winston."

Both turned around with shocked expressions. Aunt Hillary's face turned white while Uncle Winston's face turned red.

"What in thunder? How is it possible?" the aunt stammered.

"I'll be damned!" Pamela's uncle exclaimed. "How did you know that we moved here?"

Pamela ignored their questions. "We found out just in time to invite you to our wedding." She nudged Andrew gently forward. "Please meet my fiancé, Andrew Prescott."

"I'll be damned," her uncle repeated.

Andrew laughed. "I hope not!" He extended his hand. "I am pleased to meet you, Mr. Payne." Then he smiled at Pamela's aunt. "And you, Mrs. Payne. Pamela has told me about you. We hope you both will be able to attend our wedding on December 31."

"So soon?" Aunt Hillary asked.

"Yes," Pamela nodded. "Will you be able to come back to Farmington?"

Uncle Winston pursed his lips. "You don't give us much time, do you?"

"Yes, I am afraid it is rather short notice," Andrew agreed. "You see, sir, it would be very nice for Pamela to have her family present."

The old woman smiled at her husband. "Say yes, Whinny! I love weddings! Please say yes," she urged.

Meanwhile, Pamela had been observing both her uncle and aunt. She felt suddenly great pity for them. *They are old, and what is their life without children and family?* She offered spontaneously, "Uncle Winston, it would please me enormously if you were to give me away by leading me down the aisle."

"I'll be damned," the old man muttered and turned toward the fireplace to stab unnecessarily at the nicely burning logs. Before he turned around, he quickly wiped away an escaped tear. He looked at Pamela's expecting expression on her face, then nodded. "I'll do it. I'll be damned!" he agreed but warned her, "Just don't go racing down the aisle because I can't walk straight anymore!"

His remark caused instantaneous laughter and erased the last remnant of tension.

Pamela went to him and gave him a hug. "Thank you, Uncle Winston. I promise to walk slowly."

Andrew was happy for her and offered, "As you know, Pamela's cottage is quite small. But we'll arrange for you to stay at the Farmington Lodge. It is a very nice place and within easy walking distance. But I'll pick you up, of course."

Uncle Winston sat down again. "I like you ... Andrew, is it? You think of details. We'll be there. As you can tell, my Hilly is eager to wear some nice frocks—"

"Gowns!" she corrected him, then smiled at Pamela. "He knows me too well." Then she chuckled. "I'll try to teach him not to swear or say other embarrassing things in front of your fiancé's family and guests." Suddenly she realized that Pamela and Andrew were still standing: "Oh, Whinny, where are our manners? Please, Pamela and ... Andrew, sit down!"

Both smiled and responded simultaneously. "Thank you."

There was a small pause in conversation until Uncle Winston asked, "How did you know we moved here?"

Pamela and Andrew exchanged glances before Pamela responded. "The fire ..."

Her uncle suffered suddenly a coughing attack, then blew his nose for a long time. He was thinking. Finally, he said, "I … that is both Hilly and me, wanted you to go away to a place where we could not trace you so that we would not have to keep feeling guilty."

"Why?" Pamela was stunned.

Aunt Hillary picked up the thread of conversation. "We were afraid that now that you are grown-up, you would come one day here and claim your old home."

"But you knew that I planned to stay at the cottage for the next three years."

Uncle Winston studied his hands while saying, "I didn't want you to stay at the cottage. I wanted you to just go away so that I didn't have to think of you and remember how we treated you when you were little. We didn't want you to know that we moved here."

Andrew watched Pamela digest this information. There was a long, awkward silence.

Finally, Pamela looked at her uncle. "We cannot change what happened. You were burdened with a little niece you didn't know what to do with. You decided to move into my parents' house because it was much bigger and better. You, Uncle Winston, mentioned that you traced my progress and whereabouts throughout the years. Were you afraid to reconnect with me, your niece? Is this why you decided to do something to make me hate you so much to never look for you." She paused before continuing. "You must know that this house is my inheritance, but I will not, or ever will, ask you to move out! You, Uncle Winston, grew up in this house, and you belong here as much as I do! Luckily, should I ever move here, the house is big enough to accommodate two families!"

She smiled first at her uncle, then at her aunt. "With Andrew in my life, I feel like whatever happened in the past is closed! A new and happier chapter is about to begin. I would be happy if you would become my family again." Her voice choked at the last words.

"You are welcome to stay here anytime you wish," Aunt Hillary offered.

Uncle Winston stood up. "I think this calls for a celebration. How about a whiskey, Andrew, and sherry for the ladies?"

"That would be welcome. Thank you, sir," Andrew responded.

"Young man, my niece has just recreated our family, and you are going to be part of it. From this moment onward, I am your uncle Winston and Hilly is your aunt Hillary!"

After all the glasses were filled, the uncle proposed, "To congenial family relations!"

"Hear! Hear"

"Now you must stay for dinner!" Aunt Hillary declared and rang a silver bell, which produced Mannon in a short while.

"Yes, ma'am?"

"Mannon, our niece and her fiancé are staying for dinner."

"Very good, ma'am."

Pamela smiled at her aunt. "Imagine, Mannon recognized me!"

"That is amazing. He is getting too old to be of much use. We are wondering where to send him."

"Oh, don't send Mannon away! He came to Chislehurst with Mama when she married my fater. Mannon worked here ever since. This is his home. Mannon was sent by Mama's mother to watch over her! He would be lost anywhere else!" Pamela thought for an instant. "If you cannot keep Mannon, we'll take him with us."

"I won't have it, Hilly! Have you no pride? What would our neighbors say if Mannon were sent away? Pamela is right. He stays."

Pamela smiled at her aunt. "Thank you for inviting us to dinner."

Her uncle responded, "We need to get reacquainted."

"Yes. Andrew has been looking forward to meeting you both."

"Now, young man ... Andrew, is it?" Uncle Winston began, "how will you support my niece? Do you have a profession?"

Pamela and Andrew exchanged amused smiles.

"I am a barrister and have my own law firm."

"And Andrew is honorary mayor of Farmington," Pamela added.

"Good." The old man nodded his approval. "A respectable profession."

Mannon knocked and opened the door. "Ma'am, dinner is served."

"Thank you, Mannon. In that case, let's go to dine," Aunt Hillary said, leading the way.

While walking through the hall Pamela looked around and found everything to be the same. Seeing the set table, she remembered the silver and china. It filled her for a moment with homesickness.

Uncle Winston sat at the opposite of the door at the head of the table while Aunt Hillary sat at the other end near the door. Pamela sat on her uncle's right side, and Andrew sat opposite her on her aunt's right side. There were two candelabras lit with seven pink candles each. The dinner was quite nice—a vegetable-onion soup, pickled Dover sole, and a small beef roast with vegetables. For dessert was a peach pie with ice cream and English cheeses.

"Tell us, Andrew," Uncle Winston began, "how did you meet Pamela?"

He explained about Mrs. Hood, her wish for Pamela to inherit her estate, and their consequent and more and more frequent meetings.

"And when did it occur to you that you might be in love with my niece?"

"Whinny! You shouldn't ask such personal questions!" Aunt Hillary admonished.

"Woman!" her husband responded firmly, "I reserve the right to ask any question I deem appropriate."

Andrew and Pamela laughed.

Andrew smiled at Aunt Hillary. "A very justified question, ma'am, from a concerned uncle regarding his niece."

Pamela observed an exchange of amused agreement between the two men.

"When Pamela came to my office after she had received my letter in which I asked to see her regarding Mrs. Hood's request, I liked her immediately." He smiled at Pamela. "To tell you the truth, sir, I believe the beginning of my falling in love with her began right then."

Pamela gasped, then laughed. "Really? I had absolutely no idea, Andrew!"

The uncle turned to face her. "I am not going to ask you the same question … so that Hilly has no reason to embarrass me further." He sent his wife a withering look.

"Aunt Hillary and Uncle Winston, would you like to come to Farmington one day before the wedding day on the thirtieth of December so that you can recover from your journey? Then return, perhaps, on the first or second of January?"

"Yes, I think we can manage that. We'll arrive in Farmington one day before your wedding and stay at the Farmington Lodge until the second of January," Uncle Winston agreed.

"You realize," Pamela cautioned, "that we may not have much time to entertain you during your stay."

"I am certain we'll endure your neglect," Aunt Hillary teased.

At the end of the dinner, Aunt Hillary gestured to Pamela to follow her. She led her upstairs to a room at the far end of the gallery. She withdrew a key from her skirt pocket and opened the door into a small darkened room. The room smelled stuffy. After her aunt had drawn the drapes and opened the shutters, Pamela recognized her mother's dressing room with several floor-to-ceiling closets. Aunt Hillary gave Pamela another key while pointing to one closet. "Open it, Pamela."

There were many long formal gowns neatly arranged and hanging from a rod inside. Near the bottom of the closet was a wide drawer.

"Pull out this drawer, and take out the box," her aunt instructed.

Pamela placed the box on a table near the window but hesitated to open it. She felt acutely that this had been her mother's domain and was reluctant to intrude.

"Open it, silly girl." Her aunt sounded almost impatient.

There were lots of tissue papers, which Aunt Hillary removed.

Pamela stared at an exquisitely embroidered pale-ivory duchesse silk bodice with tiny seed pearls. "This is gorgeous!" She touched it gingerly with one finger.

Aunt Hillary removed the bodice to reveal a cloud of matching silk skirts and petticoats. "This was your mother's wedding gown. Perhaps you wish to wear it on your wedding day?"

Still stunned, Pamela whispered, "This is the most beautiful thing I have ever seen! Isn't it too … too grand for me? I am not an earl's daughter like my mother was!"

"Nonsense, Pamela! You are the earl's granddaughter whether he acknowledged you or not! I think your mother would be very pleased for you to wear it on your wedding day." The old woman sighed, remembering. "I didn't know your mother very well, Pamela. She was a true lady, very beautiful and kind. I always felt shy in her presence. I never met her father, the earl. He was very angry with his daughter for marrying 'below her station,' but I met the countess, your grandmother, at your mother's wedding and after you were born. She looked very fragile and sad."

"Why did the earl, my grandfather, never come here?"

"Because it was said that he was so very angry with your mother that he had disinherited her, his daughter—his only child, mind you! We all thought he was cruel!"

Pamela was silent. She had heard about this, but it had never quite seemed true and had not affected her personally—until now!

Aunt Hillary went to the closet to remove another box and brought it to Pamela. This time her aunt opened the box and swiftly removed some tissues. A delicate lace veil in pale-ivory color lay carefully folded in the box. "This is Belgian lace. It goes with the Swendown tiara."

Pamela shook her head. "I cannot possibly wear such fineries in the small town of Farmington!"

Ignoring her niece's protestations, Aunt Hillary continued, "Whinny will bring the tiara down himself because it is very valuable! We keep it in our bank's safe."

"I do remember photos of my parents' wedding with Mama wearing this gown with this veil and the tiara." Pamela sighed. "It seems a whole life ago."

"Yes, my dear, it has been a very long and lonely time," her aunt agreed. Then she turned cheerful once more. "I'll bring your bridal bouquet! What kind of flowers do you like?"

Pamela thought for an instant. "It will be winter, so there isn't much choice. I love roses and lilies of the valley, but they would be very expensive!"

"Poooh!" Her aunt dismissed Pamela's doubts. "It will be white roses and lilies of the valley!" She continued in a whisper, "It will be our secret!"

When the two women joined the two men in the library, Uncle Winston addressed Pamela, "How did you find out that we moved here?"

Pamela had to reflect for a moment. "As I told you, it was the fire. Inspector Healey from Scotland Yard traced it to the man you had hired to set it."

"Hmm ..."

An awkward silence followed before her uncle asked, "One thing still baffles me. How did you find out that you inherited this house?"

Pamela nodded, then explained, "Mama had always assured me that this house would always be mine." She paused an instant. "Shortly before my twenty-first birthday, I received a letter from a Lord Edward Crighton. He had been a friend of my parents. He still works at the Home Office where my father had worked for two years. Apparently my father gave him his last will and testament, the title deed to this house, and other documents in which I was named sole heiress to his estate before leaving for India. Lord Crighton explained in his letter that he waited to send me these documents until I turned of age. In his letter, Lord Crighton mentioned that his earlier attempts to turn over the documents had been unsuccessful as they were returned to him each time unopened with the stamp Addressee Unknown on the thick envelope."

"But you have now the cottage! You don't need two houses," Uncle Winston said.

Pamela sensed his fear of being asked to move out. "No, you are right, I don't need two houses. Perhaps later Andrew and I may wish to move here. But as I said earlier to you, the house is big enough to easily accommodate two families."

"What about Scotland Yard ... and the fire?" He asked cautiously.

Pamela looked at Andrew and asked him to explain. "It is entirely up to Pamela to file criminal charges against you, sir."

Pamela had been observing her uncle and noticing his anxiety. She was silent for a long moment. "For you to arrange … to pay someone to set fire to my cottage was a real mean thing to do!" She paused before continuing. "However, I will not file charges against you. I don't think my father would be pleased if I were to sue you or ask you to move away."

Aunt Hillary sighed with great relief. "Thank God … and you, Pamela!"

Uncle Winston gazed down at his folded hands. "It is humiliating to receive charity at my old age."

Pamela got up and went over to him. "Please don't think that way! You grew up in this house with my father. It is still part of you. Surely we can live together in peace once we return here."

"And when there are children?" Aunt Hillary asked.

While Pamela blushed, Andrew chuckled. "You will be welcome to babysit them once in a while."

Later that evening Pamela and Andrew drove back to Farmington. She had been handed two large cartons after promising not to show the contents to anyone before her wedding day … least of all Andrew!

"I am so very grateful to you, Andrew, for coming with me to meet my relatives. I can tell that they like you!" After a long silence, she continued, "I think I learned today that one must not judge people by the first impression. One must reserve judgement until one has met a person more often to give them a chance to get to know him or her better. How could I ever file a complaint against them? They are old and lonely!"

"I think, Pamela, that they both feel enormously relieved and most grateful to you."

"You know, Andrew, I think, basically, they are quite good people."

CHAPTER 9

An Ancient Manor and Other Revelations

On the following Saturday—the last day in November—Andrew drove Pamela to his family in Tarrington. He was secretly amused but also sympathetic to her nervousness. "You will see they are all very nice people, like myself!"

"I am sure they are. You see, I am not used to a family relationship."

"There is nothing to worry about, darling. Just be yourself, and react to them in whatever way you feel. I know they will like you!"

"I hope you are right."

It was a four-hour drive through small forests, farmland, and small and larger towns.

"Please tell me again your parents' names as well as your brothers' and their wives' and your sister's names."

"Well, my father's names are Michael Anthony Donald Prescott. My mother's names are Priscilla Mary, and my little sister's names are Lucille Mary. We call her Lilly. Then one of my brothers' names are Tony for Anthony Henry. He is one year younger than me. His wife's name is Eleanore. We call her Elly. Then there is Scotti for

Gordon Scott. He is three years younger than me, and his wife's names are Aimée Louise. We call her Lis."

"I hope I will remember which name goes with which face." Pamela still sounded nervous, and then she realized something. "You are the eldest son. How come you are not married yet?"

Andrew laughed. Without taking his eyes off the road, he reached over to take her hand and kissed it. "It is very simple. I was waiting for you!"

While Pamela was repeating the names in her mind, Andrew drove through a wide-open iron gate into a park. The driveway was flanked by old elm trees and wound its way around small meadows and a small pond until a gray building could be seen.

"Is this Tarrington?"

"Yes. At least the building you see ahead is Tarrington Abbey." Andrew watched Pamela's surprised expression and smiled.

"I thought we were going first to your home?"

"Yes, we are. We are presently in Tarrington. This is Tarrington Abbey where my parents happen to live."

Pamela turned to him. "You didn't tell me that you live in such a huge place."

"Yes, I did! Remember, I once told you that we live in a very ancient house?" He chuckled. "I admit, I wanted to surprise you."

"Now I am even more nervous."

"You will find us very normal people, nothing stuffy or intimidating."

The moment the car reached the front steps to the house, the door opened.

A young girl of about eighteen ran to meet them. "How wonderful that you came, Andy!" She paused and looked at Pamela. "Finally, you brought your bride-to-be. How exciting!" She hugged her brother with enthusiasm the moment he got out of the car.

After reciprocating his sister's enthusiastic welcome, Andrew held her at arm's length. "Let me look at you, little pet."

"Andy!" she protested. "I am not your little pet anymore. I am quite grown up!"

"Lilly, I want you to be the first of my family to meet my Pamela."

Pamela approached the young girl. "It is lovely to meet you. May I also call you, Lilly?"

"Yes, of course. I am so glad to meet you, Pamela. Andrew has been talking about you for such a long time!"

"Has he?" Pamela was surprised. "I hope good things?"

"Yes, oh yes!" Lilly first intended to shake hands but changed her mind and hugged Pamela. "You are going to be my sister. I hope you'll come to live here!"

"Thank you, Lilly. I had no idea you lived in such a big place."

"Oh well, you'll get used to it."

"Ho, ho, ho!" Tony and Scotti arrived on horseback.

"Welcome to TA!" Tony called out his greeting after jumping down from his mount. "We have been holding our breaths to meet our new sister-to-be!" He went over to Pamela but looked over his shoulder at Andrew. "Am I allowed to offer a welcome kiss, Andy?"

"Only a very quick one," Andrew teased.

Scotti jumped also from his mount and kissed Pamela on the cheek. "It's about time that we met you, Pamela. Welcome!"

"I am overwhelmed by this warm welcome, thank you!" Pamela said while blushing.

"Father is working with the estate manager. He'll join us later," Tony told Andrew.

"But Mama is in the morning room," Lilly said, taking Pamela by the hand. They entered the house.

The morning room was sun filled. It was separated only by a double glass wall from a beautiful atrium. A fountain received bubbling water from the mouth of a small dolphin sculpture surrounded by tropical plants.

"Welcome to our home, dear Pamela!" Andrew's mother greeted her with a warm embrace.

"Thank you very much, Mrs. Frescott." Pamela took an instant liking to Andrew's family.

"Come sit down next to me." She smiled. "As far as we understand Andrew's wishes, you will be our daughter-by-love at the end of next month! May I suggest you get used to calling me Mama like my children do?"

"Thank you, Mama," Pamela responded shyly.

"You'll soon get used to our lively family."

Andrew joined them and greeted his mother with an affectionate embrace.

While they spoke, Pamela observed her. Andrew's mother was delicately built. Her blond hair was loosely tied up in a knot on top of her head, allowing a few curls to frame her oval face with even features. Her skin was like porcelain. She had striking blue eyes and a nicely sculpted nose over a mouth that was ready to smile. She wore a pale-orange dress with a large opal pendant on a gold chain. Her face radiated joy at seeing Andrew.

He smiled at his mother. "I kept TA as a surprise for Pamela."

"I don't know if you shouldn't have told her about TA before coming here?"

"May I ask, what is TA?" Pamela asked.

They laughed, but Andrew's mother explained, "I am sorry. We shouldn't have laughed. It was quite thoughtless of Andy not to tell you a bit about us. This, our house, is called Tarrington Abbey. It sounds so formal for a family home, so we simply call it TA."

"Abbey … does it mean that it had something to do with a church and monastery?"

"Yes," Andrew's mother responded. "Andy must tell you about the interesting history of TA."

"Thank you. I am looking forward to learning more about the abbey and history."

"There is a lot of history here." She turned to her daughter. "Lilly, have you shown Pamela her room yet?" She then smiled at Pamela. "You may wish to freshen up. How long was the drive up?"

"Not quite four hours, Mama," Andrew answered.

"That is what I estimated."

"Are we going to have tea or an early dinner?" Lilly asked.

"We planned on an early dinner since Pamela and Andy may wish to retire early."

After Lilly left, Pamela stood in the bedroom given to her and gazed around. The bed was covered with a soft-blue damask spread with matching pillows. The walls were painted in dark blue with ivory-colored trims and crown moldings. There was a small chandelier hanging from the center of the ceiling. Near the large gothic window, a chair in front of a small writing desk was draped with pale-blue velvet matching the curtains. *I wonder why Andrew never told me about his family. Do they belong to the nobility? They seem to be really very nice people.*

A knock interrupted her thoughts. "Come in."

It was Andrew. "Will you be comfortable here?"

"Need you ask? Look at this elegant room!"

He smiled and embraced her. "My family is very pleased to meet you, finally. You already conquered their hearts!"

"Please, Andrew, tell me honestly who you and your family are."

"Is it that important?"

"Yes, it's very important for me to know. Please tell me so that I won't make any faux pas. I called your mother Mrs. Prescott."

He nodded. "Let's sit down."

Before he was about to sit on the bedspread, Pamela removed it and sat next to him.

"Well," he began, "my family—that is to say my great-great-grandfather, Lord Michael Anthony Gordon Prescott—was brigadier general of the Royal Guards Regiment. During any kind of military confrontations, he would ride very closely but slightly one foot behind the king to protect him. It so happened that, at one time, my great-great-grandfather saw a man aiming a pistol at the king. He rushed his mount forward and took the bullet himself but saved the king. In gratitude, His Majesty bestowed the earldom of Tarrington on him."

"Was your great-great-grandfather badly hurt?"

Andrew nodded. "Yes, I am afraid so. For a year he was partially paralyzed from the waist down, which ended his military career. However, after a miraculous surgery, he recovered almost completely. He was able to ride again and took great interest in restoring Tarrington Abbey and the estate."

"I am so sorry that he lost his career but pleased that he recovered."

"Fortunately, he had already three sons, so the earldom was safe."

"Your father ... is he also an earl?"

"Well ... yes."

Pamela was very quiet for a moment, then she asked, "Does that mean that your father is a lord ... and you too?"

Andrew reached for her hand. "We don't think it is anything special."

Pamela blushed with embarrassment while admitting, "I called your mother Mrs. Prescott!"

He almost smiled, but when he saw Pamela's embarrassment, he said, "I am certain she enjoyed hearing you mention her married name."

"She asked me to call her Mama."

Andrew hugged her. "There, you see? She has already accepted you!"

"How must I address your father?"

"Why don't you wait for him to decide?" Andrew remembered why he had come and said, "I came to tell you that my room is only two doors to the right, just in case you get lonely."

"Do you dress up for dinner, like long gowns?" Pamela asked worriedly.

"Not when we are just family. You will see that we lead a very uncomplicated life here. Mama and the girls wear long skirts sometimes. Did you bring your long purple skirt with you?"

"Yes, and the long honey-colored velvet skirt."

"Those will be perfect! Please, my darling, don't worry."

"At what time do I have to be ready for dinner?"

"Today is an early dinner, at six o'clock. I'll come and get you at 5:30pm to go down to the library where we usually have a drink." Andrew noticed that she looked tired. "Why don't you rest awhile? You may wish to have a shower. Luckily, this is one of the rooms that has its own bath/shower—a very recent luxury installation in this part of the building."

"Yes, thank you, Andrew. Please come and get me at about 5:25pm."

The shower did wonders for Pamela's spirit. She combed her hair in a loose twist and fixed it with her horn clasp.

When Andrew came to pick up Pamela, he thought that she looked very charming in her pale-pink blouse and long purple skirt. She wore only pearl earrings from Mrs. Hood. He had changed into a soft-blue shirt, navy tie, and jacket with dark-gray slacks. He took her by the hand while they descended the wide mahogany staircase. Before opening the door to the library, he squeezed it to reassure her.

The earl came to hug his son. "I hear you have brought me a new daughter-to-be."

Hearing this remark erased Pamela's nervousness.

"Yes, Father." Andrew brought Pamela closer. "Please meet my Pamela."

Pamela curtsied, then found herself looking up into a finely chiseled face. The earl's hair was dark with some silver strands. His dark-blue eyes dominated his attractive face. It was a face Pamela found herself drawn to. She recognized a strong resemblance to Andrew.

"Pamela," he said in his deep voice, "we are very pleased to welcome you into our family. You must know Andy made us wait for several months before he finally brought you here."

"Thank you, my lord." Pamela turned toward Andrew's mother. "I had no idea about Andrew's family until now!" She apologized and explained, "You see, it was only two weeks ago when he admitted that he felt like I did—seriously in love!"

Lord Michael chuckled. "You are gaining three charming sisters and two mischievous brothers. They have, in my humble opinion, turned out quite nicely. The credit goes to my beloved wife. I need not mention Andy's fine qualities. You have already discovered those! In addition, you are gaining a mother and a father!"

"Thank you, my lord."

"Ah, Pamela, I propose you call me, let's see, *father*." He gave her a generous hug. "Welcome, dear Pamela."

"I ... I don't know what to say."

"You'll think of something soon enough," he teased.

During dinner, Andrew's father asked Pamela about her family. She told them about her parents—first of her father working at the Home Office before buying a commission in the military where he rose to the position of colonel. He then was appointed military attaché at the British embassy in New Delhi. She explained that after her mother had inherited Swendown, her father's estate, she had decided to sell it to start a school in a rural area in India to allow children to go to school to obtain an education.

"Pamela," Lord Michael interrupted her then, "I think I have heard of your parents' work. Even today both your parents are still held in high esteem. They could have returned to a gentle and comfortable life here. Instead they addressed a great need in India. Does the school still exist?"

"Yes. You knew my parents?" she asked hopefully.

"Unfortunately, not personally. But at the House of Lords and Home Office, I heard your parents' names mentioned. Wasn't he Colonel Adrian Payne and your mother was Lady Elizabeth Mary Rose? She was the daughter of the late Earl of Swendon, Lord William Henry Scott, yes? I have met him several times at the House of Lords."

Pamela's face lit up with joy. "Yes, my mother was his daughter." A shadow spread over her face. "My parents were killed in India."

"I am very sorry about your parents' untimely deaths," Lord Michael expressed sympathy. After a moment, he smiled. "How delightful to not only meet Lord William Henry Scott's granddaughter but even more so to welcome her into our family!"

"Thank you, Father," she addressed him for the first time.

They shared a new bond and understanding.

"Pamela, does the school still exist?" Andrew's mother asked.

"Yes. It has one fund my mother created, which should finance the running of the school for at least fifty years. A separate trust fund was created for future expansions. She had hoped to add education up to college level. I plan to visit it sometime to see how it is doing."

"Perhaps during your honeymoon?" Andrew's father suggested.

The dinner was a happy and relaxed gathering. Pamela was surprised at how comfortable she felt in their midst. She was asked to share the rest of her life story with her new family.

"Pamela," Andrew's mother spoke, "we would be delighted to have you with us for Christmas."

"Oh, that would be wonderful. Thank you, Mama! Now I am looking forward to Christmas!"

After dinner, Andrew's father asked him, "Would you like us to send out invitations to the wedding?"

Andrew looked at Pamela. "What do you think?'

"Yes, please. Thank you, Father."

They worked together to compose the invitation to the wedding.

It is with great pleasure that we

LORD MICHAEL ANTHONY DONALD PRESCOTT
and
LADY PRISCILLA MARY PRESCOTT

announce and invite you to attend the wedding of our son

LORD ANDREW EDWARD MICHAEL PRESCOTT
to
PAMELA DESIRÉE PAYNE
LADY OF SWENDOWN

daughter of the late
COLONEL ADRIAN CHRISTOPHER NIGEL PAYNE
and the late
LADY ELIZABETH MARY ROSE PAYNE.

The wedding ceremony will be held at St. Paul's Church
in Farmington, Kent, at eleven o'clock on 31 December
1980.

A luncheon reception will follow
at My Fair Lady restaurant in Newhurst

RSVP
Lord and Lady Michael Prescott,
Tarrington Abbey, Tarrington, Kent

Before wishing good night, Andrew asked Pamela if she would like to join him for a ride on horseback visiting the villages and farms belonging to the estate on the following morning.

"I have not ridden since I left college. That was three years ago."

"Don't worry, you'll soon feel comfortable in saddle."

It was still dark when Andrew met Pamela to take her to the stables on the following morning where he chose a nice mare for her.

They witnessed the tender birth of a glorious new day. Pamela very much enjoyed riding through the awakening countryside. On their way, they saw families of deer, rabbits, peacocks, and at a distance, some sheep roaming their peaceful meadows while enjoying their leisurely grazing. The horses with several playful foals were led by stable boys to their enclosed meadows to enjoy their freedom.

Andrew introduced Pamela to the farmers working in the fields, women washing laundry or working in their gardens, and children eagerly getting ready to go to school. It was obvious to her that they liked and respected their employers.

CHAPTER 10

The History of Tarrington Abbey

*B*efore their departure on Sunday morning, Andrew took Pamela to see the original foundation of the first abbey.

Andrew began by saying, "It was built by Irish monks during the early fourteenth century. During the two following centuries, the monks did not only build the abbey but also a small hospital and a distillery where they created strong potions to cure many illnesses." Pamela admired the carefully chiseled quarries fitted next to and on top of each other with remarkable precision to create a formidable foundation.

Andrew continued telling her the history. "At the end of the sixteenth century, the entire compound including the abbey had been destroyed. It was not clear who had done this shameful deed! The monks disappeared. For a long time, the whole area was abandoned and grew into a wilderness. At the end of the seventeenth century, the ruins of the foundation was first discovered by an amateur archaeologist named Eric Thompson. Soon after Thompson reported his findings, some Irish monks claimed the property. They demanded the right from the English government to rebuild the abbey, which they did. However, for unknown reasons, the abbey and additional buildings were mercilessly burned down at the beginning of the eighteenth century. Once again, the monks disappeared and were never seen again. The place was left to return into a wilderness. People had forgotten about Tarrington Abbey.

"Then in 1840, after an assassination attempt on the king that was prevented by the quick action of my great-great-grandfather, who took the bullet instead and saved the king's life, he was presented in gratitude with the earldom of Tarrington and given a large parcel of land with surrounding hills, valleys, villages, and fertile farmlands. No one remembered Tarrington Abbey. After my great-great-grandfather had recovered sufficiently and was able to ride his horse again, he roamed the land to decide where to build his future home. He discovered the foundation of the ancient abbey. He researched the history of it and decided to build on top of the sound foundation."

"What a fascinating history. One feels very respectful in a place like this as if some ghosts were still here."

Andrew laughed. "Interesting that you should say this. There are some people who claim that they have seen a monk walking the halls and library on some occasions."

"The poor monk! Perhaps he must be looking for something," Pamela mused.

"Several years ago, Father tried to talk to him when the monk-ghost appeared in the library, but the monk ignored him completely. Father said the ghost, if you believe, kept looking at the floor on the right side of the fireplace."

"Perhaps there is something important still hidden?" Pamela reasoned.

"It is possible. I know Father has often considered removing some of the flooring at that spot, thinking that, perhaps, the monk would find whatever he is looking for and then feel at peace. I am glad you don't seem scared or worried about seeing a monk-ghost."

"Not at all."

"Father will be pleased to know that you, too, suspect that there might be something hidden."

During the long drive back to Farmington, Andrew asked, "How do you feel about your new family?"

Pamela reflected a moment before responding. "Oh, it was ... I never felt so happy and included. Your family is most kind and generous in accepting me without reservations! I never knew that a family could be so warm and harmonious! I don't know how to thank you, my dearest Andrew, for bringing me into your family!"

"I am so very glad to hear you say this, my love. I know they all love you for who you are! You have no idea how very special you are!"

After a moment of silence, Pamela explained, "You see, I have never experienced being with and belonging to a family. Whenever my parents returned from India for a short vacation, they would be so busy attending and giving parties. Mama spent very little time with me. I was probably too young for her to be interesting. I saw Papa only when I would be allowed to go to the parlor to quickly greet the guests."

"How sad! You mentioned that you were six when your parents died. Do you remember them at all?"

"Yes, I remember that I was allowed to watch Mama getting dressed to go out. Watching her maid helping her getting ready reminded me of my playing with my dolls. Mama had a very large collection of silk gowns in radiant colors that were made for her in India. Much of her jewelry had also been custom-made for her by Mr. Dalal, the Indian jeweler in London. On some special occasions, she wore the Swendown tiara, which looked very pretty. She appeared to me like a princess."

"Do you remember your father?"

"I remember very little about him. He seemed to avoid me and almost never talked to me. There was one ... no, a couple of occasions, when I saw him in his full dress uniform as colonel of his regiment in a glorious red coat laden with gold braids, lots of color stripes, and several medals pinned to his chest. He did not look like my father then. He was too grand and proud. I didn't know what to do. I think he felt equally awkward with me."

"Did you feel lonely as a child?" Andrew asked with sympathy.

"Not as long as I was with Bambi, my nanny. But when she was asked to leave and an ugly and severe governess was installed by my uncle, I became rebellious! I really hated her and prayed each evening that she would die and leave me alone." Pamela chuckled at her remembering of the past. "I was so horrid to her that she resigned! As punishment I was sent to a boarding school for girls and St. Mary's College later on."

"I cannot imagine you being horrid!" Andrew teased.

She laughed. "I am certain that you wouldn't have liked me then!"

"What is important is the way you have turned out, which is quite nicely!"

"Thank you." She was silent for a long time until she looked at him. "Andrew, I would like to ask you something."

"If I know the answer, I will tell you."

"You are the oldest son of your parents—the earl and countess of Tarrington. Does this mean you are a viscount and that one day—hopefully in the far-distant future—you will become an earl?"

"Yes, but not for a very long time, God willing! Unless something terrible happens." He reached for Pamela's hand and kissed it. "Darling, there is no need to worry about this!"

"Do the people in Farmington know who you are?"

"No. I wanted to be and to earn their respect for myself, not my title. Do you understand?"

"Yes, very well. I will not disclose your secret," Pamela promised.

"It is now *our* secret!"

Andrew stopped in at her cottage for a cup of tea before he would leave for his apartment.

Pamela found with her mail a letter from her uncle. "Please, Andrew, wait so that I can tell you what he writes." She opened the envelope and read:

Our Dear Pamela,

We hope that this letter finds you and your charming fiancé in good health and spirit! You have chosen a fine young man as your future husband!

Your Aunt Hillary and I thought it would be very nice to have you over for Christmas so that we can get to know one another better. As you know, there is plenty of room to put you up! If your Andrew has no other plans, he would be, of course, most cordially invited to join us as well!

Hilly and I have so much to tell you about your parents—things we should have shared with you a long time ago!

We hope you will find forgiveness in your heart for our neglecting you during all the years you grew up without our guidance and affection.

Please call us when you receive this letter so that we can plan on a modest family Christmas! Our telephone number is 17-38-29-45.

With anticipation and affection,

Aunt Hillary and after…Uncle Winston

PS. Let us know with which train you plan to arrive so that we can pick you up at the station.

"Oh, Andrew, what should I do? I already promised to be with your family on Christmas."

After a moment of hesitation, he responded, "I have the impression that your uncle and aunt would like to make up so much lost time with you. I think they must feel very guilty. I could tell that your uncle was eager to take you back, so to speak."

Pamela contemplated for a long moment. "Perhaps it is important to them and to me as well. I would very much like to know more about my parents. Will your parents understand?"

"Oh, yes, absolutely! I know that they will understand and be happy for you to finally have a family of your own. Yes, Pamela, I think it is important that you spend this Christmas with them."

"I also feel I must. Please explain to your parents how much I appreciate their wish to include me for Christmas."

"I will tell them," he promised. "So you will be leaving the weekend before Christmas. I'll take you to the station."

"Thank you, Andrew. Is it not amazing that all of a sudden, I have two families?"

He embraced her. "Yes! I am so very happy for you … for us!"

CHAPTER 11

Reconciliation

*T*rue to their promise, Uncle Winston and Aunt Hillary received Pamela at the train station and drove her home. During the ride, Uncle Winston told her about the hidden Chislehurst caves that served as bomb shelters during World War II. The town was very pleasant as most houses had gardens around them. When they arrived at 1 Stonehenge Crest, Pamela experienced mixed feelings but said nothing.

Uncle Winston chuckled suddenly. "Oh, we forgot to tell you that we hired a young girl who would like to earn a little extra money as a lady's maid, and our old cook agreed to help out while you are here so that Hilly and I will have more time to enjoy your company."

"My goodness, there was no need. I am not used to being pampered."

"Never mind. Your aunt thought it would be nice."

"While Whinny is parking his Dragon, we'll go inside to warm ourselves."

A young girl opened the front door and curtsied. "Good afternoon, ma'am and my lady."

"Good afternoon," Pamela responded.

"This is Maddy, our lady's maid. Good afternoon, Maddy." Aunt Hillary introduced the girl.

Where is Mannon? Pamela wondered.

They gave their coats to Maddy.

"Lady Pamela may wish to rest and freshen up," Aunt Hillary suggested.

Maddy was a sweet-looking girl with a round red face wearing a black dress with a lace collar and a crisp white cap.

Pamela responded, "Yes, I think I would like to rest and freshen up a bit."

"I thought you might enjoy staying in your mother's bedroom."

"Thank you, Aunt Hillary. Yes, I remember her bedroom." Pamela followed Maddy upstairs, then through the gallery, but she wasn't prepared for the initial shock of remembering the room without her mother in it! Pamela found that she had to swallow tears.

"Would you like me to unpack your suitcase, my lady?" Maddy asked.

"No, thank you, Maddy. Please don't call me my lady. I am not yet married to Lord Andrew."

"But Mrs. Payne said that you were a lady born from your mother's side."

Pamela was surprised that her aunt would even remember this. She smiled at Maddy. "If you like to call me thus, you are welcome."

Maddy beamed. "You see, you are the first lady I am serving as a lady's maid! Is there anything I can bring you? A cup of tea?"

"No, thank you, Maddy. I'll just rest a bit and freshen up."

Maddy walked to the bed. "Here is the bell-pull if you need me." She curtsied quickly and left Pamela alone.

Her favorite painting—a triptych—was still hanging over the low dresser. Pamela remembered when she was little how she used to stand in front of it and gaze at it with the feeling that she was witnessing the painted scenes.

On the left panel of the triptych, Saint Elizabeth is depicted wearing a dark-purple gown and a light-gray apron filled with food. She is distributing it the poor who are huddled on one side outside the castle wall. On the right panel, the painting depicts her tyrant husband and his soldiers approaching the castle, surprising her by returning early from a journey. On the center panel, which is the largest painting, Saint Elizabeth's husband is sitting on a black stallion dressed in armor and helmet with fierce-looking bodyguards and soldiers. His hand is pointing to Saint Elizabeth's apron, challenging her, "What do you have in your apron? If it is food from my table for these wretched creatures, I will kill you!" Saint Elizabeth stands serenely while replying, "I have only roses." She opens her apron and beautiful white roses tumble to the ground.

Pamela smiled. The painting still exuded magic, and she liked it still!

She looked around her mother's bedroom. It was still the way she remembered it. "Mama," she whispered, "I am back. How I wish you were here with me!"

Suddenly Pamela felt exhausted and intended to only lie down for a few minutes but must have fallen asleep. Her watch told her it was five o'clock. After washing and exchanging her travel clothes with a deep-blue velvet dress from Mrs. Hood's collection, she then combed her hair and added one string of pearls.

Pamela found her relatives in the library. They had moved a third chair near the fireplace to allow all of them to sit close enough to enjoy the warmth generated by the gentle fire. "I am terribly sorry if I kept you waiting! I didn't intend to fall asleep."

"Don't worry, dear, you are on vacation!" her aunt assured her.

Uncle Winston cleared his throat before speaking. "Pamela, thank you for coming. Hilly and I are very pleased that you came. We have much, so very much, to make up for!"

She smiled at him. "Yes, I, too, am glad to get to know you better."

She paused then chuckled, "I am certain you remember me as an absolutely horrid little girl!"

"To tell you the truth," her uncle sounded amused, "we really didn't know what to do with you. Here we had no children. Then all of a sudden, we had this little niece to take care of. It didn't work out so well, did it?"

"Yes, Uncle Winston," Pamela confessed. "You looked so very imposing in your black coat and hat that I was really scared of you. When you told me that Mama and Papa had died in India, I didn't believe you! I thought you made it up to punish me and because you didn't like me!"

"It was such a tragedy," Aunt Hillary added. "We felt very sorry for you but didn't know what would be best for you."

"And your nanny treated you like a baby. That is why I fired her," Uncle Winston explained. "But the governess didn't turn out so well either."

Pamela laughed. "Ah yes, I remember her! I prayed each night that she might die!"

Her uncle nodded. "I suspected that much. Did you also pray that I and Aunt Hillary would die?"

"Funny!" Pamela chuckled. "That didn't occur to me."

"You must know, Pamela," Aunt Hillary said, "that your uncle kept close track of your grades at your school and St. Mary's. He wanted to know how you were doing. The headmistress asked him repeatedly to come and visit you, but we were afraid."

"Why?"

Uncle Winston answered, "I was afraid that you might want to come home. We would be at a loss once again what to do with you. Also, we didn't want you to know that we had moved into your home."

There was a long moment of silence until Pamela asked, "Was I really that horrid a child?"

Her aunt hastened to explain. "Oh no! You were actually a nice little girl. At least, most of the time. But when we first sent Bambi away and then took you to the boarding school, you displayed quite a temper tantrum!"

Pamela smiled. "I am glad that all that is behind us! It is very nice to meet you both as adults."

During dinner Aunt Hillary said, "Pamela, you look so much like your dear mother! She seemed to be always dreaming and living in another world!"

"There are so many things you need to know about your parents." Her uncle had turned serious. "I don't know how much you remember. It is hard to know where to begin!"

"And there are a lot of things from your mother you may want to have!" her aunt added.

"Well," Uncle Winston began, "let me start with your parents' wedding. Your mother was the only daughter of the last Earl of Swendown, Lord William Henry Scott. An unreasonably strict gentleman, if I may so!" He paused an instant. "When your mother fell in love with your dashing father, Colonel Adrian Christopher Nigel Payne, my brother, she announced to her parents that she was going to marry the colonel. The earl grew very angry. He didn't want his only daughter to marry below her station and threatened to disown her. He assumed that her love was only an infatuation and that she would soon realize her mistake and heed him. But it didn't turn out that way. They eloped to Gretna Green and got married. Adrian asked for and received transfer to the British embassy in New Delhi. When my brother was posted in India, your mother went with him. Meanwhile, your grandfather, the earl, in retaliation, disinherited your mother. Only shortly before his death did he write a new will to reinstate your mother as sole heiress to his earldom and estate. Therefore, she and her future descendants will inherit the titles of *lord* and *lady*.

"While your father stayed in India for a long time, your mother would sometimes return here for some months and stay alone in this house before joining your father again in India. One day, Lady Elizabeth your mother, found out that she was pregnant."

Aunt Hillary interrupted her husband. "I must give Whinny credit for persuading your mother to go home to her parents. Her father, the earl, was ailing and was not told that his daughter had returned home and was about to give birth to a baby! You were born at the Swendown Manor in hiding!"

Uncle Winston resumed. "Then you arrived—a darling bundle but also a big problem."

"Whinny, you make it sound as if you blame Pamela!"

"I only wanted to tell Pamela that her mother wanted to go back to India, but she knew that she couldn't take the baby with her!" Uncle Winston argued.

"That is when your nanny, Bamb , was engaged to take care of you."

"Yes. Your mother didn't know until her father, the earl, had died that he had reinstated her in his last will and testament as sole heiress to his entire estate."

"Your parents were able to come home on home leave every fourteen months. Do you remember them at all?"

Pamela smiled. "Yes, I remember Mama mostly getting ready to go out. I also remember my parents having lots of strange people over. I think I was too little for them to take much interest in me or spend some time in the nursery."

"You see, they were very popular," her uncle explained. "And whenever they left again for India, Adrian, your father, turned over to me the responsibility of supervising your development. He had appointed me as your legal guardian. As such, I recognized that your nanny protected and kept you safely in the nursery. She was a good nanny, but when you had turned six years old, it was time for you to start schooling."

After dinner, they returned to sit near the fireplace in the library.

Pamela turned thoughtful before admitting, "I realize only now what you have done for me, believing whatever you decided was in the best interest for me for my benefit. I am grateful to you! I have to apologize for my childish behavior. I hope to be, from now onward, a more understanding and appreciative niece to you and Aunt Hillary."

"Oh, we loved you even then!" Aunt Hillary tried to reassure Pamela. "It was just … your mother was such a lady, always very kind but distant. Whinny and I felt totally inadequate in her presence as we both were not born into nobility."

Uncle Winston changed the subject. "My father, your paternal grandfather, was an investor. He was a good man! He was particularly interested in mines. He owned several in Wales and one in Africa. For many years, he had tremendous good fortune and made a handsome amount of money. However, after he had visited and closely inspected some of his coal mines, he realized the atrocious working and living conditions of the miners and their families. He spent a lot of money to improve the safety constructions in the mine shafts and tunnels. He strictly forbade that children be sent to work underground! Instead he built and opened schools and hired teachers for them. He also insisted that none of his workers spend more than eight hours in the mines. My father was the first mineowner to introduce three shifts of working crews for every twenty-four hours. He also built better cottages with fireplaces for which he would give the families free coal to keep them warm during the mean winter months. When he realized the need for an infirmary, he installed one for the miners and their family members to be treated free of charge. All this reduced his profits drastically.

Some of his fellow-mineowners called him a communist and an idiot, arguing that there were always more than enough miners to replace the sick or dead ones.

Pamela's uncle continued telling his father's history. "Your grandfather wanted to return to Africa to inspect his mines again, but he suffered a heart attack and died shortly before his planned departure. So I went instead to see the conditions. It was a lucrative mine but, the treatment and working conditions of the workers were abominable! I tried to stop the beating of workers when they dropped exhausted to the ground, but the managers were unwilling to stop it, arguing that they would have mutiny on their hands. I wondered many times what Father would have done. Finally, I decided to sell the mines in Africa. All of a sudden, we had a lot of cash! Your father and I decided to invest in railroad companies here in England and America."

Aunt Hillary reminded her husband, "Don't forget to tell about our house."

"I was just getting to that, Hilly."

Pamela was observing her relatives and felt amused at how her aunt was eager to contribute to the story, thinking that her husband might forget.

"Yes, yes!" He nodded and resumed. "Your father, being the first son, inherited this house. But your father, bless him, insisted that I and Hilly should also have a comfortable house. So Hilly and I set out to look for property. We soon found a pretty house that she liked. So we moved to Windsor Road, 30 Horseshoe Crescent, here in Chislehurst. Pamela, do you remember the house?"

"Vaguely. I think I visited only a couple of times."

"After we sent you to boarding school, Hilly and I decided to move into your father's house and sell ours. As you know, this house is really far too large for just the two of us. But we thought at that time, perhaps one day, you may wish to return here. By then, you might have a husband and children. This is, after all, your inheritance!"

A moment of awkward silence followed before Pamela gathered her courage to ask, "Uncle Winston, you sounded so angry when you came to Farmington. Why?"

"Yes," her uncle nodded gravely. "I am afraid I wasn't very nice to you."

"Your uncle wasn't very pleased when he found out that you had studied and graduated at the academy without his consent. He traced you to the pension at Shrewsbury and later heard that you had moved out. He grew worried that you would want to return to your home and force us to move out! But when he was informed that you had inherited a cottage in Farmington and moved there without letting us know, he was furious at your acting independently. He said that you need not return to Chislehurst ever!"

Uncle Winston admitted, "Well, yes that's, true! I got angry when you didn't tell us during our surprise visit that you owned the place. You gave vague answers open to interpretation!" He paused, then continued. "Perhaps I ought to apologize for having threatened you. Of course, I knew that you had come of age and that my guardianship had expired, if you will. Of course, we know that this house is yours! In my anger, I said things I hope you have forgotten!"

After a brief silence, Pamela said, "There is one thing you said that hurt me deeply. You said that I wasn't worthy of the Payne family name! Do you still think so?"

Her uncle pulled out his handkerchief and wiped his forehead before responding, "No, not at all! I admit it was a mean thing to say. This is precisely what I want you to forget! I must tell you that your parents would be very proud of you! And so are Hilly and I. I must tell you, Pamela, that I regretted threatening you immediately afterward. Can you forgive your old uncle?"

"But then you had the fire being set ..."

"Ah, that! Yes." Uncle Winston stared at his hands. "I didn't want you to stay there. I wanted to scare you enough to leave so that I could never trace your whereabouts again. I felt guilty and wanted

Hilly and myself to forget about you." He shook his head in disbelief. "I really cannot explain. It was a crazy thing to do!" He looked at Pamela. "I hope there was not too much damage done?"

"It was mostly the backs of books that burned. Andrew found a man who does those kinds of repairs. We'll have them restored."

"I am glad to hear. Pamela, you must send me the bill for all the repairs. I won't hear any argument about this!" he insisted.

She smiled and went over to him. "Thank you, Uncle Winston." She hugged him. "Andrew will take care of everything." She went over to her aunt and gave her a hug also. "Let's not mention this episode ever again, please."

Both her relatives sighed with relief. "Thank you, Pamela."

"Do you think my parents were happy?" Pamela asked.

Aunt Hillary responded immediately, "Yes. I guess at least for a couple of years. But I always wondered why she would return here and stay for months alone in this big house."

"Hilly, you forget Pamela was there with her nurse! She must have been pleased to have some peace of mind for some time," Uncle Winston suggested. "One thing I cannot understand is why her father, the earl, never told her that he had reinstated her as his sole heiress. He did not even attend your parents' wedding! We saw the earl on a couple of occasions from a distance. He was probably a decent chap, but he always appeared distant and proud, totally unapproachable."

"Because he was an earl after all!" Aunt Hillary explained.

"In my humble opinion," Pamela's uncle argued, "that is no excuse for not attending his only daughter's wedding!"

"Please tell me more about Papa. I never got the feeling that he cared for me."

Uncle Winston began by saying, "Adrian had worked at the Home Office for two years but never cared very much for his work there.

He was shy. He never went out of his way to get to know people. I think that is why he chose the military. It gave him a structured way of life. He felt secure within the rules and rose to colonel! Quite an achievement! We were stunned how many military brass and dignitaries attended his memorial funeral service in London. The Royal Regiment had arranged for it. There was a pillow on his flag-draped coffin with five medals. He had been well-liked and held in high esteem by his peers."

"We have a beautiful case with all five medals upstairs in your father's room!" Aunt Hillary informed Pamela.

"How about Mama? Was she well-liked?"

"Oh, your mother was like a fragile doll!" Pamela's aunt smiled. "She was very beautiful and charming with her friends. Whinny and I were not moving in the same circles, but I liked your mother … from a distance."

"When did they decide to open the school in India?"

"While Adrian, your father, was stationed as military attaché with the embassy in New Delhi, he had to travel throughout India. He took your mother with him whenever she was in India." Uncle Winston explained. "During those trips, your mother was most distressed at the lack of access to education—schools so many rural children didn't have. But when your grandfather, the earl, died and your mother inherited, she sold the entire estate and decided to open one school in a rural location in India that would be within reasonable distance from various villages. In India, in those days, women, especially a foreign lady, weren't able to start any kind of business on their own! So Adrian resigned from his military position to help your mother to create a school in India on their own. Your mother found the ideal village called Dhalarnabad. She founded her school, which she called Lady Elizabeth Mary Rose School. She had great hopes to not only create an elementary and high school but possibly also a college at a later date. She used all proceeds of the Swendown estate's sale to set up a fund to finance the school for the next fifty years. She also created a separate trust fund to be used only for future expansions. It was not to be touched by anyone except herself, her husband or you, her heiress Pamela Desirée Payne."

Aunt Hillary sighed. "And then they were killed by an idiotic truck driver!"

"What happened to them? Were their bodies sent home? Where is their grave?" Pamela asked with intense curiosity.

Both her relatives exchanged glances. They were hesitant to tell her.

"I am sad to tell you," Uncle Winston began, "but your parents were cremated like Hindus. It was impossible to preserve their bodies for shipment. After eight weeks, we received one urn with the explanation that both your parents' ashes had been combined in that urn."

Pamela shook her head. "But didn't you tell me a moment ago about my father's memorial funeral in London with all the military brass and dignitaries attending?"

Her uncle nodded. "Yes, I did. And yes, there was a funeral officially for your father in London. But the flag-draped coffin contained only one cup of your father's and your mother's ashes. The ceremony of honor was offered by and for the military and Home Office."

"Where is the urn now?"

"It is buried here in the garden. We had a private memorial service here in Chislehurst. Our vicar said blessings and prayers before the urn was set in the earth. We planted a gorgeous rhododendron over it with a marble stone bearing their names and dates."

"Where was I during that time?" Pamela asked urgently.

Her uncle replied with reluctance, "You had just started at the boarding school. The headmistress said you had a very hard time adjusting to your new environment and did recommend that you not attend your parents' burial. She said that it would be impossible to explain to you how both your parents ended up in one small urn. She said it might be too upsetting for you."

Aunt Hillary added an indirect apology, "Having no experience with children, we accepted the headmistress's advice."

"I see ..."

After another awkward silence, her aunt tried to sound cheerful, "We have a whole drawer full of letters, souvenirs, and medals for you!"

"Tomorrow we will show you their grave and lots of interesting things."

It was late by the time they wished one another good night.

Pamela tossed and turned in bed, hoping to find sleep but her mind was racing. It was barely dawn when she went into the garden to look for her parents' grave marker. It was on a slightly elevated lawn section with the rhododendron bush placed like a crown just behind the marble plate. She knelt down and traced the engraved names with a tender finger, caressing it. "Goodbye ..."

She returned to her room, undressed, and went back to bed. Finally, she was able to fall asleep. To her surprise, it was ten o'clock when she woke up.

"Ah, good morning, Pamela!" Uncle Winston greeted her when she entered the small dining room. "Hilly told me not to wake you for breakfast. Did you sleep well?"

"Yes," she lied. "Thank you." She felt embarrassed. "It is almost too late to wish you both good morning. I am sorry to be so late."

"Don't be silly, Pamela," her aunt responded. "It just so happens that we, too, are late. Therefore, we can all have breakfast together." She moved the various dishes closer to Pamela. "What would you like to do today?"

Pamela reminded her aunt, "Didn't you mention yesterday that you would like to show me some things of my parents?"

"Yes, of course. I don't know how much you remember about your parents and this house though."

"I would be interested to see more. It is possible that I may remember things when I see the rooms."

"Good. Your uncle has his solicitor coming this morning. I think this is a very good time for us to explore, don't you agree?"

It was bittersweet for Pamela to go from one room to another as memories became alive in her mind. The grand concert piano was still there at the same corner in the music room. It was covered with a large white sheet like most of the furniture in the other rooms. She wanted to pull down the sheets, which seemed to her like sleeping ghosts! She would have liked to open the drapes and shutters to allow sunlight and fresh air to enter this slumbering tomb! But she didn't mention this to her aunt.

Next to the long dining room was a smaller one closer to the butler's pantry and kitchen. The heirloom china, crystals, and some candelabras were neatly displayed in glass vitrines. Aunt Hillary opened one wide double-door wall closet where silver platters, trays, bowls, and countless additional candelabras had been carefully placed on silver-tarnish-retardant velour-covered shelves with equally lined walls and doors to keep them shiny and ready for the next formal occasion. Pamela remembered having seen some of them on the splendidly prepared dining table before a grand dinner. The three crystal chandeliers were shrouded in thin cloths. The long dining table and chairs were also covered with overlapping white sheets.

In contrast, the kitchen was old with a huge hearth, blackened hooks, and one large grate. It had been sealed off by glass to prevent draft and dust. "This is just to remember old times!" Aunt Hillary chuckled.

Against the other walls were modern appliances still sufficient to create feasts for a large crowd. Two walls were covered with once-shiny copper pots from the smallest butter heater to the largest turkey pans. They were covered with a thin layer of dust, hiding their beautiful, rich color.

"Would you like to see your nursery?"

Pamela hesitated for an instant. "Later perhaps. However, I would like to see the atrium."

"Ah, I am afraid that atrium is not doing very well. Nobody knows enough about plants to keep them healthy. We have asked Mannon to care for the plants, but he is too old to do the work, I am afraid."

"I meant to ask about Mannon."

Aunt Hillary seemed evasive: "He ... he had a cold and decided to spend Christmas with his sister in Dorking."

Pamela didn't believe her but replied, "I hope he'll recover soon! Perhaps I'll see him before I leave?"

"I think he plans to spend New Year's Eve also with his sister."

Even with the cautionary introduction about the condition of the atrium, it was a shock for Pamela to see the chaos of half-dead plants fighting for space while some had completely dried out. She didn't comment and left the veranda room.

Aunt Hillary rushed after her. "I am sorry, Pamela."

"I remember Mama saying that the atrium required more care than the rest of our garden. It is not your fault nor the fault of Mannon!"

After lunch, Uncle Winston suggested they visit the Chislehurst Caves to where the emergency shelter during WW II were.

Pamela was amazed how well and thoughtful the sleeping quarters, the eating areas, the kitchen, the toilets and washrooms, the storage rooms as well as the hospital facilities, the pharmacy, and not least, the supply lines for and countless tanks of oxygen were arranged to provide efficient service. There were even small cribs for babies. The only section that was closed off was the radio and communication center within the cave.

"I most sincerely hope there will never be cause to have to use these again!" Uncle Winston commented in a solemn voice as they were leaving.

Back at the manor, while Pamela's uncle prepared drinks, she explored the bookcases. She remembered this room only as having been allowed in simply to quickly say good evening and curtsy to the guests her parents were entertaining.

Touring the house, she found so many fragments of memories tumbling loose in her mind. Sometimes she felt like laughing, and other times she felt like crying. *What would my life be like if my parents were still alive?* she wondered, then decided, *I must chase all painful memories out of the windows and fill the house with sunshine and music! It will be a happy place once Andrew and I come to live here!*

After retiring for the evening, Pamela found that she wasn't yet ready to go to sleep. She climbed up to the nursery. She wanted to do this alone as she was uncertain how she would feel seeing her first world without Bambi. The rooms were on the third floor in another wing. She went to her own bedroom first and turned on the light. In one corner was her small crib, and next to it was a larger bed. Both were covered with ghostly sheets. There was a square low table with two small chairs near the windows. She discovered framed photographs of her parents hanging over two bookcases. One was at a garden party at Buckingham Palace with Queen Elizabeth II. Another showed her mother in a gorgeous purple sari while Papa wore the Royal Regiment's dress uniform. It looked like that one had been taken in India, probably at an embassy function. Then there were several formal photos of her parents' wedding. Her mother was wearing the gown, veil, and tiara that Pamela would be wearing in a week for her own wedding! *I am going to take these with me!* she decided while continuing her former-nursery exploration. Well-used books of nursery rhymes and Beatrix Potter's stories lay dormant on the shelves between some of her favorite dolls, rabbits, and well-loved teddy bears. It seemed such a very long time ago! In a small cabinet, she saw painting supplies and more children's storybooks. One of her favorites was *The Tale of Peter Rabbit*! She imagined Bambi reading it to her. It was then that she broke down in tears.

Later she didn't know how long she had wept until the deep hurt of losing Bambi was soothed. She didn't know if she mourned for herself or for the loss of Bambi or her parents. *My dearest Bambi, wherever you are, I hope you are happy!* Even though Bambi had protected her as much as she could, she could not prevent the pains of separation. Pamela realized that she did miss her parents, especially her gentle mother! After she calmed down, she reminded herself that after her parents had died, it was her uncle who had made all his decisions with his best intentions! She dried her tears and removed all the photographs of her parents. She found behind one of the framed photographs a surprised spider that scrambled to save itself. It was the only thing alive in this room of eternal slumber!

CHAPTER   12

Pamela Finds Her Mother's Letter

*H*aving returned to the main wing and her mother's bedroom, Pamela still couldn't sleep. She went to her mother's dressing room with the floor-to-ceiling wall closets. In one were many day dresses arranged according to their pastel colors, light and winter coats, jackets, and one long almost-black sable coat. From a higher rod were blouses and sweaters with matching jackets also arranged according to their colors. Underneath on another rod were skirts and kilts neatly arranged. The clothes seemed to have been chosen to match into sets. In the next closet, Pamela found long gowns from the deepest velvet black to gray, white, ivory, pale to dark blues, soft to rich yellows, orange to red, scarlet, and then purple. Many had beads or seed-pearl embroideries on the bodices. On a shelf below were neatly folded shawls. In yet another closet she discovered silk saris of all rainbow colors decorated with imaginative designs with broad gold and silver borders woven, each with a matching blouse and petticoat. Below was a shelf that stored dainty slippers to evening high-heeled shoes. In the last closet were boots, sensible walking shoes on the bottom shelf, then handbags for travel and smaller purses for daily use. On two higher shelves were a couple of tropical helmets and hats in all shapes, sizes, and colors. *When could Mama wear all these things?* Pamela wondered.

Inspired by her discoveries, she went to explore her mother's vanity. Arranged in front of the triple mirror were a few fancy perfume bottles. She opened the top of one and found it had a very strong tropical scent. An antique brush, comb, and hand mirror set with engraved silver handles and backs were set out on the glass top. In the small top drawer she found cosmetic jars of various sizes, a couple of perfumed powder jars, an open tray with charcoals, pencil eyeliners, and brushes and lipsticks of many colors. In the lower drawer she found nail polishes from transparent, pale-pink, to deep-dark-red colors. Sets of nail scissors, files, and sand brushes were set in another tray. Pamela shook her head in amazement. She remembered watching her mother getting ready to go out, but she had no idea how elaborate her preparations for her appearances had been!

Led by curiosity, she went to her mother's dresser. In one of the two top drawers she found small elegant evening purses in all possible colors, short and long gloves, and lots of dainty handkerchiefs with laces. The other contained various jewelry cases for rings, brooches, necklaces, and bracelets. Pamela opened a couple and found that they were for everyday use, nothing expensive. In a drawer below were carefully folded delicate silk lingerie in pastel colors and black. She didn't touch those and was about to close the drawer when she noticed a corner of paper sticking out from underneath a pile of petticoats. She pulled it out and was shocked to see her name on the envelope. "Mama," she whispered in awe. She went to the bed and sat down. For a long moment, she didn't dare to open it. Finally, she gathered enough courage, opened the envelope, and started to read:

January 1965

My sweet little darling girl, Pamela Desirée,

Each time we come here for a visit and I see you, I fall in love with you! You have no idea how very desperate I feel each time we have to return to India and leave you behind! I am only grateful for our dear Bambi who is protecting you! But even then, it breaks my heart when we have to leave you behind! My husband tells me that I should not grieve as we have so many children in India. He does not understand that you are the only treasure I love with all my heart and soul! I try to be very brave and not cry. God only knows how terribly I miss you!

I have no idea when you may find this letter, if at all! I do hope it will remain safely sealed because it is for you only! I do hope by that time you will be quite grown-up and understand.

I want you to remember always that your father—even though he doesn't know—and I love you very, very much! I have no idea what will happen to us in India. It is a restless country with many unhappy and neglected people! The future is most uncertain for everyone!

I want to explain to you why we have returned to India (after my husband had resigned from the Home Office and military service). After my father, the late Lord William Henry Scott, Earl of Swendown, your grandfather, had passed away, I had inherited his entire Swendown estate. My husband persuaded me to sell it so that we were able to establish trust funds to create a school for rural children in India. With a heavy heart, I agreed to the sale. I knew we would never be able to live there! But I must secretly confess that it was dreadfully sad to leave my beloved home to strangers! I had always hoped to show you the beautiful old manor and park! My husband must never know of this … this … my profound sorrow! But I must not think of this!

The school is named after me. I would have liked to name it Swendown School, but my husband and some Indian friends suggested that my name should be given. It is now named Lady Elizabeth Mary Rose School. It is located in a small village called Dhalarnabad. With the proceeds from my father's estate, we built a large main hall with an auditorium, a dining hall, and a kitchen. We have thirty students at the moment. There are, so far, two school buildings—one for first through fourth grades and the other for fifth through tenth grades. I hope that, one day, we can expand our curriculum to college level! We have one dormitory for those children who live too far to walk to and from their homes each day. They return on weekends. Then we have two buildings with several bright and airy classrooms and study halls with a well-stocked library next door (I had shipped most English classic literature, several world atlases and world maps from my father's library here, and all my favorite great novels!) Then there is a laundry, and next to it are shower rooms. Before we started building, we explored the water tables. As a result, we have three very deep wells to assure adequate water supply for the entire campus. We also have a small infirmary just in case a student gets hurt or sick. I have my office in a small separate building. Our teachers live in several small cottages adjacent to the campus. Then there are modest cottages for our employees. My husband and I live in a two-story house also adjacent to the campus. It is very modest! I am still hoping to bring you with us to India when you are a bit older so that you can meet our children and study with them. I have shown them photographs of you, and they are very eager to meet you!

Imagine, some of our students walk five kilometers from their homes to school in the mornings and return in the late afternoons! Luckily, we have very good cooks who provide healthy and nourishing meals for them! We have our own tailors, gardeners, cobbler, plumber, and mechanics to keep everything in top shape!

Last year we decided to have uniforms made for the students—navy-blue skirts and white blouses for girls and navy-blue slacks and white shirts for boys. For the colder season, they have matching navy-blue jackets. I designed and had a clever tailor make labels with (this time I insisted as I am entitled by birthright to the name!) the Swendown arms for the jackets! They look very handsome, and the students are so happy! Then, of course, we had our cobbler make very good walking shoes!

My husband teaches reading, writing, and geography and conducts study hall so that each student has access to assistance as needed. I teach Western and Asian history (my favorite subjects!) next to my running the office. We found a wonderfully gifted musician who teaches all students various instruments. He knows Western and Indian classical music. In addition, we have a small chorus, and I play an old piano (from the British embassy in Delhi). So you can see, we have a small orchestra! We just hired four new teachers to instruct hygiene and nutrition, arts, sciences, and mathematics.

I forgot to mention earlier that the location for our school was chosen to be in the center of several rural villages to offer as many children as possible the opportunity for a good education and to better their futures!

But there is one thing that scares me to death, and I simply cannot accept it nor get used to. It is the lorry drivers! The trucks are always overloaded and chronically in very bad mechanical condition. But what is worse is that the drivers speed on our extremely uneven country roads with lots of potholes! Recently, we had two people from one village killed by such a truck! Luckily, our students walk and, therefore, are able to jump to the side when they see a lorry driver barreling toward them! Still I am worried all the time! But please, do not worry, my darling, my husband does not drive himself! He has hired a former employee of the British embassy, an Indian, who had been hired to drive the ambassador and his staff. He is very experienced, careful, and reliable! He drives us wherever we have to go.

Whenever we are here in England—home—I take photos of you to treasure and keep them with me until our next reunion! I miss you most dreadfully, my darling Pamela Desirée! But I must not end this letter with something sad!

I bought in Delhi, on our way home to you, some lovely silk materials for you to have dresses made. I hope you will like them!

I kiss your photograph as I say "Goodbye" and "May God bless you"! My sweet darling Pamela Desirée, always remember that you are closest to my heart wherever I am!

I am so very sorry that we will miss your sixth birthday celebration, which is in one week!

Your loving mother

Pamela felt numb. After a long while, she opened the window and gazed at the moon and wondered, *Mama, can you see me? How I wish you were here! I, too, miss you dreadfully! Do you know what happened to me after your accidents? It was a long and lonely life until I found the Maria Montessori Academy for Teachers. But even then, inside I felt lonely and abandoned. But then two miracles happened! Mrs. Henrietta Spencer Hood and Andrew Prescott! Mrs. Hood gave me her cottage after she passed away, and this is how I met Andrew! He is a barrister and mayor. He is very kind and thoughtful. We are going to get married on the last day of this year! How I wish Papa were able to lead me down the aisle, but Uncle Winston will do it. Andrew has a large and lively family who live in a nice old manor called Tarrington Abbey. They have accepted me as I am! Andrew's father had heard of you and Papa at the Home Office. Then his father mentioned that he had known your father from the House of Lords! How small the world is! Mama, please do never leave me so I can talk to you when I miss you so terribly!*

The hooting of an owl interrupted Pamela's thoughts. She smiled when she realized that she suddenly felt peaceful and decided to return to bed.

To her surprise, she woke up at ten o'clock!

CHAPTER   13

Christmas at Tarrington Abbey

*I*t had always been a tradition at Tarrington Abbey that on the first Sunday of December, the family would gather whenever possible so that each member could draw a straw with a name of one of the other family members. It was only for that person that a gift was to be selected. The limit was fifty English pounds. This way, each had to give only one present. Andrew's straw had Lilly's name! He was undecided about what to give her. When he asked Pamela, she suggested a cashmere scarf or leather gloves or a book on horses, which Lilly loved. He bought at Harrod's an elegant fountain pen.

This would be the last Christmas Andrew would celebrate without Pamela! It was a lively time of celebration with lots of teasing and laughter and, of course, guessing who had selected his or her gift! It was a very sensible agreement to give one present only. The donor was supposed to remain a secret.

It was only on Christmas morning when it was permissible to come downstairs to the library in dressing gowns and slippers to open the gifts. Then it was tradition that the youngest be the first to open his or her gift. It was always Lilly! When she saw the pen from

Harrod's, she was thrilled and tried immediately to guess who had selected her present, but nobody admitted!

Andrew was the last before his parents to open his gift. It was a large nicely wrapped box. He shook it, but there was nothing moving inside. Finally, he opened it to find an old *pot de chambre*! Everybody screamed with laughter. He detected a small box attached to one side. After opening it, he found an envelope inside with two fifty-pound notes with a note: *For dear Pamela and Andrew to help fulfill small wishes, perhaps during your honeymoon!* Andrew was very touched by the gesture of including Pamela and, although he strongly suspected his parents to be the generous spenders, thanked the unknown gift-giver!

Even though everybody was in great spirits, Andrew missed Pamela. He knew that she was returning on Boxing Day and decided to return to Farmington late on Christmas Day. His family understood that there were still many preparations to be made before their wedding day. He called Pamela's home early on the following morning, but she hadn't returned. He took a chance and went to the railway station, parked the car, and entered the hall when Pamela got off the train.

She was surprised and overjoyed to see him. "Oh, Andrew, my darling, what a beautiful surprise! How did you know when I would reach Farmington? I missed you so very much!"

He hugged her tightly. "It was pure luck! I tried to call you at home, but since you weren't there yet, I thought I would try my luck. And here you are! I missed you too! The family is fine and sends you their love!" He hugged her again. "Just think, from now onward we'll not be separated for Christmas, Easter, or any other day!"

"How was your Christmas?"

"It was nice. Everyone enjoyed it. But I was always thinking of you! How was your Christmas?" Andrew asked.

"Aunt Hillary and Uncle Winston hired a young girl as a lady's maid and had their former cook take over the cooking. The cook was very good. However, Maddy, the lady's maid (as she called herself) didn't have much to do. Aunt Hillary suspected that we would meet today. She gave a fresh loaf of bread, a large cut of roast beef, some cheese, and other things for supper."

On the drive to the cottage and later when they were sitting on the sofa in front of a lively fire, Pamela told him about her visit, her recollections of the house, and especially her mother. She showed him the photographs of her parents that she had removed from the nursery, and then she gave Andrew her mother's touching letter to read.

After reading the letter, Andrew was silent for a long while. *There is something wrong with this letter. I cannot figure it out right now. I have to think about it.*

Pamela waited patiently for his reaction.

Finally, he asked, "How would you like to go to India on our honeymoon?"

"Honeymoon! Oh, Andrew," she giggled, "I have not even thought of it!"

"That is what I suspected. Well, I had an idea while driving here. How would you like to visit India and see your mother's school, which is now your school, to see how it is doing?"

She turned thoughtful, then smiled. "My school! I haven't even realized this!" She then remembered. "We can use the coins to finance the trip!"

"Yes, perhaps."

"If I remember correctly, Mama always said January and February are good for travel within India. Could we really go there?"

Andrew laughed. "I would not suggest it if I didn't mean it. We can go to the travel agent in London my father always uses to see how soon he can arrange a tour."

"What about your work?"

"It so happens that at this moment, I have no case pending. Since it is my own law firm, I am free to close it temporarily. Come to think of it, I have not taken a vacation for the last two years!

"I have no passport. We need passports and possibly visas!" Pamela worried.

"Yes, you do need a passport and visa." Andrew remembered something. "I'll call Father. He has a friend who can speed up the process of issuing a passport for you. Hopefully, he also knows the First Secretary of the Indian ambassador who could expedite the issuing of a visa. Do you have photos?"

Pamela chuckled. "Yes. Luckily, I had to have some photos made for my new teacher's and driver's licenses. I have several."

"May I call Father from your phone to see if we may impose on his friend with our passport request?"

Andrew's father offered to call his friend and inform him of the situation and that the couple would stop by on the following day. His friend graciously agreed.

They went on the following morning to London. First Pamela submitted her application for a new passport. They met the gentleman friend of Andrew's father who was willing to arrange for a most urgent processing. He said it would take a couple of days and that he would send it by special courier to Farmington on December 30.

Andrew mentioned, "It is too bad that Pamela cannot use my last name as we are going to get married on the following day."

The gentleman thought for a moment, then suggested that Pamela fill out another application form with her married name. He explained that since all the other information remained the same, he would mark the date of issue in the passport as December 30. He would also issue a backup document with her newly married name with issue date as December 31. To Pamela's great relief, he promised that he would still have a courier deliver the documents on December 30.

They had lunch at an Indian restaurant. "Just to introduce you to what is in store for you!" Andrew teased. He ordered one tandoori shrimps dish, lamb curry—medium mild, naan, rice, and dahl. For dessert they enjoyed halwa with Indian tea.

Pamela had brought along one gold coin to find out its value. After lunch, they went to a reputable coin dealer.

Initially, the coin dealer stared at the coin. He reached for a magnifying glass and carefully studied the coin on both sides. Finally, he asked, "Where did you get this coin?"

"I inherited it," Pamela replied.

"Please give me a moment. I have to look it up in my history register of rare coins. It has never been traded. It is in mint condition!" He went to a small desk.

Pamela and Andrew observed the dealer reading the index by year then the place the coin had been minted. He studied and compared the relief on each side of the coin and then shook his head before he joined them at the counter. "This is a museum piece! There are very few of those known to still exist."

"We thought so," Andrew agreed.

"Is it possible to estimate its value today?" Pamela asked.

The dealer hesitated a moment before returning to his desk and looking through several other books until he seemed satisfied. "I am only guessing, mind you," he cautioned. "This coin, according to my estimation and evaluation records, is approximately ninety-eight English pounds worth."

Pamela gasped. "I had no idea!"

"You may consider having it made into a pendant," the coin dealer suggested.

Andrew smiled at her. "Yes, I think that is a lovely idea!"

"Thank you very much." Pamela smiled at the coin dealer before they left his store.

"My God, Andrew." Pamela was stunned. "How is it possible?"

"I cannot say—only that you are a very fortunate young lady."

"Perhaps we ought to give some of the coins to a museum?"

"You must think about it carefully. Don't rush to any decision."

Pamela smiled at Andrew. "We can definitely pay for a marvelous honeymoon in India with some of the coins!"

CHAPTER 14

Planning the Honeymoon in India

*T*hey took a taxi to the travel agent, which was owned by Mr. Ravi Gupta. Being Indian, he was familiar with travels within India.

Mr. Gupta invited Pamela and Andrew to sit at his desk and ordered tea for them. When Andrew introduced Pamela and himself, Mr. Gupta recognized him as the son of his client, Lord Michael Prescott. Unknown to Andrew nor Pamela, Mr. Gupta had been instructed by Andrew's father, Lord Michael, not to disclose a secret agreement that had already been reached between the two gentlemen.

Andrew explained their wishes and situation—the travel must begin as soon as possible!

Mr. Gupta smiled. "How long are you planning for your tour?"

Pamela looked at Andrew as they had not discussed this.

"We have six weeks. We leave as early as possible in January and return sometime mid-February."

"You would start in Bombay, yes?"

"Yes. Bombay seems like a good starting point." Andrew agreed when Pamela nodded her agreement.

Mr. Gupta typed something into his computer. "You would be flying from London to Bombay. You are lucky, British Airways just started nonstop flights to Bombay! I strongly suggest you fly first-class so that you may be able to sleep and arrive in Bombay less fatigued." He continued to advise them to stay in Bombay for at least the first two or three days to get adjusted to the time change and climate.

"Can you recommend a hotel?" Andrew asked.

"Yes, sir, there is the Taj Mahal Hotel, which is the favorite of British travelers. It is rated five stars. The staff is outstanding and understands what will make your stay memorable. It has several very good restaurants, but there are other good restaurants nearby."

"Yes, that sounds sensible," Andrew agreed.

"Where else do you wish to go?"

Pamela responded, "We have to go to a small place called Dhalarnabad. I think the closest town is Lonavla."

Mr. Gupta nodded. "I know where Dhalarnabad is and how you can get there."

"Oh, good!" Pamela felt relieved. "I was afraid you might not know it since it is a very small place."

Mr. Gupta smiled. "It is my duty to find whatever place you wish to visit." He proceeded to tell them of the necessary train journey to Lonavla. "I recommend you travel first-class because the coaches are less crowded and have air-conditioning." Lonavla is one of the popular hill stations for vacationers in the Western Ghats (mountains). From there they would have a driver with an air-conditioned car to take them farther up to Khandala and Dhalarnabad.

"Is there a hotel in Dalarnabad?" Pamela asked.

"I am afraid not, my lady. It is a small village. You will have to return to Khandala or Lonavla. The drive in good weather is less than one hour. In Lonavla, I can recommend a good hotel. It is not fancy, but it is clean. The food they serve is very good. If I may suggest, wherever you are in India, drink only bottled water from a sealed bottle or, if you like, beer. Tea is always safe! How long do you plan to stay in Dhalarnabad, Lonavla?"

Pamela looked at Andrew and suggested, "Two days, I think. There is a school I—we—have to visit. It will be our first stop on our honeymoon after Bombay."

"Ah," Mr. Gupta chuckled, "congratulations are in order! May I wish you great happiness and success?"

"Thank you very much, Mr. Gupta," Andrew and Pamela answered simultaneously.

"Do you have any particular places in mind you wish to visit?"

"We would like to see the Taj Mahal, New and Old Delhi, Jaipur ..." Pamela started.

"We should definitely see Udaipur, the Ajanta Caves, Calcutta, and it would be fun to stay on a houseboat in Kerala," Andrew added.

Mr. Gupta nodded. "Yes, those are places well worth seeing! May I suggest that I compose a comfortable travel plan for you with all hotels, drivers, and sightseeing included so that you may select what you prefer. Lord Andrew, if you can give me your telephone number, I will contact you by tomorrow morning around ten o'clock, if this is agreeable with you?"

Andrew gave his business card and Pamela's telephone number.

After they left Mr. Gupta's office, Pamela smiled. "Just imagine, Andrew, I have read about all these exotic places but never dreamt to actually see them!"

On their drive home, Pamela asked Andrew, "Should we telegraph the headmaster of the school to inform him of our upcoming visit?"

Andrew thought for a moment. "Perhaps it might be more interesting to see how the school is being run when they don't expect any visitors."

"Yes, but wouldn't it be terribly rude to just show up?"

"Pamela, my love, isn't the school yours now? Part of your inheritance?"

It took a moment for Pamela to respond. "Yes, now that you mention it, I should be able to visit my school at any time without prior notice!"

"But promise me that you won't be too disappointed if the school has deteriorated," Andrew cautioned.

"I will not expect anything. It should be doing well because there is a generous budget for paying salaries and monthly maintenance fee. There is even a separate trust fund for expansion of the school. I will be grateful if you can help me study the financial situation."

"I promise to help and support you in every way possible."

After a short pause, Andrew started laughing. "Pamela, do you realize that we haven't even made certain that we can have the church and vicar for the wedding? Our parents have already sent out all the invitations, but we forgot the most important thing—the wedding ceremony! Also, we have to first register at the town hall! I can ask Inspector Healey or anyone else you like to witness the civil marriage! I think I can act as mayor for my own marriage as long as there are witnesses."

"Oh my god, Andrew! How could we forget? What if we cannot have the church ... or the vicar?"

"I'll call the vicar the minute we get home!"

Andrew called the vicar from Pamela's cottage. To their great relief, the church and the vicar would be available!

"I know, if necessary, Uncle Winston and Aunt Hillary will be happy to act as witnesses."

The telephone rang just as they entered the cottage.

"Good evening, Pamela, this is Marion Thrifoot. How are you?"

"Thank you, Ms. Thrifoot, I am fine." Pamela chuckled. "Just very busy."

"Pamela, I received your request for a two months leave of absence at the beginning of the new year. We can grant this leave to you with your understanding that you will not receive a salary during that time. Luckily, we found an elderly lady who used to be a teacher and is interested in the Montessori method. We'll muddle through without you.

"The other reason for my calling you is to thank you for the wedding invitation! My goodness, I had no idea! Please accept my congratulations! Now, as you can imagine, the news spread like wildfire through our campus! The children would like to do something with flowers in the church for your wedding, if you agree. Of course, they are all excited and looking forward to seeing their teacher as a bride!"

"Oh, how awfully sweet! We would be happy and honored to have the children at the church. Thank you for such a thoughtful gift!"

After Pamela hung up, she smiled at Andrew. "Our problem for flowers at the church is solved! Ms. Thrifoot said that the children will do something. Isn't this sweet of them?"

"Yes, that is very nice. It shows how much they love you!"

"I want to call the vicar's wife to request her to arrange for a little party for them after the church wedding. I know they love lemonade and chocolate cookies! What do you think?"

"I am sure they'll be thrilled!"

CHAPTER 15

An Amazing Itinerary

*A*t nine o'clock on December 29, Andrew rang the doorbell at the cottage. When Pamela opened the door, he waved several sheets of paper in triumph. "Our honeymoon trip to India! Mr. Gupta faxed them to my office this morning! A very impressive itinerary, I must say! He must have worked all night with his agents across India. All we are waiting for now are the passports with the visas and the airline tickets, but Mr. Gupta assured me that they will be sent by December 31!"

"When will we be leaving here?"

"We'll leave here on the second of January, stay in London one night, then fly to Bombay on the third of January and arrive there on the fourth!"

They sat on the sofa and began to read.

Travel Itinerary for Lord and Lady Andrew Prescott

January 3, 1981	Depart London (Heathrow) at 11:00 British Airways, flight no. 3, seats nos. 3-A and 3-B
January 4, 1981	Arrive Bombay (Santa Cruz) at 23:15 Meet Mr. Kumar Patel—your personal guide (who will travel with you throughout India) Reside at Taj Mahal Hotel, suite no. 10 (Separate suggested sightseeing)
January 8, 1981	Depart Bombay for Lonavla at 11:30 (by train) Train no. 5, first-class, coach no. 57, seats 19-A and 20-A Arrive Lonavla at 16:27 Reside at Lonavla Palace, rooms nos. 12 and 13 (Separate itinerary for visiting the Lady Elizabeth Mary Rose School in Dhalarnabad) (Sightseeing open)
January 12, 1981	Depart Lonavla at 9:20 for Aurangabad (Ajanta Caves) India Jet, flight no. 18; seats nos. 2-A and 2-B Arrive at Aurangabad at 14:00 Reside at Royal Ajanta Lodge, suite no. 5 (Visit Ajanta Caves, other sightseeing options open)
January 16, 1981	Depart Aurangabad for Udaipur at 9:20 India Jet, flight no. 30, seats nos. 1-A and 1-B Arrive Udaipur at 12:03 Reside at City Palace Hotel, suite no. 7 (Separate suggested sightseeing)
January 21, 1981	Depart Udaipur for Jaipur at 11:00 India Jet, flight no. 21; seats nos. 3-A and 3-B Arrive Jaipur at 13:00 Reside at Rambagh Palace, suite no. 9 (Separate suggested sightseeing)
January 28, 1981	Depart Jaipur for Agra by car around 9:45 Arrive Agra around 15:00 (lunch stop on the way) Reside at Royal Taj Mahal, suite no. 15 (Separate suggested sightseeing)
January 30, 1981	Depart Agra for New Delhi around 10:00 by car Arrive New Delhi around 14:00 Reside at Mumtaz Mahal, suite no. 7 (Separate suggested sightseeing)
Febuary 4, 1981	Depart New Delhi for Calcutta at 10:35 India Jet, flight no. 89; seats nos. 3-A and 3-B Arrive Calcutta at 1:27 Reside at Imperial Palace, suite no. 3 (Separate suggested sightseeing)
Febuary 7, 1981	Depart Calcutta for Cochin at 11:15 India Jet, flight no. 391; seats nos. 5-A and 5-B Arrive Cochin at 18:45 Reside at Empress Jasmine. Two bedrooms, indoor and outdoor living/dining room, shower, separate toilet, open deck and roof terrace
Febuary 10, 1981	Depart Cochin for Bombay at 9:30 India Jet, flight no. 375; seats nos. 3-A and 3-B Arrive Bombay at 16:25 Reside at Taj Mahal Hotel, suite no. 10 (Possibly some more sightseeing)
Febuary 12, 1981	Depart Bombay for London at 00:35 British Airways, flight no. 79; seats nos. 9-A and 9-B Arrive London (Heathrow) at 10:35

Suggested Sightseeing—Visits—Shopping

Mr. Kumar Patel, our experienced and trusted guide, will travel with you.

A car and driver will be at tour disposal throughout your travels.

Bombay

A leisurely stroll on Marine Drive—often called the Queen's Necklace

Visit Haji Ali Mosque at Worli—architecture is Indo-Islamic

Chatrapati Shivaji Temple

Jehangir Art Gallery offers distinguished art—classic and modern

Art and History Museum

Reach Elephanta Caves by small tourist boats (or private)

Stroll at Collaba, savor freshly prepared Indian snacks from stalls

Shopping at Breach Candy for saris or fine Indian silks, antiques

Fine jewelry and bookstores at Taj Mahal Hotel

Restaurants in Taj and Khyber Pass in vicinity are excellent!

Lonavla—Khandala—Dhalarnabad

Depart from crowded and unique Victoria Terminus (railway station)

Journey to Lonavla will show you glimpses of rural India

Lonavla is largest town of this hill station

It is a popular vacation place that is easily reached by train

We chose Lonavla Palace because it has air-conditioning as well as adequate heating (nights are cool!)

Drive to Dhalarnabad via Khandala to visit Lady Elizabeth Mary Rose School

Dhalarnabad and other villages are situated on the Western Ghats (mountain range). They form a large plateau surrounded by deep canyons with lush tropical vegetation and wildlife

Visit Rajmachi Point, a famous fort, by car

Visit Tiger's Leap with a sheer drop of approximately 450 meters

There are also ancient caves and temples in the area

Aurangabad—Ajanta Caves
Tour and sightseeing in and around Aurangabad
Drive to Ajanta Caves—there are thirty Buddhist temples cut
into rocks situated in the Waghora Valley carved by the ancient
Waghora River, creating a wide horseshoe turn
Recommend for following day—return to Ajanta Caves
Souvenir shopping

Udaipur
Drive/walk through city—often called Jewel of Rajasthan
Visit some of the eleven palaces
Visit City Palace Museum (used to be *zenana*—ladies' chambers)
Visit Jagdish Temple, seventeenth century with iconic carvings
(located outside City Palace)
Drive to the white marble Monsoon Palace on hilltop with
panoramic view!
Jag Mandir, a small palace on Lake Pichola
Seventeenth-century Moghul architecture—luxury palace hotel
Visit artisan studios where miniatures are being copied
Rajasthan is famous for precious stones. Local jewelers create
original and replicate ancient jewelry in silver and gold.

Jaipur
Jaipur is called the Pink City as most of it is built with sandstones
See Hawa Mahal (Wind Palace) with windows of the harem
carved out of stones like filigree so that the ladies could look out
without being seen
Nahargarh Fort above Jaipur is magnificent!
It is like an ancient palace city
Birla Mandir is a modern Hindu temple/museum
Albert Hall Museum is rich in art, arms, jewelry, etc.
Jantar Mantar is an eighteenth-century astronomical observatory
Amer (or Amber) Fort is a sixteenth-century fortress on a hilltop

Agra
Taj Mahal was built by Shah Jahan for his wife, Mumtaz
It has an imposing white marble mosque-like tomb structure with exquisite inlay of flower motifs and scriptures from the Quran.
We suggest a visit at sunrise and at sunset.
Drive to Qutub Minar—once a vibrant city until the wells dried out.
Drive to Fatehpur Sikri to see the highest (seventy-three meters) brick minaret built in 1193 BC.

New and Old Delhi
Red Fort was a sixteenth-century residence for Moghul emperors
Fortresses in the center of New Delhi are now several museums
There are parliament buildings along wide boulevards
India Gate war memorial for WW I
Jama Masjid was built in the seventeenth century with Moghul architecture
Humayun's Tomb was built in 1572
Chandni Chowk is a sprawling bazar with spices, produce, jewelry etc. It is very crowded!
Meena Bazaar, Old Delhi indoor shopping—confusing and overwhelming, but fun to browse and splurge!
Browse through crowded streets of Old Delhi—stay close to Mr. Patel!

Calcutta
Victoria Memorial Hall is an imposing palace museum
Dateshives Kali Temple is a spiritual Hindu center
Marble Palace Museum offers interesting exhibitions
Jorasanko Thakur Bari is the ancestral home of Rabindranath Tagore
The Indian Museum houses the largest collection on Asian art
St. Paul's Cathedral is Anglican in Indo-Gothic architecture
Visit sculptures craft shops where artisans build voluptuous sculptures of the goddess Kali and others from mud/clay to be decorated and offered to the sea through extreme crowds of humanity, trucks, cows, trams, etc.

Cochin

Kerala is on the Malabar Coast in southwest India
The backwaters are calm rivers and lakes interconnected by
canals that irrigate the rice paddies and other vegetations
Stay on comfortable houseboat with attendants
Enjoy the visits by fishermen, peddlers, flower and other
merchants who will approach in their boats laden with their wares.
This is the ideal place—surrounded by tropical vegetations—to
relax after a hectic trip!

Return to Bombay

Stay again at Taj Mahal, suite no. 10
Visit the Dhobi Ghat—giant laundry center
Perhaps final shopping?

We wish to thank you for the pleasure of assisting you during your
travel within India!
Mr. Ravi J. Gupta, manager, Reliable Travels, London, UK

"Will we see all these places?" Pamela asked in awe.
"Well, there are more suggestions we can possibly see, but it is a
helpful way to select and decide. I must say Mr. Gupta did a very
good job!"

CHAPTER 16

Preparations and the Wedding

"Now we have to go and see Mr. Gather, the owner of the My Fair Lady restaurant to decide on the wedding menu," Andrew reminded Pamela.

As they were about to leave to drive to Newhurst, a special courier arrived with Pamela's passport and the other document with her married name. She felt greatly relieved. "All we need now are the tickets for India."

During the drive to Newhurst, Pamela mentioned, "Andrew, do you realize that Mr. Gupta didn't mention the price of our honeymoon trip?"

"Yes, I noticed too but didn't want to worry you about it. Don't worry, I have some savings, and if absolutely necessary, you have more than enough coins to pay for it."

After inviting them into his office, Mr. Gather welcomed them. "I am honored that you decided to celebrate your wedding luncheon at my restaurant! Thank you."

"You are most welcome." Andrew nodded.

"I took the liberty of suggesting a wedding menu. You are, of course, free to reject it and decide on whatever you prefer."

The menu was projected on a screen, so it was easy to read.

WEDDING MENU FOR MR. AND MRS. ANDREW PRESCOTT
31 DECEMBER 1980

SALMON-WASABI MOUSSE ON CUCUMBER WHEELS
ACCOMPANIED WITH VOUVREY
LEMON SORBET

CREME VICHYSSOISE WITH CARAWAY MELBA TOASTS
CRANBERRY SORBET

ROASTED SUCKLING PIG WITH CHAMPAGNE-SORELLE
GLAZE
AND CHAMPIGNONS
ACCOMPANIED WITH RIESLING D'ALSACE
GRAPEFRUIT SORBET

CHATEAUBRIAND WITH SAUTEED FENNEL, CARROTS, AND
SPINACH
POMMES DE TERRE A LA DUCHESSE
ACCOMPANIED WITH LALANDE DE POMEROL
KIWI SORBET

CREME DES MARRONS GLACEES WITH VANILLE
GAUFRETTES
ACCOMPANIED WITH ZINFANDEL
RUM-RAISIN ICE CREAM WITH HOT CHOCOLATE SAUCE
WHITE-RUM SORBET

WEDDING CAKE (ALMONDS, CARROTS, LEMON,
SULTANINES, GINGER)
WITH ROSE OR WHITE CHAMPAGNE
HOT COFFEE, TEA OR CHOCOLATE

OPTIONAL
SHERRY, PORT, COGNAC, SCOTCH, GIN, OR VODKA

"How could anyone eat so much food?" Pamela asked.

Both men chuckled. Mr. Gather explained, "I imagine you and your family and guests will arrive around 13:00. By the time everyone is seated, it will be 13:30. We would start with the salmon mousse and allow thirty minutes with the lemon sorbet. The vichyssoise and cranberry sorbet another thirty minutes. The roast and sorbet we'll allow another thirty minutes. During the main course—the chateaubriand—I expect there will be speeches given. With the kiwi sorbet we allow forty-five to fifty minutes. Let's see … it is already almost four o'clock! The marrons glacés and ice cream could be served simultaneously if time is a factor. That will bring us closer to five o'clock. I expect more speeches when the wedding cake arrives, is cut, and is served, so I add another forty to fifty minutes. Families and guests often like to linger after they have waved the newly-married couple off on their honeymoon.

"So you see, Ms. Payne, the wedding luncheon won't be over until sometime before six o'clock! By the way, Mr. Prescott, how many people do you expect in your party?"

"It's a small family wedding," Andrew responded. "There will be maximum of thirty to thirty-two people."

"How do you wish the tables to be arranged? Horseshoe is a favorite way for most people to see the head table. We can have eight people at the head table with the bridal couple in the center. Then the tables at left and right can have twelve each or more."

"You have obviously done this before!" Pamela said.

Mr. Gather laughed. "Oh yes, many times. Would you like us to do the table decorations?" He projected different table settings. The one with silver candelabras with white candles and white carnations on a pale-pink tablecloth with matching napkins elegantly folded into swans was selected.

"Andrew, I think it would be nice if we asked our local baker to do the wedding cake," Pamela suggested.

"Do you think he is up to it? He doesn't bake cakes, only breads."

"Yes, come to think of it, you are right. Perhaps it is best to have you, Mr. Gather, create the wedding cake."

They selected one three-tier cake with white frosting and pale-pink roses of marzipan with two white doves rising in the air at the top.

Pamela spent the remaining time cleaning the cottage. At noon on December 29, the courier from Mr. Gupta's travel agency arrived with a heavy envelope. She didn't open it as she wanted to finish her housecleaning first and wait for Andrew. She had prepared the king-size bed with brand-new sheets and planned to sleep the night in the guest room. The windows sparkled clean with newly washed curtains, and the floors and furniture smelled of beeswax. Both bathrooms displayed new towels, soaps, and lotions. The kitchen was shiny and bright. At the grocery store she found a bouquet of pink carnations with holly and ivy and was able to make two arrangements, one for the coffee table in the living room and one for the dining table.

Andrew had gone to the Victoria Hotel in Newhurst, where his family would stay, to welcome their arrival. He was bringing them to her cottage around six o'clock for drinks. There was just enough time to take a wonderfully rejuvenating shower and put on a new long turquoise velvet skirt with a lace blouse in matching color from Mrs. Hood. She left her shoulder-length hair free because it was still damp from the shower.

It was a lively chaos for a while when Andrew's family and friends arrived. There were not enough sofas and chairs to seat everyone. The younger gentlemen decided to sit on the carpeted floor. Andrew had foreseen the need for additional glasses and had brought a box of them from his apartment.

Most likely the cottage had never before been filled with so much laughter!

At one point, Andrew's mother took Pamela discreetly aside and asked if she had a wedding gown. Pamela took her upstairs to show her the wedding gown of her late mother. She felt relieved when her future mother-in-law agreed that it was most lovely indeed!

There was a vote for where to have dinner. A modest place for tasty pizza won! After dinner Andrew's family and friends returned to Newhurst.

It was ten o'clock when Andrew and Pamela returned to the cottage. She gave him the envelope from Mr. Gupta. They studied the neatly printed itinerary and were very impressed. Andrew kissed Pamela good night and left so that she would get some sleep before her relatives would arrive on the following day.

After Aunt Hillary and Uncle Winston had settled down at the Farmington Lodge, Pamela arrived with Andrew and his large family. Aunt Hillary wore an elegant dark-plum dress with a matching coat and a matching colored hat, which half-leaned like a flat planet on her head but looked amazingly chic on her. Uncle Winston wore a dark navy suit with a plum-colored tie on a white shirt.

The mutual introductions went smoothly as everyone went by their first names. The party of thirty-one people enjoyed a delicious and relaxing dinner at the Farmington Lodge with lively conversation. Quietly observing her relatives, Pamela was surprised how sophisticated they were in manner and speech. They had traveled the world over to oversee Uncle Winston's small businesses in Asia and the Continent. Pamela was relieved to notice that Andrew's family and relatives felt very comfortable in one another's company.

After dinner, the men excused themselves and went somewhere to celebrate Andrew's last evening as a bachelor.

Meanwhile, the women spent the evening at Pamela's cottage until midnight. Her aunt was in great spirits. She and Lilly volunteered to dress the bride on the following morning. At first, Pamela suggested that both be her maids of honor.

But Aunt Hillary said, "I am far too old to be a bridesmaid! I think it would be much nicer to have just you, Lilly."

Lilly shook her head. "I can't because I didn't bring a long gown suitable for a bridesmaid."

"Come look." Pamela showed Lilly Mrs. Hood's gowns. They selected a long pale-peach-colored silk gown that, after tucking it in here and there, fit very nicely! And so it was agreed that Lilly was to be the only maid of honor. Pamela lent her Mrs. Hood's pearl necklace to wear for the wedding.

Pamela meant to sleep in the guest room, but sleep evaded her. Finally, at dawn, she soaked in a fragrant lavender bath. By the time her relatives and Lilly arrived, she had already had her breakfast but insisted that they all should have something to eat with tea or coffee. She needed to be busy to prevent herself from getting too nervous.

As promised, Aunt Hillary's bridal bouquet was delivered at nine o'clock. There were fifteen white roses surrounded by delicate lilies of the valley. It was gorgeous and dew fresh with a wonderful perfume! Even Lilly received a small bouquet with the same types of flowers that made her feel very important.

The two ladies dressed the bride with great care. Lilly liked the wedding gown so much that she asked if, when her time came, she could borrow it! Aunt Hillary insisted that Pamela wear some pale-pink nail polish on her fingers as well as on her toes, which she applied with a secure hand!

When Uncle Winston knocked on the bedroom door, Pamela was ready. "May I come in?"

"Yes." Aunt Hillary opened the door for him.

"I brought the tiara for the bride." He held a large purple leather case with the Swendown arms engraved in gold. He opened it to show to Pamela. "Dearest Pamela, as you know, this was your mother's by inheritance. It is yours now!"

Lilly was surprised. "How did you get such a lovely tiara? You are not—" She stopped herself.

Uncle Winston straightened up and explained almost solemnly, "Our Pamela's mother was the only daughter of the Earl of Swendown, William Henry Scott. Pamela is a lady by birth. This is the Swendown tiara. Pamela inherited the title of Lady of Swendown. The tiara belongs now to her."

"Does Andrew know?" Lilly asked with surprise.

Pamela laughed. "I have never thought of telling him. We never talked about it. Like Andrew didn't think it was important to let me know in advance that your father is an earl. I really don't think it makes much difference."

While the two were chattering, Aunt Hillary knew exactly how to fix, with tiny clips, the Belgian lace veil with the tiara on Pamela's head. One section of the delicate veil she draped lightly over Pamela's face. She studied her creation carefully before leading her niece to the full-length mirror.

"I didn't know how beautiful the gown with the veil and tiara would be! Do you think I can really wear this? Here in Farmington?"

"You silly goose!' Aunt Hillary chuckled. "You are the most important person today!"

"On par with Andrew, of course!" Lilly added loyally.

Pamela smiled while turning toward Lilly. "Yes, you are absolutely correct! If it were not for Andrew, nothing like this would happen today!"

"Stop your chatter, it is time for us to go!" Uncle Winston reminded. He insisted that Pamela go alone with him in his rented car to the church while he requested Lilly to drive his wife.

During the short drive to the church, Uncle Winston turned emotional. "Pamela, my dear, I so wish that your parents were here to see how beautifully you turned out! They would be so very pleased and proud to welcome Andrew to the family!" He was wiping away an escaped tear before he continued. "You have chosen a fine young man! But what I really want to say is, can you ever forgive me … us, your only relatives, for having neglected you during your formative years?"

Pamela put her hand gently on his arm. "Please, Uncle Winston, I can understand now to a great extent how reluctant you must have felt to accept the responsibility and burden of guiding a little girl to adulthood. Now that we have found one another, everything will be so much more enjoyable. The past is over. We are beginning a new and happy chapter in all our lives!"

Her uncle was silent for a while, then smiled at her. "Just look at you!"

Pamela blushed. "Thank you." She paused an instant: "You know, Uncle Winston, I have been thinking, especially since our Christmas time together, that, perhaps, if you had coddled and spoiled me, I might have turned out far less sensitive to others, especially toward children at the school."

"And now you are giving me the honor to lead you down the aisle to give you to your Andrew! You have no idea what this means to me … and Hilly. Thank you, my dear Pamela!"

They reached the parking lot behind the church where Pamela was assisted out of the car. Aunt Hillary and Lilly came rushing over to adjust the gown and straighten out the veil. They were ushered into a small room at the back of the church to await the signal for Uncle Winston to lead Pamela to the altar. He hugged his niece and kissed her on the forehead. "We are so very proud of you, Pamela Desirée Payne … for the last time!"

Pamela blinked away some tears. "Thank you, Uncle Winston."

"Just remember, don't race down the aisle with me."

They all laughed.

Before leaving to sit on the first bench row, Aunt Hillary kissed her niece on the cheek and whispered, "Be happy, sweet Pamela!"

It was a relief for everyone to hear the organ start playing J. S. Bach's beautiful hymn "Jesu, Joy of Man's Desiring." This joy-filled cantata embraced the waiting congregation who stood up and turned toward the entrance.

Holding her pretty bouquet, Lilly, in her pale-peach gown and with a shy smile, walked slowly at a ten-foot distance in front of Winston Henry James Payne. His face had a solemn expression while leading his niece down the aisle. The veil enhanced the shy but happy smile on Pamela's face.

Just before reaching the altar, Pamela noticed her kindergarten children assembling quietly in front of Lilly. The girls were wearing white blouses and skirts with pink ribbons while the boys, also dressed in white, wore blue ribbons at their waists. Each child was carrying a pale-pink carnation with a white silk ribbon. When they offered their flowers to Pamela, Lilly took the bridal bouquet so that Pamela was free to accept the carnations. She was deeply touched. "Thank you, my little sweethearts! How very lovely your flowers are! Thank you!"

After the children were settled on their benches, Pamela could feel her uncle starting to tremble with emotions. She looked at him and smiled. "We are almost there. Thank you."

And then she had only eyes for Andrew, who was standing in front of the altar with his two younger brothers as best men. She had never seen him in a gray formal morning tailcoat with matching vest over a white shirt with a high starched collar and light-gray bow tie and striped dark-gray trousers. He looked very handsome indeed!

His expression seemed almost stunned while watching Pamela approach. It was only when she reached him at the altar and Uncle Winston offered Pamela's hand to him that a brilliant smile lit up his face while he accepted her hand and kissed it.

Uncle Winston went to sit beside his wife next to some of the schoolchildren.

The vicar began reading the short liturgy. "Dearly beloved ..."

Somehow Pamela could not pay attention to the ceremony until she heard the vicar coaching her to say her vows. She managed to repeat them correctly and say yes. She waited for Andrew to repeat his vows and confirm with a yes. When Andrew slipped an antique platinum ring with a small diamond on her finger, Pamela panicked for a split-second, realizing that she had completely forgotten about a ring for Andrew! To her surprise and great relief, Lilly appeared and offered her the ring for him.

"I pronounce you now man and wife," the vicar's voice concluded.

Andrew lifted the veil and gently draped it over the tiara and kissed Pamela for the first time as her husband! He whispered, "My Lady Andrew, I love you!"

Pamela felt tears fill her eyes. One escaped and was about to slide down, but Andrew wiped it gently away with one finger. "You are the most beautiful bride I have ever seen, my lady wife." He kissed her again.

She found her smile. "My lord husband Andrew, I love you more than ever."

It was at that moment that the sun sent a ray through the church window and made the tiara sparkle to the delight of the onlookers.

Only then did Pamela realize that she had been holding her breath. She inhaled deeply and felt enormous relief.

As previously arranged, the Montessori children were given a party at the church's meeting hall with lemonade and cookies and ice cream and chocolates.

The bridal couple were escorted from the church to the waiting car while being showered with rice, teasing, and laughter. As soon as the white-and pink-ribbon-decorated car started moving, it began a tremendous racket with the tins and bells attached to the rear bumper.

The wedding reception and luncheon was held at the My Fair Lady restaurant in Newhurst. Mr. Gather, the owner/manager, had been right. It took a very long time for everyone to be seated.

Andrew's parents were seated next to Andrew and Pamela's Uncle Winston was sitting next to her, then Aunt Hillary next to an empty chair. Pamela wondered if Ms. Thrifoot, the headmistress of the Montessori academy, might be seated there, but then she saw her at another table. Before the first welcome toast was offered by Andrew's father, an elderly woman was ushered to the head table. It was Bambi!

Pamela recognized her immediately and went to embrace her with tears in her eyes. "Oh, Bambi!" she cried out. "I cannot believe my eyes. Is it really you? Oh, what a fantastic surprise! How are you?" The questions tumbled out.

Tears were rolling down Bambi's cheeks. "Please forgive a silly old woman for crying on such a happy occasion. But it is such a joy to see you so happy and ever so beautiful—like your mother was!"

Once again Pamela hugged her old nanny. "In that case, I am a silly young woman crying with joy. Now we have found one another again. How are you?"

"I am fine, thank you. You must know that it was your uncle and aunt who searched for me. They eventually found me in my tiny one-room cottage in the Lake District. Not only did they invite me to your wedding, but they came to fetch me! Your uncle said to make absolutely certain that I would be at your wedding!"

Pamela led her nanny to the empty chair at the head table then walked over to her aunt and uncle. "Dear Uncle Winston and dear Aunt Hillary, you have given me the most nostalgic present! Thank you both from the bottom of my heart!"

After the first course was served and enjoyed by everyone, Andrew's father stood up while holding his glass. "Here is to my eldest son, Andrew Edward Michael Prescott, who has found and fallen in love with a sweetheart of a young ... very young woman, the former Lady Pamela, who is now our dearest Lady Andrew. May your love for each other increase with each new day!"

In response, everybody stood up while raising their glasses. "Hear! Hear!"

The bridal couple smiled with acknowledgement and thanks.

As for the food … each dish was delicious! The selection of fine wines accompanying them contributed no doubt to the jovial and sometimes lively conversations among family and guests!

At one point, Uncle Winston stood up and offered a toast. "I have the feeling that there are two invisible family members with us here—Pamela's late parents, who would be enormously pleased for their daughter, their beautiful Pamela Desirée, the brand-new Lady Andrew who is now the newest member of the distinguished Prescott family, for having found a fine young man, Andrew Edward Michael! You all heard him promise today to love and cherish Pamela for the rest of their lives! I not only lift my glass but, foremost, my heart to the bridal couple. May your happiness renew with each sunrise!"

Everyone stood up and agreed. "Hear! Hear!"

Before the wedding cake was brought in, Pamela was presented with a flat silver box with a white ribbon. With surprise, she accepted it and offered it to Andrew, but he refused to take it. She looked around the tables, trying to find out who might have given it, but everyone looked innocent.

Andrew encouraged her, saying, "My darling, please open it."

She untied the ribbon and removed the lid and gasped.

Andrew leaned over. They saw the British Airways tickets and the neatly printed India trip schedule and list of sightseeing destinations with all the vouchers and additional tickets for trains and airlines within India inside. They both looked at Andrew's father.

He explained, "This is a collaboration between your two families and friends. It is our wedding gift to you both!"

Andrew asked his father, "How did you know that we planned our honeymoon trip in India?"

"Ah." His father chuckled. "It just so happened that you selected the same travel agent who does all my travel arrangements. Ravi Gupta already knew that we—that is, all of us here—wanted to treat you to your honeymoon! It was not difficult to guess where you would want to go with Pamela having inherited her mother's school in Dhalarnabad! When you visited Mr. Gupta, he was very pleased and agreed to choreograph a trip for you to and within India."

Pamela stood up to address the assembled family and friends. "I don't know what to say except … thank you! Thank you all from the bottom of my heart! It is a most wonderful gift for both of us!"

Andrew seemed equally surprised when he stood up. "We had absolutely no idea what you all were so generously scheming for us! I join Pamela in thanking each and every one of you for this amazing gift! It will enrich and bring joy to us for the rest of our lives. Again, thank you very much!"

"Hear! Hear!'

"You know," Pamela admitted laughingly, "when we received what we believed to be our itinerary, we noticed that there was no price given! Andrew assured me that he had some savings that would help."

Everybody was amused. "Now you won't have to worry anymore!"

Before leaving, Andrew invited all the families and friends for lunch on the following day at the Farmington Lodge before they would be returning to their homes. Bambi was invited to join Uncle Winston and Aunt Hillary.

It was well past six o'clock. After Pamela had received many compliments on her mother's wedding gown, veil, and tiara and lots of hugs with good wishes, Andrew took her by the hand and drew her toward the car to drive her home to their cottage. After watching with amusement the car's noisy attachments creating a racket and causing people to turn their heads, the family and friends returned to the lounge to enjoy after-dinner drinks.

Once inside the cottage, Andrew held Pamela at arm's length. "My Lady Andrew, I want to properly look at you! Your elegant gown, the delicate veil, and the gorgeous tiara! Is it your mother's Swendown tiara?"

"Yes." She smiled. "It is mine now!"

"You looked absolutely, stunningly beautiful today! I wish you could always wear it!" He chuckled, remembering. "Did you notice the children were speechless when they saw you walking down the aisle?"

Pamela felt enormously relieved. "Thank you, my darling Andrew! I am so glad you like my mother's wedding attire! I was worried that it was too grand for Farmington." She smiled too, remembering. "I have never seen you in formal dress! I thought, if I had to choose the most handsome man in the whole crowd, the choice would easily fall on you!"

"My sweet Pamela, I must tell you that this may look handsome, but the collar is suffocating me!"

She helped him to remove it. "Yes, some fashion can be very uncomfortable."

"How about I light a fire and we can study our honeymoon trip?"

Pamela brought the silver box with the itinerary for their travels within India. She joined him on the sofa. The British Airway tickets were on top. They indicated the departure date from London for January 3, 1981!

"We'll stay at the Dorchester overnight," Andrew told her. "Father offered to drive us to London, leaving in the morning of the third of January."

"Oh, that is awfully kind of him! Darling, do you realize we don't have much time to pack?"

"You won't need many things. Bring a few summer dresses and a couple of gowns. Perhaps a jacket and some sweaters for cooler nights. Comfortable walking shoes and one pair of dress shoes and then whatever toiletries ladies need!"

Pamela laughed. "You would make an excellent lady's maid! What about you?"

"My suitcase is already packed. It's upstairs in the guest room."

"Isn't it amazing that your father thought to give us this honeymoon wedding gift?"

"Remember, darling, he said it was your family as well as all our friends who contributed to it! How does it feel to be a Prescott?"

She smiled at him. "It feels wonderful! I am so very lucky to have not only you as my very own husband but also such a charming and large family!" She paused, then said, "I do hope you'll get to like Uncle Winston and Aunt Hillary ... and Bambi!"

"During the last two days, I have been observing your relatives. I believe that they are truly nice and interesting people. I could tell that they feel dreadfully sorry for their neglect. But I am very pleased for you to have reconnected and found affection. I think their searching for and bringing your Bambi to our wedding reflects very well on them!"

"Perhaps, if you agree, we can invite her to stay for a few days with us?"

"I think she would love that!" Andrew agreed.

Pamela stifled a yawn and realized that she felt tired.

Andrew noticed it. "Would you like to retire?"

"I realize that I am also hungry."

"No wonder! You hardly touched the food!"

"I was too nervous. But I am hungry now. How about you?"

Andrew stood up and gently drew her up. "Let's raid the kitchen! I would love to have a piece of the wedding cake with a brandy."

After extinguishing the fire for the night, they enjoyed sharing a generous piece of their wedding cake from one plate and brandy from the same glass.

"This cake is delicious. What do you think is in it?" Andrew wondered.

"There are lots of exotic spices, like cinnamon, allspice, nutmeg, mace, ginger, cloves, raisins, almonds, pecans, and candied fruits. Then, I think, it was baptized generously with rum!"

"It reminds me of a plum pudding."

"Yes, they are similar. I will try to bake one for you sometime."

"Please bake one for my birthday."

"Andrew," Pamela said, "do you realize that we don't even know each other's birth dates?"

He chuckled. "I think there are still a lot of discoveries ahead for us!"

"Please tell me. When is your birthday?"

"Mine was on June 8 of this year," he replied.

"Good! We'll celebrate them thoroughly each year!" Pamela promised.

"When is your birthday?"

"And mine was on March 28 of this year."

"Good! We'll have wedding cakes on yours and my birthdays," Andrew decided.

She was unsuccessful in hiding another yawn.

When Andrew noticed, he smiled. "Would you like to go ahead?"

"Yes, thank you. I would like to take a shower." Before leaving the room, she bent down and kissed him.

"Since our future lady's maid has not yet been engaged, will you need help with the tiara, veil, and gown?"

"Perhaps with the tiara and veil. I wouldn't want to damage them."

"Come sit on a dining room chair so I can study the system." With careful hands, he separated the tiny hair clips attached to the velvet bottom of the tiara from the veil and lifted both with gentle hands.

Luckily, the bodice and skirt had zippers, which Pamela was able to take care of. She used a fragrant lily-of-the-valley soap and enjoyed the shower. She had selected a long plain white nightgown, which looked brand-new, and slid it over before slipping between the sheets.

Andrew waited another five minutes after he heard the shower water stop to allow Pamela enough time to do whatever she pleased before knocking on the bedroom door. "May I come in?"

"Yes."

He found her already in bed, covered up to her neck. "Would you mind if I were to take a quick shower?"

"No, not at all. I put a sandalwood soap and fresh towel out for you."

While Andrew showered, Pamela got out of bed and lit candles on the dresser and turned off the light. The room was bathed in soft hues. She returned to bed and started worrying. *I have no idea what I am supposed to do.*

Luckily, Andrew returned soon from the bathroom. He was dressed in a dressing gown. "How is my sweet wife, Pamela?"

"She is a bit nervous."

He suppressed a smile. "My darling, there is no need to be nervous. We have no agenda."

"You see, I don't know what I am supposed to do. I have no experience."

"You don't need to do anything, my love! We'll just get acquainted as much as you feel comfortable. May I join you?"

"Yes." She added timidly, "Please."

Andrew took off his dressing gown. He was wearing pajama bottoms and got into bed. He drew her gently into his arms. It was only then he realized that she was trembling. "Pamela, what would you like to do?"

"Talk."

Luckily, she didn't notice his smile even though he felt very sympathetic. "Yes, if you like, we'll talk. What would you like to talk about?"

"I really don't know." She sighed. "In preparation for tonight, I read several novels. The problem is that they always skip to tell you what happens after one gets married."

Andrew suppressed a chuckle. "You wouldn't want an author—a total stranger who doesn't know you—to tell you what to do on your own wedding night, would you?"

"No, you are right. I wouldn't like that."

Andrew noticed that her trembling had subsided. He thought to continue their conversation. "When did you decide to become a teacher?"

"Oh," Pamela responded, "you see, with Bambi having been sent away, that horrid governess and, later, the cruel people at the boarding school made me decide to look for a way to treat and educate children in a positive and supportive way. Then, when I was at St. Mary's, by chance, I found an article in a magazine describing the Maria Montessori teaching method. I felt it was godsent! During one of my vacations, when I had, of course, no home to go to, I came here to Farmington to meet Ms. Thrifoot, the headmistress of the academy, to explore the possibility of enrolling in a teachers' training program. I was allowed to observe some classes and was convinced that this is what I wanted to do. But then there was a problem of money for my training. Luckily, Ms. Thrifoot was kind enough to arrange for a full scholarship and a modest stipend loan with a contract that after my completion of training and after receiving my teacher's diploma, I would spend three additional years for a modest salary to compensate the balance of the loan for my living expenses."

"And then Mrs. Hood happened!" Andrew nodded.

"Yes." Pamela smiled. "She became my savior! I will always be most sincerely grateful to her! I must tell you that only last week I reimbursed the entire cost of my scholarship and loan to the school from Mrs. Hood's savings. This freed me up to take leave until March. Little did I know then that I would be spending my honeymoon during that time!"

"It is admirable what you have achieved on your own, Pamela. You should be very proud of yourself!"

"No, Andrew, not all on my own! If it hadn't been for Mrs. Hood! I suspect that she paid for my scholarship in the first place, and Ms. Thrifoot took a chance with me. I don't know what would have happened to me after St. Mary's."

"Still, I think you have achieved a great deal! I am very proud of you and so very happy that you are my wife!"

"Oh, Andrew, you are so very nice, thank you." She put her hand on his chest and felt a fine layer of hair, but underneath, he felt solid. Suddenly, she started chuckling.

"What is it?"

"I just remembered. One of my children asked me once why his dad was growing beard and chest hair but not his mother."

There was amusement in Andrew's voice when he asked, "How did you explain?"

"I couldn't. I tried to explain that most mothers are softer because they have to hold their little babies. Beards and chest hair would scratch their soft skin. But I suggested he ask his father."

She could feel Andrew shaking with laughter. And then he asked, "Was he satisfied with your answer?"

"For the time being."

Andrew felt her completely relax. "Well, I shaved to make sure I won't scratch your delicate skin." His kisses traveled over her face, neck, shoulders, and gradually lower as the nightgown slipped away.

At first Pamela held her breath, amazed at the wonderful feeling, but soon she responded instinctively to his love giving. During that night she discovered a world of new emotions she had never known existed!

CHAPTER 17

" You Got Us Fooled Good!"

*T*hey slept until the doorbell woke them up.

"Who could that be? I don't think Uncle Winston and Aunt Hillary would come so early," Pamela said.

"Nor any of my family!" Andrew agreed while quickly slipping into his dressing gown and going downstairs. He opened the front door.

It was Inspector Healy holding out the latest newspaper. "Good morning, Lord Andrew," he greeted with a smile spreading across his face.

For a second Andrew was surprised by the inspector's greeting because he was used to being addressed by him only as Prescott. "Good morning, Inspector. How are you?"

"Oh, I am fine, thank you … my lord," he added, teasingly.

"I am afraid I am not yet presentable. How late is it?"

"Ten o'clock but never mind that! After all, I just thought you might be interested to know and see that you and Lady Andrew made front page." He waved the couple of newspapers in his hand.

Andrew accepted them and stared at the picture of their exiting St. Paul's Church with a large headline "Viscount and Lady Andrew's Surprise Wedding!"

"You had us fooled good, Prescott ... my lord." Inspector Healy grinned.

"It was never my intention to fool anyone. I just wanted to be me for a while, a regular barrister doing his job in a little town."

The inspector nodded. "I can understand, but your secret is out! Will you continue your services here?"

"Yes. I hope so. Once we return from our honeymoon, I know that Pamela intends to continue teaching at the academy for some time."

"I am glad to hear it, my lord."

"Please, Inspector, keep calling me Prescott. I like the name!"

"Very good, Prescott. I leave you now to read all about your wedding!"

Pamela appeared in a sweater and skirt and smiled at the inspector. "Good morning, Inspector Healy. Would you like to come in?"

"Thank you, Lady Andrew, but I better hurry back home. My wife is waiting."

She looked at the man with surprise, then at Andrew, who laughed. "Our secret is out. Look at the newspaper!"

"Oh my goodness! What do we do now?"

"Unless you like to be addressed as my lady, Lady Andrew, or your ladyship ..." Andrew teased her.

"How about Mrs. Prescott?" Pamela interrupted.

"Well done, Mrs. Prescott!" Inspector Healy praised. "I am off now. Have fun reading the newspaper!" he called over his shoulder while leaving.

"Let's take a shower and get presentable in case someone

else comes," Pamela suggested.

They found time before leaving for the family luncheon at the Farmington Lodge to read the amazingly detailed story about their wedding and several additional photos, including one with the schoolchildren, on an inside page!

"We'll save this for our own children," Andrew said to his blushing wife.

The families had already seen and read the newspapers and were equally amused at the people's surprise. They were a bit noisy during lunch as they were sharing photos—laughing at some and admiring and making fun of some individuals' expressions.

After a well-fortifying lunch, the various families left to allow the honeymooners to do their final packing except Andrew's father, who had promised to drive them to London to stay one night at the Dorchester. Pamela insisted he stay with them in the guest room. While she and Andrew were still packing, changing their minds, unpacking and exchanging clothes, their father enjoyed browsing Mrs. Hood's remaining books in the music room. For dinner they went to the little pizza place and enjoyed themselves.

Mr. Ravi Gupta met them on January 3 at the London hotel. He and his driver took Pamela, Andrew, and Lord Michael to Heathrow. On arrival, they were ushered to the first-class lounge while their passports, tickets, and luggage were being checked. It had comfortable sofas and chairs and small tables. There were interesting paintings of different parts of the world and several fresh flower arrangements. They were served high tea and drinks.

When the moment arrived for their father to leave, Pamela said, "I wish you could come with us!"

"Thank you, my dear Pamela Prescott, but you just concentrate on enjoying Andrew's loving company while you have him all by yourself!"

CHAPTER 18

Flying to and Visiting Bombay (Mumbai)

This was Pamela's first trip on an airplane. She was happy to sit at the window watching the preparation for takeoff. The pilot and head steward came to greet them before the pilot disappeared into the cockpit with some other personnel. They were offered champagne and pecans. It seemed to take forever until the entrance/exit doors were closed and everyone was reminded to fasten their seat belts.

Finally, the sound of the engine started out gently as the plane reversed slowly away from the gate, turned, and moved toward the tarmac. After a moment of pause, the engines started to roar while the speed increased until … it was then that Pamela's hand slid into Andrew's hand for reassurance.

"My darling, don't worry." He smiled. "The jet engines are supposed to gain full thrust to lift this giant plane off the ground in order to climb higher and higher … to about thirty-six thousand to forty-thousand feet to reach cruising altitude." He squeezed her hand. "Isn't it exciting?"

Trusting Andrew and the pilot, Pamela smiled. "Yes … it just sounds so forceful and loud!"

"Just think how heavy the plane must be with all the passengers and their heavy luggage! It requires enormous power to lift a plane off the ground."

"You are right. It is amazing when you think of it!"

Andrew smiled. "Here we are between heaven and earth. We are beginning our honeymoon!" He leaned over and kissed her.

"You know, Andrew, it is still like a dream how everything happened! You, your family, my relatives, Bambi, the dream wedding, the cottage … and now this fantastic honeymoon to India!"

"Dreams come true!"

"But I never dared to dream for anything so wonderful!" Pamela admitted.

"Then accept it as a blessing."

"Thank you! Yes, it is!"

Except for one elderly couple, they were alone in the first-class cabin.

Pamela remembered that Andrew had been looking forward to reading some legal articles. She had brought a book to read, a book she had wanted to read for a very long time—*To Serve Them All My Days* by the wonderful English author R. F. Delderfield! But before indulging in reading, she first gazed out of the window.

The plane had reached high altitude. Suddenly, she felt thrilled to watch the Continent far below with tiny towns, rivers, forests, hills, and fields visible between shredded clouds.

The head steward offered drinks. Andrew asked for a double scotch, and Pamela requested a gin and tonic. They were served with caviar, smoked salmon, and cucumber sandwiches. Later a delicate salad was followed by filet mignon with vegetables. There was a fine selection of white and red wine. A chocolate-mousse tarte, coffee, tea, and a choice of after-dinner liquors were offered.

After the rich and enjoyable dinner, Andrew suggested, "You may want to try to sleep."

"Yes, I'll read a bit and then try to sleep." Pamela closed the window shade and was amazed how quickly Andrew fell fast asleep. She observed him and thought, *He looks so young and handsome. And he is my husband!*

Whenever she closed her eyes, she felt as if she was falling backward. Even with repeated attempts, she was unable to sleep. Once in a while, she opened the shade to peek out. Far below were the eccentric shapes of snow-capped mountains and valleys. The Mediterranean Sea shores were the last sceneries before a thick blanket of clouds hid the earth below. Later she could not see anything through the increasing darkness of the night.

Still, sleep evaded her. Whenever she opened the shade, it was pitch-dark below. Once in a while, she could see fires burning from oil fields, probably in Saudi Arabia. She became familiar with the even vibration and rolling sound of the engines, which turned into a reassuring rhythm.

Andrew woke up. "How are you doing, Pamela?"

"I still can't sleep. But I am enjoying the story of David Powlett-Jones, a teacher first, then headmaster at Bamfylde."

"How very appropriate a topic for you!" He checked his watch. "Do you have any idea where we are?"

"I think we are flying over Saudi Arabia, judging from oil field fires."

"Oh, in that case, we'll land in about two to three hours! Darling, did you sleep at all?"

"I am afraid not."

Andrew withdrew some articles from his briefcase. They both read.

It was about two hours later when Pamela noticed that the sound of the engines and speed changed. "We are descending," she announced.

Andrew laughed. "Yes, we are. You are already an expert flyer!"

Peering through the window, at first Pamela could only vaguely make out, here and there, open fires with huts of villages.

The head steward offered an English breakfast, but both Pamela and Andrew chose croissants and pastries with coffee and orange juice.

Each time Pamela peeked through the window, the earth drew closer!

Now there were many more small open fires and lots of dwellings with winding alleys between them. They were flying low enough to see people huddled around the fires. Even cows and stray dogs could be seen!

"We are almost on the ground!"

"Hopefully on the tarmac." Andrew chuckled.

A slight bump, and the engines raced in reverse to slow down the speed, then came to a very slow run.

Andrew reached over and hugged Pamela. "Pamela, we landed in Bombay!"

"Yes! Yes! Isn't it exciting, we are here?"

While the plane was taxiing toward the gate, Pamela said, "Oh, Andrew, never in my life, after my parents died, did I dare dream of flying to India to visit my mother's school! My parents used to sail on Cunard ships."

At the airport were long lines for immigration checking for foreigners, Commonwealth passport holders, and Indian citizens. Other long lines were for customs. Finally, they reached the exit where a throng of noisy people were waiting to receive and welcome passengers, probably family members and friends. There were some men holding up signs with names. To their relief, among them they recognized their name, Prescott. They approached the person.

"I bid you welcome to Bombay, Lord and Lady Andrew. May I introduce myself? I am Kumar Patel and will be your guide during your trip within India." He was of medium build with raven-black hair and an impressive moustache. His eyes were black and alert while his smile was friendly. He wore white slacks and shirt with a small maroon vest. He had an assistant and a porter with him. There were two cars waiting. In one, their luggage was stowed efficiently into the trunk while Mr. Patel introduced Pamela and Andrew to Mr. Dalal, their driver. He invited them to take their seats in the second car, a solid-looking ambassador car made in India!

The drive from the airport to the city was a culture shock, especially for Pamela! She gazed with utter disbelief at the shacks. Most were composed of cardboards, pieces of plastic, and some aluminum boards. Bare bulbs shed weak lights on groups of people huddled around open fires to keep warm. Half-naked children ran around while stray cows and dogs roamed freely, some onto the road, in search for food that brought the traffic to a halt. What astonished her most were the TV antennas and even a few satellite discs attached to many of these primitive dwellings.

"Andrew, what do these people do when it is raining? Surely these … structures will collapse!"

Mr. Patel, who was seated next to the driver while his assistant drove in a car behind with the luggage, turned around. "May I answer Lady Andrew's question, my lord?"

"Yes, please," Andrew replied.

"These people are amazingly resilient, my lady. They find additional plastic or whatever to stop the leaks."

"I am surprised," Andrew said, "to see all the TV antennas and even some satellite discs!"

"My lord, you would be astonished if you knew how many of these people are reasonably well-off! Many of them make more money by begging than if they had a modest job," Mr. Patel explained patiently. "Besides, they don't have fixed working hours!"

"But there are people lying on the ground sleeping." Pamela was puzzled.

"Yes. Some of them have been born in these sheds. Others have lived all their lives on the streets and are accustomed to sleeping wherever they are."

Pamela shook her head. "I cannot imagine ..."

Mr. Patel was eager to explain. "My lady, I must tell you that, when Prime Minister Indira Gandhi was in power, she had barracks built for people in the slums and for the homeless. But they didn't like to be ordered around to do what the supervisors were demanding. Very soon the people left and returned to their own primitive dwellings to be free to do whatever they wanted. So you see, my lady, the housing project failed most unfortunately."

The car had to stop at a red light. Even though it was past midnight, it was approached by several small children extending their hands, begging.

Mr. Patel opened his window and told them in a severe voice, "Go away! Do not harass foreigners!"

Reluctantly, the children moved away.

"They looked hungry," Pamela commented.

With a patient voice of a schoolteacher, Mr. Patel said: "Believe me, Lady Andrew, they are clever enough to find food."

She was not reassured, but seeing Andrew slightly shaking his head, she understood and remained silent. However, quietly, she felt disturbed by seeing so many people sleeping on the streets.

By the time they reached the Taj Mahal Hotel, it was exactly twenty-four hours since they had left London. They were assisted by handsomely uniformed guards with fanlike turbans. Mr. Patel had made all preliminary check-in arrangements so that the reception needed only their passports and credit card information. Another uniformed valet, with an equally elaborate turban, accompanied Pamela, Andrew, Mr. Patel, and h s assistant to a spacious suite in the original palace-like building. The valet offered to unpack their suitcases, but Pamela thanked him and said that they would do it themselves.

"I hope these accommodations are satisfactory, my lord and lady?" Mr. Patel inquired.

"Yes, they are fine," Andrew responded.

"Yes, Mr. Patel, they are lovely. Thank you." Pamela smiled at him.

"At what time would you like me to meet you tomorrow ... or, perhaps, even later today?"

"I have no idea," Andrew replied. "My wife was unable to sleep on the plane. We'll call you when we feel rested."

They enjoyed a leisurely shower and collapsed into the beds. They slept through the rest of the night until ten o'clock the next morning.

In spite of going to bed late, Pamela found Andrew awake when she opened her eyes. He leaned over for a kiss and smiled. "Good morning, my lovely Pamela."

She returned both his kiss and smile. "Did I sleep too long?"

"Oh, no, my love. How are you feeling?"

Pamela sat up. "Wonderful!"

"Ready to conquer India?"

"Absolutely ... after a quick tub bath. Did you see how wonderfully deep the marble tub is and all the lotions and soaps?"

Andrew laughed. "No, I did not. I am sure you know how to use them!"

"I hope you are hungry ... because I am!"

"How about having breakfast here in the room? You can have your bath while we wait for it. I also have to call Mr. Patel. How long would you say until we'll be ready to go out?"

She glanced at the clock over the fireplace. "It is ten o'clock now. We need to unpack. How about noon?"

A small table with a crisp white tablecloth was wheeled in, laden with a silver bowl filled with fresh croissants, scones, danish pastries, toasts, butter balls, marmalade, and strawberry jam. There was also a silver pot of strong hot coffee for Pamela and a silver teapot with a pitcher of hot milk, raw sugar cubes, and white sugar. A pitcher with a generous portion of orange juice and some lemon slices were neatly arranged with fine china and silverware. The valet moved the table near one of the windows overlooking the Bay. He then removed a plate cover and served Andrew scrambled eggs with two bangers!

While eating their delicious breakfast, they watched people promenading along the shore. Some were jogging, and others walked briskly while a couple of men were leisurely sitting on the low stone wall munching on buns. A large and a small dog of unidentifiable races tried to keep up with the joggers.

"Bombay is welcoming you to a beautiful afternoon, Lady and Lord Andrew!" Mr. Patel greeted them at noon in the hotel lobby.

"Good morning, indeed!" Andrew nodded. "Where do you suggest we go today?"

"Good morning, Mr. Patel. Thank you for bringing us to our hotel so dreadfully early in the morning." Pamela smiled at their new guide.

"You are most welcome! How are you, my lady? I know Mr. Gupta has made some suggestions, but you are, of course, free to select whatever you prefer."

"Pamela thought we might go to see the Haji Ali Dargah mosque at Worli. Then my father mentioned to also visit the Mahalakshmi Temple, if possible."

To reach the mosque they had to walk along a long narrow pier reaching far out into the Arabian Sea. The tide was high, which sent in rolling waves that crashed their white foam crowns into the rocks, at times splashing people who were walking near the edge. Children especially enjoyed running near the rocks and shrieked with delight whenever they got sprayed. Most women were wearing either black or colorful salwar kameez the knee-length shirts with long trousers below—preferred by many Moslems, with their heads discreetly covered by veils. Most men wore crisp shirts, sweaters, or vests with trousers. Some parents were pushing prams. The crowd was in a festive and playful mood.

A marble gateway led into the mosque square where musicians sitting on a carpet played pretty tunes on drums and flutes. One old man sat with them, perhaps a retired member, who joined his flat palms together in the lovely gesture of greeting—namaste—and thanks whenever someone put a coin in the copper plate before him.

At the entrance of the mosque everybody had to leave their shoes in the care of an attendant to whom one also gave a coin while hoping that when they exit, their shoes would still be there.

The white marble building was covered with mosaics of delicate flower motifs and inscriptions from the Quran. It was refreshingly cool inside! Even though there was a crowd, the pilgrims were respectful in the sanctuary. A magnificent golden dome stretched out over the worshippers and admiring crowd. It was supported by a canopy and surrounding marble walls. The architecture was Indo-Islamic with harmonizing proportions. Tourists were ushered to a separate section in order not to disturb the men and women who were kneeling on prayer rugs. The beauty of the surroundings created a solemn but festive atmosphere. There were moments when Pamela felt she was intruding into sacred moments of prayers that should be most private.

Before driving next to the Hindu temple, Mr. Patel suggested they taste some snacks from a little open-air stall. He selected meat samosas for each and some vegetable pakoras. Andrew tried the Indian tea, which was a mixture of tea, boiled milk, spices, and lots of sugar. After tasting it from his cup, Pamela selected a ginger beer, which she ended up sharing with him. To change their taste, Mr. Patel recommended *gulab jamun*, which were small round cake balls soaked in a heavy rose- or almond-flavored syrup. They were extremely sweet but tasty!

In front of the Mahalakshmi Temple were lots of little stalls with trinkets for sale in all colors and sizes. Children pulled on their parents' hands to allow them close enough in the hope that there was just one special trinket for them.

Flower vendors were close to the entrance, inviting visitors to buy some for their offering to the goddess Lakshmi. Mr. Patel bought two lovely fresh jasmine garlands and gave them to Pamela and Andrew as offerings to the priest once inside the temple. There was an eager melee while people took off their slippers or shoes to store them with a custodian who nodded, pleased after he received a handsome coin from Mr. Patel.

Entering the refreshingly cool hall, they realized how hot it was outside! They waited for their turn to offer the flowers to the priests, who bowed their thanks and gave Pamela another garland, which the priest gently draped over her head. She clasped her palms together in the most graceful gesture of respect and thanks. In addition, Andrew offered some money, which brought a big smile on the old priest's face. The goddess Lakshmi was very voluptuous and richly decorated with silk scarves, flower garlands, and pearl necklaces. Her expression was severe! At the foot of the altar were bowls with food that would be eaten happily later by the Hindu priests!

"May I suggest we stop at a nice restaurant called Lotus Queen not far from here at Breach Cancy." Mr. Patel said. "Perhaps when you feel a bit rested you might wish, since we are here, to shop in this neighborhood with some of the best shops with good selections."

"What kind of shops?" Andrew asked.

"There are a couple of antique stores, carpet places, and material and sari shops. Then there are several art galleries and fine jewelers."

"What do you think, Pamela?"

"Could we decide after having had lunch and resting our feet a bit?"

"Would you prefer to return to the Taj for a nap?" Mr. Patel asked.

"Oh no, thank you! We have so little time here it would be such a shame if we were not exploring as much as possible."

In front of the restaurant, Mr. Patel suggested that he would meet them again in about one hour.

But Andrew stopped him. "I, that is, I am quite certain that my wife agrees with me that we would very much appreciate your joining us in whatever meal we are having. It would be a good time to plan our next adventures. Unless, of course, you do not wish to join us?"

Their guide was somewhat surprised. "This is very kind of you, my lord. It is not at all expected of you to do so! However, I would be honored to join you for lunch and whenever you wish. Thank you, my lord."

"Ah ..." Andrew smiled. "If you agree, Mr. Patel, why don't you call me simply sir or Mr. Prescott? *My lord* and *my lady* sound too formal. Don't you agree, Pamela? Perhaps *ma'am* or *Mrs. Prescott* would be acceptable to you."

Pamela agreed. "Yes. What about lunch for our driver?"

"Thank you, ma'am. Mr. Dalal is used to bringing his own canteen prepared by his wife."

The light vegetable dishes with naan were delicious and were accompanied into the stomachs with ginger ale, which had a more intense ginger flavor than the English version. After sharing vanilla ice cream and coffee, they felt restored and ready to shop.

Andrew decided that they would start with the materials and sari shop. The selection of types of materials from raw cotton to the finest weave—from raw silk to veil-thin silk to heavy silk in all imaginable colors—were mind-boggling to Pamela. After some hesitation, she was being measured for any gown, dress, coat, jacket, or blouse. With Andrew's advice, she selected a warm plum-colored light-silk material for an evening gown in a very plain but elegant style. Then she decided on a pale mustard-yellow wash-and-wear and a hot-pink and also a sky-blue material for dresses she could wear at school. The tailor provided a stack of fashion magazines to choose styles, but most were too fancy. Andrew, of course, offered his opinion on which style to select, and Pamela eventually agreed. The manager of the store persuaded her to look at some saris.

"Oh, I don't wear saris."

"Madam, allow us to drape one on you to see if you like the effect." He gestured to a beautiful young woman to assist Pamela in draping the sari while he watched. "With your ivory complexion, I would say a darker and rich color would enhance your beauty."

Pamela looked at Andrew. "We had not planned on buying saris."

"Come to think of it, I think it might be a nice touch for you to wear a sari when you visit your school!"

"I had not thought about this. Yes, my mother told me that she used to wear saris to the school."

"Madam, please come and look into this mirror," the manager urged.

For a split-second, Pamela thought she saw her mother in one of her photographs taken while she was in India. The final selection was made for a pale-turquoise light-crepe silk sari, a rich cobalt silk with woven silver flower borders, then a deep-purple silk sari with a broad pattern in gold at the edges and a wide design at the end section, and the last was a medium-dark-gray silk sari with beautiful woven silver threads and borders. On each sari cloth was enough material for a matching blouse. For the petticoats, she asked for matching heavier silk rather than cotton. She told the manager that she had seen some women wearing most beautiful silk saris but with cotton petticoats, the silk didn't always slide down to cover their shoes.

"Yes, of course, madam," the manager agreed. "How soon do you need the saris, dresses, and gown?"

Both Andrew and Pamela looked at Mr. Patel, who replied, "The parcel should be sent to the Taj no later than January 7 by noon."

"We will be pleased to deliver everything by January 7 noon."

Pamela smiled. "Thank you."

"It is entirely my pleasure to assist you, madam, sir."

Later, when they were back in the car, Pamela remarked, "Andrew, this is only our first day, and we already spent so much money on me!"

He laughed. "I would say that it was a good beginning. I am looking forward to seeing you in your new saris."

"Thank you very much, my darling!"

Mr. Patel, who was sitting next to Mr. Dalal, the driver, turned and asked, "How are you holding up, ma'am, sir?"

Andrew looked at his wife before answering. "I feel that we are somewhat tired. We seem to still be on British time."

"Would you like to return to the Taj? We could stroll around the Gateway of India, which is right in front of your hotel. I am sure you know that it had been built to welcome the Prince of Wales."

The place was crowded with happy people shuffling about, chatting and photographing while their children played hide-and-seek. Hundreds of pigeons claimed the monument as their home while carelessly leaving their marks on the ageing walls.

At the edge was a boat landing. There were several small boats bobbing in the water at the bottom of stairs, waiting for tourists to take them to the Elephanta Caves on a small island nearby named after the caves.

"Wasn't one of Mr. Gupta's sightseeing suggestions to see these caves?" Pamela asked their guide.

"Yes, ma'am. It is a popular attraction. It is well worth seeing. You may wish to visit the caves tomorrow. May I mention that you wear sturdy shoes as the grounds and steps to the caves are very uneven."

Andrew had been watching the little boats and looked somewhat unconvinced as to their seaworthiness and asked, "How long have these boats been serving the island?"

Mr. Patel smiled. "Please do not worry, sir. They are quite safe. They are frequently checked by the Maharashtra Tourist Safety Board."

Andrew nodded. "I am glad to hear it!"

Pamela withdrew her camera from her purse to take pictures. Almost immediately, she was surrounded by three children begging while an older boy was standing nearby, observing.

It took only a definite sweep of Mr. Patel's hand to chase them away. "They are such a nuisance," he grumbled apologetically. "Best thing is to ignore them. But you need to be alert around them, especially while you take photos! I am afraid some are expert pickpockets."

"Thank you for the warning. We'll remember!" Andrew responded. "Can you recommend a place to have dinner?"

"The Taj has several restaurants. There is the Seaview Lounge on the second floor, which is casual but offers a nice selection of lighter fare. It is a favorite spot where you can enjoy a leisurely meal. Then there is a very good Chinese and French restaurant as well as a very informal snack place. Of course, you can always order room service."

"Thank you, Mr. Patel." Pamela looked at Andrew. "If you agree, Andrew, I would prefer to stay in and make it an early night."

He smiled at her and nodded. "I do agree with you, darling."

"At what time would you like me to meet you tomorrow?" Mr. Patel asked, then added, "If you would like to visit the Elephanta Caves, I would suggest meeting at eight o'clock at the pier. The earlier we leave, the better as it will get quite hot later on. I'll have the tickets for you."

"Very good." Andrew nodded. "We'll be at the pier at eight o'clock."

When they were getting ready for bed, Pamela asked, "Are you satisfied with our excursion today?"

"Yes, for the first day, I think we did rather well. Not too much exertion! An interesting contrast between the Muslims at the mosque and the Hindus at the temple."

"I am so glad that most people of these major religions are getting along now, most of the time. They seemed content, happy, and enjoying themselves, especially the children!"

"Yes," Andrew responded with some hesitation. "I do hope the two major religions in India will learn to remain and live in peace."

In spite of the continuing traffic outside, they slept well.

"I am looking forward to visiting the Elephanta Caves," Pamela said during their breakfast at the lovely Seaview Lounge.

Mr. Patel had already purchased the tickets and secured two seats at a window in the small boat. Very soon the small boat was filled almost shoulder to shoulder with Indian and foreign tourists. Immediately after a sharp whistle pierced the air, the boat engines started rumbling and shaking as it moved sideways away from the landing.

The sea was relatively calm, but Pamela felt a bit queasy. She tried to breathe evenly and not look at the water. After a while, she got up and moved through the crowd toward an open space in the floor of the boat where one could see the engine room below. The engines worked in a synchronized rhythm. Soon she noticed, to her shock and horror, that there were two workers on opposite sides continuously scooping up seawater that had flooded the engine room floor and emptying the buckets through open holes back into the sea!

She nudged her way back to Andrew. "We are sinking, Andrew!"

He noticed that she had turned white with fear and reached for her hand. "What are you saying?"

"I saw the engine room floor flooded with water, and there are two men pouring the water back into the sea. This boat is leaking!"

Mr. Patel overheard Pamela's comments and quickly reassured her. "No, ma'am, this happens all the time. Please believe me. This boat is not sinking!"

Concerned, Andrew reminded Mr. Patel, "You mentioned that the condition of these boat are being frequently checked for safety by the authorities."

"Yes, my lord," he responded a touch nervously. "I assure you that the boat is safe. We have never had an accident."

The crossing seemed endless to Pamela. She kept focusing on the island, which seemed only very slowly to be coming closer. When the boat reached the landing, Pamela felt relieved to be back on solid ground. She didn't want to think about the return trip on such a boat.

To her surprise, Andrew embraced her in front of the crowd. "Are you all right, my darling? Do you want to stay or return?"

She smiled at his concern. "I am fine now, thank you, my love. We'll go to the caves as planned."

The Elephanta Caves had been carved out by devoted Hindu priests during the ninth and eighth centuries. However, when the Portuguese took hold of the island, the soldiers destroyed a great deal of the carvings and paintings on the walls. Today, the caves are still a popular place for pilgrims and tourists who enjoy the island for a pleasant picnic outing. The most famous sculpture is the Trimurti—a large three-headed carved bust. One face is reflecting the god Siva (the Destroyer), then the god Vishnu (the Preserver), and then the god Brahma (the Creator). The caves are deep, and some have amazingly high ceilings.

The adult visitors from many religions, when they see these works of devotion, surely must feel admiration and respect for the priests of so long ago! Some children found the heavy supporting pillars a wonderful place to run around while trying to catch one another.

At noon Mr. Patel suggested they have something to drink at a small open-air refreshment stand with a few folding tables and chairs arranged under bright-red umbrellas that provided welcome shade. Various salty snacks and cookies were offered as well as some sandwiches. They had a choice of tea, coffee, ginger ale, or beer and several flavors of ice cream.

Before the next boat was due to depart, there was enough time to visit one other cave. By the time they reached the harbor, it was quite hot. Luckily, the boat was not very crowded. Most tourists preferred to spend more time exploring the island.

Pamela had decided not to sit at a window nor look into the engine room below. She had decided that it was not her destiny to drown!

Andrew was pleased when he heard Pamela ask, "What could we do this evening, Mr. Patel?"

"Perhaps, when it is cooler later on, we could drive to see the lighthouse at Nariman Point?"

"That sounds sensible," Andrew nodded.

"If you will excuse me for a couple of hours, I would like to go to my office to check and confirm all your travel arrangements. Sometimes things change," Mr. Patel said.

Before meeting Mr. Patel, Andrew and Pamela shared a cup of coffee. It was a wonderfully long drive to Nariman Point. Mr. Patel pointed out various buildings of interest. From the congested buildings and crowded streets that seemed to be filled with cars, trucks, buses, and some stray cows and dogs, people wound their way courageously between the traffic, ignoring the angry horns of drivers! As soon as they approached Colaba, the southernmost tip of the Bombay Peninsula, the scenery changed. The old and newer villas were partially hidden by walls and gardens. There were street-sweepers and flower merchants near more elegant stores. Even some high-rise buildings were sheltered by walls with guards standing leisurely at the entrances. This was a section of wealth and power.

Finally, at Nariman Point, Pamela and Andrew stood at the very spot where the lighthouse warned ships at night in the Arabian Sea, which lay spread out before them. To their delight, they were allowed to climb the steep stairs up to the top to see and admire the huge source of light that was magnified by various mirrors. There was a pleasant breeze that played mischief with their hair.

After descending the staircase, Andrew admitted to Mr. Patel, "Now I feel quite content with today's excursion. I think we'll go back to the Taj and rest."

"You might enjoy a swim in the pool before supper."

"That is a tempting suggestion, Mr. Patel." Pamela smiled.

"So what will we do tomorrow?" Andrew asked.

"We could drive again across the peninsula to Malabar Hill and another section of Nariman Point, a wealthy community of mostly Parsis, and visit the Hanging Gardens.

"Parsis?" Pamela remembered vaguely. "Are they the Zoroastrians, a religious community who fled Ancient Persia? If I remember correctly, they received asylum in Bombay and became prosperous and were leaders in philanthropy?"

"Yes, those are the Zoroastrians. They fled Persia during the fifth century when the Moslems concurred Persia and forced all Zoroastrians to either convert to Islam or to be killed. Many fled to India. Here they are called Parsis. They became prosperous and are leaders in business, professions, and philanthropy. We'll pass some Parsi fire temples, where you can see some replicas of reliefs from the Persepolis palaces. We are not allowed to enter their temples where they keep the holy fire."

Andrew was impressed. "Very good, Pamela. You remember your history lessons!"

After a hearty breakfast at the Seaview Lounge, Pamela and Andrew went for a stroll along the waterfront, feeding pigeons with a smuggled bun. They enjoyed a refreshing shower and got ready to meet Mr. Patel for the drive across the Bombay Peninsula to the famous Marine Drive.

"What a shame," Pamela commented. "Look at all these mansions that must have been beautiful once but are being terribly neglected."

"It is the sea air that corrodes them. The upkeep is very expensive," Mr. Patel explained. "The owners know how valuable the land is and wait to sell them at a handsome profit."

The scenery changed when Mr. Dalal drove through a hilly section called Malabar Hill. The mansions were surrounded by lush gardens and some high walls. There were not only guards but gates to the properties to ensure privacy. Judging from the types of cars, one could conclude that the residents were wealthy. More street sweepers made certain that any garbage was swept away immediately.

At one point, in front of a Parsi fire temple, Andrew asked the driver to stop the car. He and Pamela got out to approach and study the carved relief facade. It depicted winged lions with human heads. Even though the lions' bodies were heavy, the graceful wings made them look elegant! Over the entrance was an intriguing carved disc from which a priest or a king in long robes was standing between two extended elegant wings. An elderly priest dressed in a long white robe and a white cap on his head descended the well-used stone steps. He nodded to them. "Good morning."

Pamela approached him first. "Good morning … priest?"

He chuckled in response. "Yes, I am a priest, a *dastur*. Where are you from?"

Pamela pointed at Andrew. "He is Andrew Prescott, and I am Pamela. We are on our honeymoon. We live in a small town in Kent, England."

"Welcome to Bombay."

"Thank you, Dasturji," Andrew responded. "Our guide tells me that we are not allowed inside Parsi temples."

"Yes, you have been correctly informed. Only born Parsis and Zoroastrians are allowed inside to worship at the holy fire."

"I am sorry," Pamela said, then smiled. "At least we got to see this beautiful facade of your temple."

"Thank you, ma'am. Yes, we are very proud of our temples. May I wish you a pleasant honeymoon?"

"Thank you, Dasturji," Pamela and Andrew said simultaneously.

At Malabar Point they enjoyed once again, the expansive view of the Arabian Sea.

On the way back to Marine Drive, they stopped at a Jain temple with rich stone carvings. Monks in bright-yellow and bright-orange robes were either busy performing tasks or huddled in prayer. Mr. Patel led them to the entrance where a priest welcomed them and offered to show the interior. He told them about the history of the Jain religion. It amazed both visitors to see the carved ceilings and solid columns and walls. There were no flower vendors, so Andrew offered some money to the priest, who bowed his thanks.

When Andrew saw the Oberoi, he persuaded Mr. Patel to join them for lunch. A uniformed waiter led them to a window table and handed over the menu folder. There were so many tempting dishes promised. It was hard to decide. There was a shrimp tandoori, another with the exotic name *roghan josh*, then a cauliflower with cumin dish was added on to one shajahani biryani, which was an elegant dish of spiced rice with saffron, almonds, and light and dark raisins. There was also dahl and naan. There was no doubt that beer was the only possible drink accompaniment! The waiter was astonished when Pamela asked him to pack up the leftovers. She had a plan! Even though their hunger was well satisfied, they ordered almond pistachio ice cream, which they enjoyed with coffee and tea.

The leftovers were discreetly handed over to Pamela at the exit. She gave them to Mr. Patel after exiting the restaurant. "This is for your family."

"But I could not, ma'am."

"Of course you can."

Waiting at the entrance for the car, Andrew suppressed a yawn. "I think I would like to go back to the hotel and rest for the remainder of the afternoon. How do you feel, darling?"

"The same. I am not used to such rich lunches. Besides both you, Mr. Patel, and Mr. Dalal have not had much rest since we arrived."

"There is a Western classical music concert this evening. If you wish to go, Mr. Dalal could pick you up at seven o'clock."

Andrew looked at Pamela, but she shook her head. "No, thank you. I think we would prefer just a lazy evening."

When they entered their suite, the sari parcel was waiting for them. If Pamela had not felt so tired, she would have tried on the gown and the dresses. But she examined the saris carefully. They were done beautifully!

While Pamela soaked in the marble tub, Andrew showered with his favorite sandalwood soap.

"May I join you and help you sleep?" Pamela asked when she came out of the bathroom accompanied with a cloud of jasmine scent.

Andrew chuckled. "By all means!" He moved over to allow her to join him.

"We'll soon have to leave Bombay."

"Yes. But remember, darling, the most important reason for coming here on our honeymoon is seeing your school in Dhalarnabad!"

"You are right of course."

They slept, then made love and slept again. It was wonderful to be lazy and not have to worry about time.

"Am I glad we didn't arrange to go to a concert this evening," Pamela confessed.

"So am I. Incredibly, I feel hungry."

Pamela sighed. "Do we have to get dressed?"

"We can have room service, and you can hide in the bathroom while the valet delivers the food."

"Great idea!"

Andrew enjoyed an omelet called akoory with caramelized onions, ginger, and cilantro while Pamela nibbled on a cucumber sandwich.

"Good morning, Lady and Lord Andrew!" Mr. Patel greeted them. "My wife asked me to thank you for the wonderful food. She said that they will inspire her to try out new recipes."

"I am glad."

"Did you rest well?"

"Yes, thank you."

Pamela laughed. "We were even too lazy to go down for dinner."

"It seems the time difference and climate change affected you. I must say I was surprised with how well you both held up so far."

"Any suggestions for today?" Andrew asked.

"Yes, if you are interested in contemporary Indian art, you may wish to visit one of the best gallery museums called Jehangir Art Gallery."

"Yes, we would like to see paintings by Indian artists," Andrew said.

At the gallery were some handsome abstract paintings, but what Pamela and Andrew liked best were the stunning portraits of Indians of all ages and some stylized paintings of Indian women in brilliant saris along with some scenes of villages and landscapes.

"Would you like to see an Indian movie?"

"If we have time on our return to Bombay," Andrew responded with some hesitation.

"The reason I suggested it is that the audience is as much a spectacle as the movies themselves. They demonstrate freely their emotions—crying, laughing, dancing as much as possible in their seats and often calling out their opinions, which can create reactions from other people in the audience."

On their last evening, Pamela couldn't resist browsing in the bookstore at the Taj. She saw a good number of illustrated books on India that she planned to ask Andrew if they could have some of them shipped home.

The valet offered to pack their suitcases, but Pamela thanked him and explained that she wanted to do the packing according to the next places they would stop at. They had one large suitcase that was very heavy. Pamela had a smaller travel bag that she intended to carry and keep with her. Even though Mr. Patel repeatedly offered, Andrew insisted on carrying his heavy briefcase. It contained important personal documents and several legal articles. Everything was packed before they went to the Seaview Lounge for breakfast.

CHAPTER 19

Journey to Lonavla

*A*s previously arranged, Mr. Patel was waiting for them at nine o'clock in the Taj lobby to take them to the railway station. The luggage was quickly stowed away in the trunk.

When Mr. Dalal stopped in front of a palace-like building with lots of people rushing around, Pamela asked, "Is this the railway station?"

Mr. Patel smiled at her. "Yes, ma'am, this is Victoria Terminus. Please stay close to me."

Immediately several porters approached, hoping to carry their suitcase. Mr. Patel informed the chosen porter the train, coach, and seats numbers.

Pamela watched with trepidation as the porter settled the heavy suitcase on his head and disappeared between the hurrying crowd of travelers, thinking, *There go most of my shoes and clothes for the trip.*

Mr. Patel had a keen eye and guessed what she had been thinking. "Please do not worry, ma'am, you will find your suitcase at your seats."

The travelers seemed to move together like a river in the center hallway. Toward the walls were vendors offering cards of Indian monuments, tiny statuettes of Mahatma Gandhi and all kinds of Hindu gods, glass bangles, bead necklaces, plastic watches, alarm clocks, etc. Other vendors offered sodas. Still, at another corner, a vendor offered ice cream from a refrigerated cart on wheels while next to him a man offered hot Indian tea. There were some families settled down on small rugs while waiting, perhaps, for relatives or friends arriving today. Even small children seemed oblivious to all the strangers rushing around them.

When they reached the platform, Pamela saw their suitcase swaying on the head of the porter far ahead of them. She felt overwhelmed by so many people bumping into her while rushing by and reached for Andrew's hand while trying to keep up with Mr. Patel, who walked ahead of them.

"If our suitcase gets lost, we can always buy the necessary items."

But Pamela thought to herself, *Yes, but what about my beautiful saris?*

Of course, Mr. Patel had been right. The suitcase was securely stored above her seat. He tipped the porter, who smiled and left in search for the next customer. Andrew had insisted that Mr. Patel travel with them in the same coach. When they discovered a cart with newspapers and magazines, Andrew asked Pamela if she wanted anything, but she preferred to read her book. The two men stepped out to buy newspapers. For Andrew, it was the *Times of India* and a one-day old *London Times,* and it was two newspapers in Gujrati for Mr. Patel.

"Pamela, which do you prefer, looking forward or backward?" Andrew asked thoughtfully.

"I'd like to look forward, thank you."

Mr. Patel took the seat next to Andrew. The seats were quite comfortable, and the coach was blessedly air-conditioned!

From the safety of her window seat in the train, Pamela watched amusedly the chaos of people going this and that way. Some were hurrying, while others stood in the way or moved along leisurely. The vendors managed to maneuver their carts while offering food and drinks to passengers leaning out of the windows. The voices of vendors, travelers, useless loudspeakers and the sound of engines, hissing brakes, and shrill whistles combined reminded Pamela of a very modern concert with challenging harmonies and discordants!

The moment a train pulled in on the opposite platform, Pamela was amazed at how many people were squashed into the coaches, and some were half-hanging out of doors. "Is this not dangerous, Mr. Patel?"

He chuckled. "They are used to it. This is the way they commute to work in Bombay each weekday.'

Andrew looked up from reading the newspaper and suppressed a smile. Although all the seats were filled, there seemed to be lots of air and space. Finally, their train started moving—at first very slowly before gaining some speed Mr. Patel opened the window so that Pamela and Andrew could watch people waving goodbyes and calling out their last reminders and greetings. But soon the station was out of sight, and they closed the window and settled down in their seats.

Pamela had started to read but was unable to concentrate while a new world for her glided by the window. At first the train passed through incredible slums. Even there she could see women crouching near the rails and half-naked children playing precariously close to the moving train or climbing over other rails. *Why is this being tolerated?* she wondered but didn't want to ask Mr. Patel.

She felt relieved when the train passed through rural areas. Small villages and towns were scattered across the wide-open fields, some cultivated and others eft for cows, goats, and donkeys to roam freely. At some construction sites she saw women carrying baskets with bricks on their heads while men stood on fragile scaffolds placing bricks on and between mud, building houses. At other places Pamela observed women in colorful saris gracefully carrying clay or copper jugs on their heads and going or coming from cisterns. In some villages men were gathered in the shade under stretched canvases, probably discussing politics or local problems. Along rivers women were busy washing, actually beating clothes against stones, while small children kept close, amusing themselves. Sometimes she glimpsed old people sitting in front of huts grinding spices or grains.

"Aren't you getting tired looking out of the window?" Andrew asked.

Pamela smiled. "No, it is interesting to see the towns and villages and how people work and live. I have seen pictures in books and newspapers, but it is very different to actually see it myself."

At one point, a dining-car steward announced that lunch would be served in fifteen minutes.

"Would you like to have lunch?" Mr. Patel asked. "I will stay here while you dine."

"Are you hungry, Pamela?"

"No, thank you. But I'll come with you, if you like, to eat something."

"I am also not very hungry. You are welcome to go and have lunch Mr. Patel," Andrew offered.

"Thank you, my lord. There will be tea when we reach Lonavla."

The landscape changed as the train started climbing the hills. The vegetation became lusher. Deep canyons carved by rivers during thousands of years wound around hills. Uncaptured wells gushed from high ridges over bare rocks glistening in the sunshine, creating illusions of floating veils before reaching the flowing streams on the valley floor. Tropical forests offered welcome refuge to the remaining wildlife.

"What kind of wildlife is still living in these dense forests?" Pamela asked.

"We have very few panthers, leopards, and lions left. But there are monkeys galore. They are the mischief-makers and often thieves!"

"Can they be restrained from leaving the canyons?"

"You mean like a fence?"

"Yes."

"No. A fence would be useless because these monkeys climb, jump, and leap from any high fence, rock, or tree."

"Is there a way to safely observe the animals in their habitat?" Andrew asked.

"Yes and no. Sometimes there are hunts arranged, but it is risky."

"I can imagine. Especially when an animal is wounded but not killed! What happens when the hunters kill a panther or lion?"

"It depends. If the hunter is a VIP, he or she gets to keep the head and fur as a gift and souvenir. The meat is usually distributed among the drivers. I have never tasted any of it."

"How do they hunt?" Andrew continued asking.

"There are the drivers—hired men who stalk the animal and lead it with the noise of drums and sticks into a trap where the hunters, usually on horseback, wait until they spot the animal. They use rifles to kill them."

"I do hope we'll not see any hunters while we are here. I very much dislike killing animals!" Pamela said.

The train stopped in Lonavla where a new driver, a Mr. Soli, and a porter were waiting.

The Lonavla Palace hotel was a generously spread-out lodge at the edge of a steep drop into the canyons. The bedroom was large with two twin beds. The curtains and bedspreads had bright floral prints in blue, turquoise, and orange colors, which rendered charm to the otherwise modest room. The living/dining room was connected by a double door and a balcony. The curtains were of the same material, and the furniture was solid and practical.

Pamela found not only some soap and lotion but also mosquito spray in the bathroom. "Can we use this?" she asked Mr. Patel, who had come to check the accommodations to assure himself that his clients were satisfied.

"Yes. It is meant for the occupants of these rooms. I am afraid during evenings the mosquitos grow hungry."

"Ah!" Pamela understood. "It is thoughtful of the management! We'll use it whenever necessary."

Andrew asked Mr. Patel, "Is there a restaurant we can have a lunch-tea combination?"

"Yes. It is next to the lobby. It's called Eaglehurst."

After the suitcase had been put in their bedroom, they went to have lunch. "You will join us, I hope?" Andrew invited their guide.

The waiter led them to a table at the very edge of a wide terrace that extended over the deep drop into the canyon. It created the impression of floating high in the air. At first Pamela was given a chair directly next to the railing. When Pamela looked down, her stomach felt queasy, and she got up. "I would prefer a seat on the other side of this table."

During a hearty lunch Pamela asked Mr. Patel, "Where is your room?"

"My room is in the basement. I'll give you my extension number."

Andrew asked their guide, "Have you been to Lonavla before?"

"Yes, with my parents when I was twelve years old."

"Has it changed much since then?"

Before responding, he looked around. "No, not really. You see these hill stations are mostly visited by foreigners and city people who come for holidays. Many wealthy people have their own bungalows here. They like these places to remain the way they are. The villagers are mostly farmers who tend to their livestock and grow wheat and other vegetables. They sell their products to the few hotels and vacationers. Then many are employed by the hotels or owners of the mansions. The women weave and sew wool items and sell them at fairs. Unfortunately, many of the younger generation leave to work in the city."

From the menu Pamela and Andrew selected a dish with chicken in a creamed curry gravy and goat meat with lentils and biryani with dahl while Mr. Patel chose a spicy eggplant dish with naan. They tasted local beer, which was quite refreshing. With the tea and coffee, baklavas and halvahs were served.

"How far is Dhalarnabad from here?" Pamela asked.

"Approximately twenty kilometers."

"I understand that some children walk up to ten kilometers to school."

"Yes. It is the way of life here. Most villagers walk for kilometers to their fields and flocks and carry their harvest to villages, hotels, and mansions. Not each village has a school or even a pharmacy. Doctors travel far to reach their patients. Here in Lonavla is a small infirmary with a few rooms for very sick patients."

"This is why my mother chose Dhalarnabad for her school to enable more children access to a good education."

"This was most admirable of her!"

"What do the people do for amusement?" Andrew asked.

"Some better-off villagers have TVs. In more remote villages, during fairs that are called mela, Indian movies are projected on a stretched white sheet used as a screen. It is usually the highlight of a fair and well attended! For such occasions, villagers dress up and wear their jewelries."

"What do they sell at a fair?" Pamela asked.

"The men bring their livestock and produce while women bring baked goods and their handicrafts. For the young ones, there are always peddlers with cheap toys and candy. Food that is not produced locally, toiletries, pharmaceutical items, and household goods are being trucked in to small stores."

"Can we go to one of these fairs?"

Mr. Patel asked the waiter and was told that there would be a fair in Khandala tomorrow.

"Oh, Khandala!" Pamela recognized the village name. "Isn't it on our way to Dhalarnabad?"

"Yes, it is. We'll pass by tomorrow."

After the combination lunch-tea, they agreed to meet one hour later so they could refresh and unpack their suitcases. The plan was to explore Lonavla. In the center of town were several shops. In one grocery store Pamela was surprised to find Scottish bitter-orange marmalade, her favorite! There was an amazing selection of video tapes and CDs with mostly Indian films! There was also a stand with magazines with the most beautiful Indian women on the covers that were mostly in Hindi. To Andrew's delight, he found several late issues of the *London Times,* which he bought at reduced price. In a refrigerated section were all kinds of Indian and foreign beers, Coca-Cola, and other sodas. Trays of eggs, milk cartons, fresh butter, and jars of ghee (clarified butter for cooking). Fresh produce were neatly piled up on flat wooden crates.

Next door was a cobbler sewing custom-made shoes, nice leather purses, and briefcases. The smell of leather was nostalgic for Andrew as it reminded him of the tack room at his father's stable. When they learned that the cobbler would be willing to sew walking shoes for them both, Pamela and Andrew had their feet carefully measured. The cobbler promised that he would deliver them and make certain that they were satisfactory!

The pharmacy was another store of interest. Behind a high counter worked a pharmacist who wore dark-rimmed glasses. On long bookcase-like shelves were glass jars arranged carefully by sizes, each carefully labeled. The rest of the store shelves were devoted to foreign as well as Indian beauty products that promised "wrinkle-free aging"! When Pamela discovered sandalwood, lavender, and jasmine soaps, she bought several of them.

"Would you like to go and see the Tiger's Leap? It is only about three kilometers from here."

"Does it have a barrier?" Pamela asked.

"I am not sure what you mean, ma'am."

"A railing or fence where one can hold onto? Looking down into the canyon makes me feel dizzy."

"Oh, I am very sorry! Would you like to change your room?"

"No, I love the view! I won't go all the way to the railing."

"At the Tiger's Leap, there are railings. You will be quite safe, ma'am."

As it turned out, Tiger's Leap was a huge granite rock that seemed to have been cut in half. There was no vegetation around it. About one meter before the drop was a double fence with wires.

"Did a tiger really leap from here into the canyon?" Pamela asked.

"It is what the villagers claim from generation to generation."

"How deep would you say this drop is?" Andrew asked while leaning over the fence to peer down into the dense forest below.

"About 400 to 450 meters." Mr. Patel pointed at a small copper plaque. "Here it says that one tiger kept returning to this spot, then jumped down. Obviously, it didn't get killed!"

"The treetops must have buffered the impact. Still, if it is true, it is amazing!"

The plateau was treeless, but the rocks had beautiful colors of orange, purple, copper, and some turquoise traces … probably rich in minerals!

Pamela picked up a stone, rubbed it, and showed it to Andrew. "Look what beautiful colors this stone has. One could sand it and make a tile of it."

Andrew chuckled. "Are you going to take it home?"

She smiled at him. "I don't know yet."

Mr. Patel advised that they leave Lonavla at seven o'clock on the following morning.

When they returned to the lodge, Pamela selected a video to watch on TV in their room. It was an Indian classic movie in bright colors. Of course, the story was overly dramatic with lots of mind-boggling dances and wailing songs but gorgeous costumes!

Finally, the day arrived when Pamela would see her mother's school!

In front of a full-view mirror in their bedroom, Pamela draped her new turquoise sari carefully over the matching petticoat and short blouse. She didn't even need the instructions, but she remembered that she had to tuck in tightly the wrapped sari end and pleats at the waist, then drape the remaining material from behind across her chest and attach the folds with a gold brooch, allowing the decorated end to fall freely behind her back.

It was the first time Andrew saw her in a sari. "Pamela, you look beautiful in a sari. I think you were born to wear saris!"

"Thank you, Andrew!" She smiled at him.

Even Mr. Patel and Mr. Soli, the driver, smiled and praised her.

The drive took them through some hamlets, abandoned dwellings, open fields, and a small village where she observed people doing their daily chores. The only thing that scared her were the trucks, called lorries, which were often driven too fast for the uneven country roads, threatening roaming cows, dogs, bullock carts, and pedestrians! Andrew had briefly told Mr. Patel of the fatal accident of his wife's parents here and had instructed the driver to pull over whenever possible when trucks were approaching.

While sitting tensely in the back seat, Pamela remembered her mother's letter in which she had expressed her constant fear of those trucks.

Being enormously sensitive, Andrew knew what she was thinking and reached out to take her hand in his to reassure her.

CHAPTER 20

Discoveries at Pamela's Inherited School in Dhalarnabad

They didn't stop in Khandala to see the fair. Mr. Patel recommended this so that they could reach the school as early as possible. However, when they approached Dhalarnabad, they noticed villagers draped in white saris—the color of mourning! They were headed toward the center of the village.

"What is happening?" Andrew asked Mr. Patel. "It looks like a funeral."

"Yes. Let me inquire what happened," he replied and got out of the car. When he returned, he explained that a panther had attacked and killed a boy on his way to school.

Pamela felt tears flooding her eyes. "That must have been one of my schoolboys," she stammered.

"Yes, I am afraid so." Andrew put his arm around her shoulder. "We must go to the school and find out how we can help."

"Yes." Pamela nodded.

A moment later, they saw the gate with a wide arch. At the top, in the center, was the Earl of Swendown's coat of arms over a large sign saying "The Lady Elizabeth Mary Rose School." She wanted to rejoice, but the news of the tragic death of the boy was far too shocking!

A guard was sitting at the gate. When he saw the car approaching, he got up and saluted smartly. He informed them that the cremation was about to take place near a small Hindu temple a few meters ahead.

"Darling, do you feel up to attending the ceremony?" Andrew asked.

Pamela swallowed then nodded. "Yes, I must."

They found some priests chanting prayers while people stood patiently near the pyre, which was covered with flowers. A group of schoolchildren stood at some distance while staring ahead.

Pamela saw them. *These are my schoolchildren.* She reached for Andrew's hand and struggled not to cry, but it was difficult! The children looked so terribly sad! She decided to walk over to them with Andrew to share the silent tribute to the boy she had never met. When the pyre was being lit, it suddenly occurred to Pamela that, most probably, it was here where her parents were also laid on pyres and cremated. She felt an overwhelming sadness filling her. She would have liked to walk away to grieve alone. But she saw the students standing there, watching in silence, and she felt that if they could watch this cremation, so must she! She felt that she received strength and courage through Andrew's firm and reassuring hold of her hand.

It was a while until she noticed two women staring and observing her while talking to each other. After the ceremony had ended, the women approached. The taller one spoke. "I hope you don't mind my asking, but you do look familiar. Have you been here before?"

"No, this is the first time," Pamela replied. "Perhaps you knew my mother?"

"Ah, yes, Lady Elizabeth!" the older woman nodded.

"Yes." Pamela smiled. "May I introduce my husband, Lord Andrew Prescott. I am Pamela."

The younger woman smiled politely. "We are, of course, honored that you came, even though this is a very sad day for us all at the school."

"Yes." Andrew nodded. "We were told of the tragic death of the poor boy."

"We are terribly sorry," Pamela added.

The older woman responded, "Thank you, my lady, my lord."

Pamela greeted them with "Namaste" then extended her hand. "Are you connected with the school? May we know your names, please?"

The younger woman introduced the older woman first. "This is Mrs. Chowdry, and I am Ms. Bannerji, headmistress of the Elizabeth Mary Rose School."

"We are pleased to meet you, ladies. We had hoped to visit the school and meet the children," Pamela said.

"Perhaps," Ms. Bannerji responded, "you could have informed us of your visit ahead of time. We could have arranged for a proper welcome."

Both Pamela and Andrew understood the not-too-subtle reproach.

"We didn't want to disturb the school routine," Pamela explained.

The headmistress laughed. "Our children love disturbances. Of course, not the kind we experienced today."

"Of course not."

"If you can afford the time, you are welcome to join us for lunch. We will eat with the students, so you will meet not only them but also our faculty," Ms. Bannerji informed them.

"This is very kind, Ms. Bannerji. My husband and I are looking forward to meeting all members."

While they were walking the short distance back to the school, Mrs. Chowdry said, "My late husband was appointed headmaster by Lady Elizabeth. We all loved her. She was such a gracious and generous lady! May I mention that you resemble her a great deal?"

"Do I?" Pamela smiled with delight. "I am so glad that you knew my mother and father."

"But we didn't know they had a daughter," Ms. Bannerji remarked.

"Well, I am the daughter!" Pamela felt disappointment but tried to ignore it. "I was six years old when they were killed. Somewhere here! But I remember my parents well, especially my mother."

Mrs. Chowdry shook her head with sympathy. "Yes. It was a dreadful day, the accident! We were all shocked and deeply saddened."

"Thank you, Mrs. Chowdry. My mother mentioned in a letter to me how terribly scared she had been of the lorry drivers on the road."

"And they are still driving recklessly!" Andrew added.

"I am afraid you are correct, my lord," Mrs. Chowdry agreed.

The headmistress suggested, "We have a guest room if you wish to freshen up before lunch."

"Thank you."

They reached the main building. A young servant came and was asked to take the visitors to the guest room.

Meanwhile, Mr. Patel informed Ms. Bannerji that her guests were to be addressed as Lord Andrew and Lady Andrew.

It was five minutes to one o'clock when Pamela and Andrew were escorted to the dining hall. The tables were arranged like a horseshoe. The students stood somewhat stiffly at their chairs, waiting for permission to be seated. Ms. Bannerji accompanied the visitors to the head table and indicated chairs on either side of her sitting in the center. After all the faculty members found their chairs, the headmistress gave a signal, and everybody sat down.

There was complete silence until Ms. Bannerji addressed the assembly. "We have two honored guests with us today, Lady and Lord Andrew Prescott. Lady Andrew is the daughter of the late Lady

Elizabeth, the founder of this school. I would like you to sing our school hymn for them."

The students stood up while an old man, the music teacher, stood in front of the head table and sounded the key. The children picked it up while he was indicating the rhythm. It was truly a lovely song, a blend of English and Indian tunes.

Both Pamela and Andrew smiled at them when they had finished singing.

"What a lovely hymn! Thank you very much," Pamela praised.

After everyone was served, Pamela asked Ms. Bannerji, "How many students do you have?"

"At the moment, thirty-nine. Two are too sick to come to school today."

"What subjects do you teach?" Andrew asked.

"We teach a full curriculum directed by the state of Maharashtra's Ministry of Education. In addition we teach music, dance, poetry, drama, creative writing, and hygiene." Ms. Bannerji sounded boastful when she continued, "We pride ourselves of a higher standard in all mandatory subjects! My faculty was carefully selected to keep enhancing our previous achievements."

"We also have a pretty good cricket team!" Mrs. Chowdry, who was sitting on the other side of Andrew, added, smiling.

"Ah, very important!" Andrew nodded approval. "How about vacations?"

Mrs. Chowdry chuckled. "Absolutely! It is the favorite time of our students!"

"I have been trained as a Montessori teacher," Pamela told Ms. Bannerji.

When Mrs. Chowdry heard, she smiled. "That is wonderful! I hope you will come here and teach some of our students."

Pamela looked at Andrew, who looked back at her with a blank expression. "Thank you, Mrs. Chowdry. You must know that we are newlyweds and are on our honeymoon here in India. I also have a contract in England to teach for the next three years at the academy. I will, however, be very pleased to pass on your suggestion to the headmistress there."

After lunch, Ms. Bannerji invited her guests to have tea in her office. The moment they entered, Pamela saw a large framed photograph of her mother behind the headmistress's desk. It was a lovely photo she had never seen before. Her mother wore a turquoise sari, which amused Pamela since she, too, was wearing a turquoise sari.

Andrew had also noticed the photograph and smiled at Pamela.

"May I compliment you, Mrs. Prescott, for wearing a sari? Did someone help you put it on? It must seem awkward for you," Ms. Bannerji remarked.

For an instant, Pamela was taken aback by the rather personal remark, then she put on a smile. "On the contrary! It is surprisingly comfortable and"—Pamela wanted the headmistress to know—"I had no help in draping it. It is quite logical."

Eager to change the subject, Ms. Bannerji asked, "Has there been a recent change in ownership of the school or financial arrangements?"

"Why do you ask?" Pamela responded with a question.

"I am afraid that the expenses of our school have exceeded the monthly income from the bank. To meet the present needs, we must appeal to whoever owns the school now to increase the monthly allowance."

Pamela looked at Andrew, sending a silent message. He understood and replied, "In order to study the budget for the school and related expenses, perhaps a financial consultant would be able to advise you."

Pamela felt uneasy with Ms. Bannerji. She had an idea. "Could we invite Mrs. Chowdry to join this discussion?"

"Mrs. Chowdry takes naps in the afternoon" came the prompt reply.

"I see." Somehow Pamela didn't believe her. "Do you have a treasurer?"

The headmistress replied too quickly. "No, we don't need one! I am perfectly capable to do the work. A saving, you might say!" She smiled slyly.

"You must have a board!" Andrew said. "Perhaps someone from the board could join us in this important discussion?"

"Mrs. Chowdry is a board member."

"Are there others?" Andrew asked.

"Our board is very small since we are a small school. Why would we need a large board?" Ms. Bannerji sounded somewhat defensive.

"Who else is on the board?" Pamela asked her.

"We had two more members, both died."

"How long ago?" Andrew grew suspicious.

"One was Mr. Murti. He died two years ago. He had been appointed by Lady Elizabeth. He was too old, in my opinion. The other was Mr. Pano. He died about one year ago."

"Do I understand correctly that Mrs. Chowdry and you are the only remaining board members at present?" Pamela asked with concern.

"Well, yes."

"Then there is a serious conflict of interest!" Andrew said firmly. "A board must be completely independent!"

Pamela happened to glance out of the window and saw Mrs. Chowdry walking in the garden. "Look, there is Mrs. Chowdry. She isn't taking a nap! We can ask her to join us." She stood up and opened the window. "Mrs. Chowdry! Would you like to join us for a cup of tea?"

When the elderly woman sat down, Pamela said, "We are glad you didn't take a nap this afternoon so you are able to be part of our discussion."

"A nap? I never nap in the afternoon." The moment Mrs. Chowdry said this, both Pamela and Andrew realized that it was Ms. Bannerji who wanted to meet alone with them.

"Ms. Bannerji informed us that the school has some financial difficulties," Andrew told her.

Mrs. Chowdry nodded while studying her hands in her lap. "Yes, it seems so."

Ms. Bannerji frowned and asked in a challenging voice, "Who are you? How dare you ask all these questions! You may be the daughter of Lady Elizabeth. Still, that does not give you the right to barge in, unannounced, and question me as if I were a criminal!"

Pamela controlled her increasing anger. "We told you, Ms. Bannerji, as the daughter of Lady Elizabeth Mary Rose, I feel responsible."

The headmistress shot out of her chair. "But who owns the school now?"

"I do."

There was a long moment of silence while the face of Ms. Bannerji reflected surprise, anger, and fear. She sat down. "I should have guessed!" she muttered to no one in particular.

"Ms. Bannerji," Pamela said calmly, "do you realize that I have the authority to stop all payments to the school? I must demand a detailed accounting of all monies spent over the last five years. I want to take them with me when we leave here on the morning of January 12. We are staying at the Lonavla Palace."

"That is too soon!" the headmistress protested.

"It shouldn't be. Surely, you yourself said it was a small school and that you have been acting as treasurer! You must have all accounts from 1976 to 1979 at hand. There is only one year, 1980, left to be accounted for."

"I have been too busy to keep financial records." Ms. Bannerji pointed at Mrs. Chowdry. "She is of no help. She is too old to do anything!"

Hearing the accusation, Mrs. Chowdry looked ashamed but kept silent.

"I know that there is a separate trust fund that was set up exclusively for the eventual expansion of the school. I hope that is still intact!"

"Well, no," Ms. Bannerji admitted. "We had to borrow against it to pay bills."

"For how long has this been going on?" Andrew asked.

"For the last two to three years at least," Mrs. Chowdry volunteered.

Ms. Bannerji turned toward her. "Mrs. Chowdry, you will keep out of this! I am handling this discussion, not you!"

"It is vital," Pamela said with a firm voice. "The survival of this school is at stake! I will need all the financial records turned over to me by January 11."

Mrs. Chowdry looked shocked. "Oh no, please, my lady, if the school were to be shut down, it would devastate the students! They are good children and deserve the best!"

Pamela went over to her and took her hand. "It is important to clear up this unfortunate situation. We'll be leaving on the morning of January 12. I need to know the financial situation. I only hope it isn't too late."

"My wife was hoping to observe some classes today," Andrew reminded the headmistress.

"Well, there are no classes today. The older students will play cricket."

Mrs. Chowdry explained, "Since it was such a sad morning for the children, we allowed some to play this afternoon."

Pamela smiled. "Yes, of course, that is a very good idea. What about the little ones?"

"They went on a nature walk on the plateau," Ms. Bannerji answered.

Pamela was shocked. "Are they safe from wildlife?"

Mrs. Chowdry assured her. "They went out with our strongest teachers! The students love it because they take tins and drums with them to create a racket to scare away any animals."

"That brings me to ask about the parents of the dead boy. How are they?"

Again, it was Mrs. Chowdry who answered. "They are hurting badly. You see, my lady, the boy, little Ashok, was handicapped but had a brilliant mind! He was in a wheelchair, which he could manage most of the time though hills were hard for him. But he never complained. He was the first in all subjects. I used to tease him by calling him my encyclopaedia. His parents expected him to go to university and get a good job that would help him support them in their old age. But now ..." She was almost in tears.

"I would like to visit the parents, if possible."

"How long did you say you are staying here?" the headmistress asked, grateful for the change of topic.

"I told you, Ms. Bannerji, that we'll leave on the morning of the twelfth. Please remember, I will need the financial records by the evening of the eleventh."

The headmistress kept quiet.

Mrs. Chowdry asked, "Could you perhaps see Ashok's parents today?"

"Yes, if someone can come with us to show the way. We have a car and driver."

"I would like to go with you, Lady Andrew," Mrs. Chowdry volunteered.

Pamela smiled at her. "Yes, of course, I'll need a translator! I would appreciate that. Thank you."

Andrew asked Pamela, "Would you mind terribly if I were to watch the cricket game?"

She laughed. "Not at all, darling. Have fun!"

It seemed a long drive to the next village, but Pamela welcomed the opportunity to talk to Mrs. Chowdry alone. When they passed a flower stand in a small village, Pamela asked the driver to stop so she could buy flowers.

"May I say something, my lady?" Mrs. Chowdry asked shyly.

"Yes, of course."

"Ashok's parents are very poor. They would welcome food rather than flowers."

"I am so glad you told me Mrs. Chowdry. Where can we buy food?"

"A few houses down this road will take us to a grocer."

"What kind of food do you think would be best?"

"The basics like flour, sugar, salt, tea, condensed milk, lentils, peas, nuts, grains, eggs, oil, butter, and perhaps some meat?"

"Please help me select."

The grocer was surprised when Pamela piled up the items on a side counter. It occurred to her that she should also buy some airtight containers to keep the food dry. She could tell that the grocer was very happy to help pack the groceries into the plastic containers. When she received the bill, she was surprised at how modest it was! She paid while Mr. Patel and Mr. Dalal stored the containers in the car trunk.

At first nobody responded to the knock on the door. It was only when Mrs. Chowdry called out her own name that a middle-aged man with white hair opened the door. He spoke in Hindi, "Ah, Mrs. Chowdry, it's you. Come in. My wife is feeling poorly."

"Good afternoon, Mr. Bindhi. I have a visitor with me. May we come in?"

When Mr. Bindhi saw the English woman approach, he hesitated, "We are not able to receive visitors."

"It is Lady Andrew, the daughter of Lady Elizabeth from the school."

"I really don't know ..."

Pamela came closer and greeted "Namaste" and waited for the father's reaction.

"Lady Andrew attended Ashok's funeral this morning. She is very sad and wishes to pay her respects."

The father relented. "In that case, she can come in." He stepped aside.

The woman lying on a low canvas bed asked, "Who is she?"

Mrs. Chowdry explained again. "She is the daughter of Lady Elizabeth of Ashok's school."

The woman stood up while clasping her palms together. "Namaste."

Pamela responded in the same way then said, "We do not wish to disturb you at this time, Mr. and Mrs. Bindhi. But I had to come to tell you how terribly sad we all are."

Mrs. Chowdry translated. When the men brought in the containers of food, Mrs. Bindhi dried her tears. "Thank you."

Mr. Bindhi crouched in front of the containers and stammered, "I have never seen so much food. Thank you, my lady! Perhaps I ought to call you an angel."

After Mrs. Chowdry had translated for Pamela, she smiled. "You are so very welcome."

Mrs. Bindhi made some tea. Pamela knew that she must not refuse and looked around the room, but there were no chairs. She saw Mrs. Chowdry sitting down on a rug in the center of the small room, indicating to Pamela to join her. They were served the very sweet tea in small glasses with some kind of spiced cookie.

Mrs. Chowdry was very sensitive toward the grieving parents, asking, "Will you be able to maintain yourselves?"

Both Mr. and Mrs. Bindhi nodded. "Yes, we will work on construction sites."

When Pamela heard the translation of the conversation, she felt terribly sorry for them. She looked at their faces. They were carved with deep lines of grief and appeared much older. She tried to remember how much cash she had left in her purse. She passed very quietly the money to Mrs. Chowdry to give to Ashok's parents.

"Lady Andrew shares your grief and would like to give you a small consolation." While she was speaking in Hindi, she offered the money.

But Mr. Bindhi shook his head. "No, no! We cannot accept this lady's money! We will work." He sounded very proud.

Mrs. Bindhi stood up and inspected the food in the containers while shaking her head. "It must have been Ashok's spirit that led this lady to bring all this food."

Pamela smiled. "Yes, it was Ashok's spirit!"

Before leaving, she slipped the money under the carpet for the Bindhis to find after they had left.

During the drive back to school, Pamela asked Mrs. Chowdry, "How long has this financial difficulty at the school been going on?"

The woman was silent for a moment. "Since my husband, who had been the headmaster appointed by your lady mother, passed away three years ago. Ms. Bannerji"—she hesitated—"somehow, she received the position she holds today."

"Do you know if has she had any previous experience as a teacher, a business manager, or any other responsible position?"

"I am afraid her appointment is to some extent my fault," Mrs. Chowdry answered. "I was deeply grieving my husband's unexpected death. After he died, the other two board members hardly ever attended meetings or took interest in the welfare of the school. To make a long story short, it seemed that Ms. Bannerji applied for the job and was appointed headmistress."

"Does she have a resume?"

"If she has one, I have never seen it."

"Interesting. You are a board member! How were the two previous gentlemen board members selected?"

"During my husband's time, they were very active and truly interested in the welfare of the school, faculty, and students. With Ms. Bannerji, things changed. There had been more board members during my husband's time. But little by little, they all withdrew or, as you know, the last remaining two died."

"Is there anyone here who can challenge her?" Pamela asked.

Mrs. Chowdry hesitated a moment. "I am afraid she rules unchallenged."

"Who lives now in my parents' house?"

"Ms. Bannerji. No member of the faculty has ever been invited inside."

When they reached the school, they found a slightly disheveled Andrew. He had taken part in the cricket games and was in high spirits.

Before leaving the school, Pamela and Andrew were served tea in Ms. Bannerji's office. During that time Pamela reminded Ms. Bannerji that she expected the reports before leaving Lonavla, latest by the evening of January 11.

During their drive back to Lonavla, Pamela told Andrew what Mrs. Chowdry had told her. The information confirmed Andrew's suspicions.

"I know I cannot close down the school because too many students would be hurt." Pamela sighed deeply. "But Ms. Bannerji's head may topple! I will wait until I receive the financial budget reports."

"Don't be surprised if there are no reports produced before we leave."

"This is all so very disappointing!" Pamela sounded dispirited.

Andrew drew her closer. "I know, my darling. I wish I could help. After we leave here our real happy honeymoon will begin!"

They returned to the school on the following morning. Ms. Bannerji was nowhere to be seen. Pamela and Andrew went from classroom to classroom, observing. They were impressed by the teachers.

Pamela visited one classroom where the students stood up immediately when they saw her and greeted politely, "Good morning, Lady Andrew."

"Good morning, students. Please sit down."

One boy raised his hand, then stood up. "Someone said that you are a teacher."

"Yes," Pamela smiled. "I am a Montessori teacher in England."

"Do you like being a teacher?" another student asked.

"Yes, I do." Pamela smiled. "Not so much when I was young child and had mean teachers!"

The students laughed.

"Then why would you want to become a teacher?" a girl stood up and asked.

"To take revenge!" a boy said promptly, and again the students laughed.

"Actually, quite the opposite!" Pamela explained. "Because I suffered injustice and cruelty from my teachers and classmates, I wanted to find a way to teach—a method—that emphasizes patience, openness, tolerance, understanding, and kindness."

"We have some very nice teachers here," a girl offered.

"I am very pleased to hear this because my late mother, Lady Elizabeth Mary Rose, founded this school in the hopes of offering good education to as many rural children as possible to give them a better future."

"Are you also a Lady?" a boy asked.

Pamela smiled. "Yes, I am."

Another boy stood up and recited, "King, queen, prince, princess, marquess, marchioness, duke, duchess, earl, countess, viscount, viscountess, baron, baroness, lord, lady, sir."

Everyone laughed.

"Can you, please tell us which one you are, Lady Andrew?"

"I am married to Lord Andrew, who is the oldest son of an earl, so his title is *Viscount*, but he is addressed as *Lord*."

"Have you met Queen Elizabeth?" a girl asked.

"Yes. She is very charming and beautiful."

"There is a photograph of her with Prince Philip in the assembly hall."

"Oh. I have to look for it," Pamela responded. "My parents were very fond of the Royal family."

There was a pause before Pamela asked, "Are there photographs of your great inspirational and humanitarian leader—Mahatma Gandhi—anywhere here?"

"No."

"In that case, we will have to put some up!"

The students applauded spontaneously.

"Do you like this school?" Pamela asked.

"Yes" was the general response.

"I do not like writing. Spelling is not logical!" one student complained.

Pamela chuckled. "I sympathize with you!" Then she asked quickly, "What do you like the least?"

There was a short pause before one student responded, "The headmistress."

All eyes observed Pamela's reaction.

She nodded, then asked quickly, "And what do you like best?"

There were several students' voices.

"Food!"

"Vacations!"

"Cricket!"

"Math!"

"History!"

"Music!"

"So in general, you do like this school?" Pamela asked.

"Yes!" Shouts were accompanied with applause.

"Good. Thank you! Is there anything else you would like me to know?"

One student stood up. "I am Krishna Mauri. Lady Andrew, I would like to ask you about this school's position regarding Muslims?"

All students turned first toward Krishna, then looked at Pamela expectantly.

Pamela was surprised and thought for a moment before answering. "My late mother founded this school to offer education to all and any children from neighboring villages. This is not a religious nor political school. Therefore, I want any and all children to be welcome here! And I expect all students from any other religion to be treated equally with respect and honor for their religious practices, the same as we honor your Hindu religious practices."

While Pamela was speaking, she had an idea. "There is a room adjacent to the assembly hall. I will have it arranged and dedicated for prayer and meditation. Meanwhile, I want your promise that each one of you will treat children of other religions the way you wish to be respected and treated! Do I have your promise?"

There were murmurs, some stronger, then nodding of heads with a final "Yes, Lady Andrew."

"Thank you. I think we have a good understanding of each other. My husband and I wish for each and every one of you every success in your studies and a rewarding future! Again, thank you." Pamela walked to the door. As the students filed out, she shook hands with each of them.

Mrs. Chowdry persuaded Pamela and Andrew to stay for lunch, but they declined and returned to Lonavla for lunch.

During lunch in Lonavla, Pamela suggested that Andrew visit the Rajmchi Point, a famous fort, with the driver by car while she wanted to go with Mr. Patel to the village where the Muslim family lived so he could translate.

Mr. Patel had to ask several people before they found the modest dwelling at a distance from the village where the Muslim family had found shelter.

Pamela learned that the family had fled from abuse but had found work recently at a nearby construction site. It was an ancient-looking grandmother who introduced the children, Abdul, Farouk, and Farida.

With the help from Mr. Patel, Pamela asked the children, "Would you like to go to school?"

The children stared at her, then nodded shyly.

Pamela smiled at them. "Very good. Do you know a boy called Krishna?"

Abdul nodded.

Pamela explained, "Krishna, who lives not far from you, will take you to school tomorrow."

The grandmother shook her head. "We have no money."

"The school is free," Pamela explained. At that moment she felt very proud of her mother for having founded her school!

The grandmother looked scared and frowned. "We are Muslims."

Pamela smiled at her. "Yes, I know. My school is not religious nor political. We welcome all children."

"What about prayers?" the grandmother asked.

"We have a private room where children can observe their prayers anytime."

Abdul, who seemed to be the oldest, asked, "Do we get to wear the same beautiful clothes like Krishna?"

Pamela couldn't suppress a chuckle. "Yes. Tomorrow when you, Farouk, and Farida come to school, you will receive the same clothes."

Abdul turned to his grandmother with a wide smile. "Mawa, we will look beautiful and become very intelligent!"

"Insh'Allah!"

Mr. Patel was happy to join Pamela and Andrew for supper and accepted their invitation to watch an Indian movie in their room.

On their last day in Lonavla, Pamela and Andrew explored the stores and bought whatever they thought might please the students—water and oil paint, canvas, lots of books, some toys and puzzles for the smaller students, and empty notebooks for the students to use for dairies or creative writing.

They delivered the items, but once again Ms. Bannerji was invisible! No one knew where she was.

There were no financial reports delivered by the morning of January 12!

"What should we do now?" Pamela asked Andrew.

"I suggest we give Ms. Bannerji a few more days. We leave our forwarding addresses with her. If she doesn't come up with any kind of satisfactory information, you will have to decide if you want to have her investigated."

"What an unpleasant situation!"

The airport in Lonavla was small. Therefore, the boarding of the two-props plane was efficient. The flight to Aurangabad was short. Since it was a small plane, it flew at low altitude, and Pamela was delighted to look out of the window.

CHAPTER 21

Exploring Ajanta
Caves Near Aurangabad

*M*r. Patel introduced the new driver, Mr. Sharma. He was young with a ready smile. From the airport they were driven to Ajanta.

Pamela's and Andrew's hotel, the Royal Ajanta Palace, was surrounded by lush bougainvillea in glorious colors and little fountains. Their suite was generous with a large balcony connecting the living room and bedrooms. The view was toward the lush green hills. The furniture was plain teak but all cushions and bedspreads were in bright orange-pink colored brocade. The drapes in both rooms were of orange raw silk. On the coffee table in front of a comfortable sofa was a card of welcome by the hotel manager with a bottle of champagne in an ice bucket with four glasses and some roasted almonds and sweets.

"Oh how lovely!" Pamela smiled when she saw the welcome card. "Mr. Patel, you must share this welcome with us. Please be seated."

Andrew suggested to order an early lunch in the room while enjoying the champagne and planning the afternoon excursion. By the time they left the hotel, it was already two o'clock—still enough time to visit some caves!

But it was very hot, and the climb over rugged ground was slow. There were several large groups of tourists, which made access to the caves difficult. After struggling to see one cave and being somewhat disappointed, they decided to return to the hotel.

"We should leave tomorrow at six o'clock to reach the caves before the tourists arrive," Mr. Patel recommended, and both Pamela and Andrew agreed.

Early on the following morning, when Pamela and Andrew reached the entrance of the hotel, both Mr. Patel and the new driver, Mr. Sharma, were ready with the car.

Mr. Patel knew an entrance to the caves that was not known to most tourist guides. They were the first to climb the ascent.

The temple caves had been cut into rocks situated in the Waghora Valley. It was mind-boggling and utterly amazing how, even before 300 to 100 BCE, such magnificent art was achieved! The caves had been created by carving. Actually it was by cutting, chiseling, splitting, and hammering into the iron-hard granite rocks to form these secret places of worship! The hill range with the caves embraced the ravine of the Waghora River in the form of a horseshoe. Not all caves were open to the public. Some were too fragile, and others had paintings that were too light-sensitive to be shown.

There were two distinct architectural styles. The Vahiras had been monasteries with veranda-like entrances and wide-open halls leading to the back of the caves where the actual altars were kept. They had a solid but somewhat heavy appearance. The other type of caves were the hidden temples of Buddhist monks. These caves had magnificent frescoes depicting Buddhist legends. They were breathtakingly beautiful in their aesthetic presentation. One could admire voluptuous courtesans with their rows of gleaming pearls and precious stones, which were enhanced on the dark skin color of the beautiful women! The high ceilings were supported by fluted pillars often forming a row in the hollowed space.

Each time Pamela, Andrew, and Mr. Patel exited a chillingly cold cave to climb to the next, they enjoyed the glorious sun, which seemed to play with the water of the Waghora River and greeting the surrounding landscape and hills.

At three o'clock Andrew decided that it was too hot to continue their exerting adventure. On the way back to the hotel, they saw a village fair where Pamela bought some glass bangles. Ten bangles for one rupee!

During dinner, Pamela asked Mr. Patel about his family.

"My father was a cobbler. A very strict man! He saved every penny to allow me, his only son, to go to school and later to a business school. My mother," Mr. Patel said, "was an angel and protected me whenever I got into some kind of trouble with my school friends and Father would threaten to beat me."

"Did you have any sisters?" Andrew asked.

"Yes, one, Almira. She was, as you say, the apple of my father's eye. She was sneaky, but my father would never punish her. I think it was because she was very beautiful. She married a pharmacist and moved to Delhi. To provide her with a respectable dowry, my father took a loan." Mr. Patel hesitated a moment before continuing. "It may sound boastful but my father could never have paid back the loan if I had not been able to help out. You see, the wedding and especially the dowry reflect honor and the worth of a family."

"Do you have any children?"

Mr. Patel's face lit up. "We are expecting our first child in two months."

Pamela was surprised because he looked like he was in his midforties. "We hope everything will go well and you will be a very happy family!"

Mr. Patel noticed and smiled. "You see, I never intended to marry, with my job that requires me so many times to be away from home.

But then, one day, I met her. When I realized that Vermathi was in love with me, an old man"—he chuckled—"I had to marry her!"

"Well done, man, one must never ignore love!" Andrew nodded.

Blushing, Mr. Patel nodded. "Thank you, sir, I agree!"

"By the way, if you wish to call your wife, you are welcome to use our phone. You must be concerned about her," Andrew offered thoughtfully.

"I was planning to call from the pay cabin in the lobby."

"It is easier here. We'll withdraw to our bedroom while you talk."

"I never expected … are you sure, sir?"

"Absolutely!"

"Please convey our congratulations and best wishes to Mrs. Patel," Pamela said.

"Thank you, ma'am, I will."

When the telephone conversation ended, Mr. Patel knocked on the bedroom door. "My wife says thank you."

"How about watching a Western movie tonight?" Pamela suggested.

After finding several in the lobby collection of the hotel, the final choice fell on *Gone with the Wind*!

It was a long movie. Before leaving Mr. Patel commented, "It was just as dramatic as Indian movies … only there was no dancing and singing."

On the following day, they knew what to expect and followed the same routine—they left at six o'clock and climbed from one cave temple to the next. Again they marveled at the beauty of the frescoes, altars, sculptures, and paintings. So much devotion and love must have inspired the monks and workers to create these halls for worship!

Shortly before four o'clock Pamela and Andrew felt exhausted and ready to return to the hotel to plunge into the refreshing pool and relax. They had an early dinner and went straight to bed afterward.

Before departing for the airport the next morning, Pamela went to the basement shops in the hotel. She saw a charming floor-length dress with tiny purple elephants printed on a lilac background between mustard-colored plants. It had a pretty border at the neck, arm openings, and bottom with larger elephants. The price tag was thirty-five rupees! She could not resist and bought it to surprise Andrew.

At the airport they said goodbye to their young driver while Andrew passed on an envelope, as he always did. Mr. Patel checked them in for the flight to Udaipur!

CHAPTER 22

Udaipur's Treasures

A new driver awaited them in Udaipur and was introduced to Pamela and Andrew as Mr. Khan. They were taken to the City Palace Hotel, which was part of the rambling City Palace.

Their suite was spacious. Deep-set windows, doors, and pillars had graceful arches in the Indo-Aryan style. With the sunlight coming through the windows, the suite created a welcoming feeling. Some of the walls were painted white, and others were in pastel colors. Beautiful orchids were artfully arranged on the coffee table next to an ice bucket with a bottle of white wine while salty crackers lay temptingly on a silver tray. A handsomely uniformed valet offered to unpack the suitcase, but Pamela thanked him and told him they would do it themselves.

"If you agree, Mr. Patel, while we have lunch, we can plot our next adventures."

This time the temptations on the menu could not be resisted! They ordered grilled lamb chops, croquettes of potatoes and lentils, a biryani, naan, and finally a coconut curry with a local fish from Lake Udaipur! Of course, Indian beer was chosen while they kept the wine for dinner. To crown this feast they tasted sesame seeds meringues with mango, tea, and coffee.

After this satisfying lunch, Mr. Patel said, "May I suggest you visit some artisan studios where ancient Moghul miniatures are copied while you watch? These artists will draw or design anything you like. Rajasthan, particularly Udaipur, is often called the Jewel of Rajasthan! And rightly so as precious and semiprecious stones are found in the hills and mines around here. Jewelers are happy to create any jewelry, especially traditional ones as well as modern styles. Depending on how much time you spend in the various studios, this may pretty much fil out this afternoon. You will also find wonderful material shops who always have tailors on hand to take your measurements."

"I don't think I need any additional clothes," Pamela explained. "As you know, my parents lived in India for many years. During those times, they had clothes and jewelry custom-made for them. At home I have closets full with saris, gowns, and dresses! But I would very much like for Andrew to have some lightweight suits and shirts made."

"We'll see." Andrew didn't seem very keen on the idea.

"Udaipur has eleven palaces." Mr. Patel resumed his suggestions. "We have the City Palace Museum, which is next door and well worth seeing. If you like, we can go for a drive along the lake to Jag Mandir. A small palace that was built on a small island for Shah Jehan as a hiding place from his father, it is on the southern end of Lake Pichola."

"I would like to see the Maharana Palace," Pamela said.

"I was thinking you may enjoy exploring it tomorrow as it is a large complex."

"If I remember correctly," Andrew said, "there is a Monsoon Palace."

"Yes, it is of white marble residing over a hill. I think you would enjoy seeing it."

"There are so many things to see! I would also like to see the famous Lake Palace Hotel," Pamela said.

"Well, there might be a problem. It depends on who is staying there. If there are VIPs, the security is tight, and only registered guests staying there are allowed to enter. I will find out for you, ma'am."

"So you suggest we visit the artisan studios today?" Andrew reminded.

The traffic was slow through the crowded city center. Pamela especially enjoyed seeing people's faces. She saw beauty in almost all of them! Beauty of youth and innocence, blossoming adulthood reflected, the joy and glow of discovered love, dark passions in eyes as well as the depth of sorrow and grief, the hollowness of hunger and starvation—they were there! She thought, *If I were an artist, I would love to paint these expressive faces!*

Few women wore saris here. Most of them wore the generous long skirts in bright colors with sparkling mirrors or embroideries with short blouses. A transparent veil draped over their heads and sometimes their faces. There was a joy and freedom in their way of wearing their clothes! There were men pushing heavily laden carts and rickshaws carrying tourists from shop to shop. One could easily distinguish professional men wearing suits in spite of the heat. When a couple of cows blocked the road and stopped the entire traffic, Andrew suggested, "We might be faster walking?"

"Yes, of course, if you don't mind the dust."

It was fun to mingle with the local people. The only thing Pamela couldn't get quite used to was their staring at her.

Most shops spilled out their wares onto the sidewalk, sometimes reaching the road. The colors of the merchandise seemed to rival the fruits and spice stands. There was one particular shop where many long skirts in lively rainbow colors in the Rajasthan style were displayed, some with mirrors or embroideries. Having seen them on the women, Pamela gently pulled Andrew to a stop. "Oh, Andrew, I would so like to buy one of these skirts!"

"Of course, which one would you like?"

Looking more carefully, it was difficult to decide. "Perhaps this blue one ... no, I think this purple one is prettier ... oh, what about this orange one? Then there is this nice black one with the silver embroidery." She sighed. "It's very hard to decide."

Andrew laughed. "Well, if you have still space in your suitcase, why not buy all four?"

"Could we really?"

Andrew asked the owner how much the skirts cost.

"Four-hundred rupees each."

Mr. Patel touched Andrew's arm. "Sir, he is taking advantage of you! You must bargain. It is expected! I suggest you counter with six-hundred rupees for all four skirts. He will counter with a higher price. Don't accept over eight hundred."

Pamela observed with amusement Andrew offering the suggested six-hundred rupees and the insulted facial expression of the seller who shook his head. 'You, sir, have no appreciation for the extraordinary handiwork of our Rajasthani women!" He swayed his head. "But I like you. Therefore, I will lower my initial price to the pitiful amount of one-thousand rupees for all four skirts."

But Andrew shook his head. "The maximum I am prepared to pay for the four skirts are eight-hundred rupees."

The owner made the face of a martyr but agreed.

Pamela was delighted. "Thank you, sir, and thank you, Andrew!"

The owner removed the skirts and was about to stash them into a plastic bag when an elderly woman, most likely his mother, appeared from the back of the store saying something in Hindi to which the owner nodded and said to Pamela, "You need blouses."

"Ah, yes, I forgot."

The woman removed a bundle of folded blouses in brilliant colors from a shelf and spread them out.

"Do you have white blouses?"

From another shelf she withdrew a pile of folded white cotton blouses. The material seemed a bit rough, but they had pretty embroideries. Pamela selected three.

"So how much do we owe you for the blouses?" Andrew asked.

"My mother speak no English. The blouses are six hundred."

"I'll give you six-hundred rupees," Andrew bargained.

"Sir, do not insult my mother." The owner made a sorrowful face. "It is an enormous sacrifice." The seller paused a moment, then agreed. "All right, it is six-hundred rupees."

"Yes, so we have eight hundred for four skirts and three hundred for three blouses. That makes the total of eleven-hundred rupees," Andrew said while counting out the money.

The owner accepted it with a grim face.

After Andrew and Pamela had walked a few meters from the store, Mr. Patel smiled at Andrew. "You did splendidly, sir! The owner made a good deal, and you got a good bargain."

At a jeweler's store their guide told Andrew that if he was interested in buying jewelry, this particular jeweler was honest and trustworthy. "But his prices are fixed. There is no bargaining."

Andrew turned to Pamela. "I would like to buy you something special."

"Andrew, you know how much beautiful jewelry I already have inherited! I don't need any more."

"Let's just go inside and look."

Built-in display vitrines along the walls and below glass tops under the counters, each with indirect lights, made the diamonds glitter and sparkle! One counter alone was for diamond rings only. Two others were for diamond necklaces, then another was for earrings. Along the walls were jewelry sets displayed that sparkled seductively. On another wall were cases with elegant gold necklaces with diamonds. In still another section were cases with sets of elaborate bridal jewelry with diamonds, pearls, emeralds, sapphires, rubies and other precious stones—necklaces, bracelets, earrings, finger rings, pendants, and some had inserts for the nose!

Looking at all this jewelry, Pamela was convinced that she didn't want any of these imposing adornments. "Andrew," she whispered, "there is nothing that would look good on me."

The jeweler noticed Pamela's reluctance. "Perhaps the lady would like a pendant?" He pulled out a drawer that was lined with black velvet. There were attractive pendants on gold chains with precious stones and diamonds.

Pamela saw one pendant that had a large deep-violet-purple amethyst set in a slightly ornamental gold frame.

"Do you see anything you like?" Andrew asked.

She pointed at the amethyst pendant. "This is the only one, but …"

"An excellent choice, madam," the jeweler praised. "This an unusually deep hue for an amethyst. The stone is twelve karats and is flawless." He reached for a couple of magnifying glasses and gave them to them.

Peering through one, Andrew agreed. "Yes, it is beautiful and precisely cut. Is it a new or old piece?"

"It is an antique. A museum piece actually! I bought it at an auction."

"How do you like it, darling?"

"Oh, it is absolutely gorgeous!"

Andrew gave a discreet nod to the jeweler to follow him to another section of the store.

Pamela and Mr. Patel returned to gaze at the incredibly rich bridal jewelry with complex designs. "Most of these are worth millions of rupees," Mr. Patel explained.

Meanwhile, Andrew asked the jeweler for the price of the pendant.

"It is ten-thousand rupees."

"I will take it."

"Thank you, my lord."

When they left the store, Pamela had no idea that Andrew had a pretty purple leather case in his pocket.

It was five o'clock when they returned to the hotel.

"You could enjoy high tea, or we could drive to the Jag Mandir I mentioned earlier."

"I would love to go for a drive. What do you think, Pamela?"

"Yes, it would be nice to drive along the lake. Jag Mandir was the hiding place for Shah Jehan, didn't you say, Mr. Patel?"

"Yes, ma'am."

Mr. Khan was a careful driver and avoided all trucks on the road, commenting, "It is always safer to have the monster drivers in front of you than behind you."

On the way they saw women washing—actually mercilessly beating clothes against stones along the lake. Others gathered water at a cistern. With their gleaming copper vessels on their heads, they seemed like graceful living sculptures. At one point, workers were mending the potholes in the road with a tarry mass of gravel, then jumping on them to tighten the fill.

When they reached the small dock where a boat was waiting to take tourists to the small island palace, it was blocked by three oxen staring at them. Mr. Khan and Mr. Patel tried to wave them to the side but were completely ignored by the beasts. In the end Pamela, Andrew, and Mr. Patel had to squeeze along a wall to the gate to reach the boat.

Jag Mandir was a pretty small palace, but it must have been an unhappy place for the Shah hiding from his father and enemies! It offered a wide-open view of Lake Pichola.

On their return to the hotel, they felt tired. Andrew invited Mr. Patel to join them for a light dinner, but the guide excused himself. The honeymooners enjoyed a light dinner in the elegant dining room in their Palace hotel.

Later they sat on their private terrace that offered a panoramic view of the Lake and the Lake Palace with lit arched windows reflecting on the smooth mirror-like surface on the water surrounded by a slumbering countryside.

"How very fortunate we are, darling Andrew!"

"Indeed! Just think, would we have chosen India for our honeymoon had it not been for your parents' love for this country, your mother's school, and her people?"

Pamela thought a moment before responding, "I have to admit that, as a child, I was often jealous of the children who enjoyed my parents' company so much more than I could. They spent so very little time at home in Chislehurst. Whenever they were, they had friends over. But most often they would go out to parties and balls. In spite of having Bambi, there were times I felt extremely lonely and sad. Even when Mama would be staying with us in Chislehurst, she seemed to prefer to be alone. I kept asking myself, what did I do wrong? Why does Mama not come to play with me or read a story? Why did Papa never come up to the nursery? The only times I remember are when I was allowed to watch Mama getting ready to go out to spend time with strangers."

Andrew reached out his hand and gently pulled Pamela up to stand in front of him so that he could drape his arms around her. "How very sad, my darling. I am deeply sorry you didn't receive loving support from your parents. They must have been unaware that you missed them. But, my sweet Pamela, all this is history. It was a time with painful memories, but they belong to the past! Since then you, my love, have come a very long way! I am going to do everything possible to make today, tomorrow, and all the following days, months, and years happy for you because I love you with every fiber of my being."

Pamela hid her face on Andrew's shoulder and started weeping.

"Hush, hush, my love," he whispered but understood and allowed her to release all her secret sorrows.

Slowly she stopped weeping, then reached for her handkerchief to dry her cheeks and blow her nose. And then she promptly started to hiccup. "Oh, Andrew, I am such a hopeless mess."

He chuckled. "You insult me. If you were anything like a hopeless mess, I probably would have never fallen in love with you!"

Pamela looked up at him. "Do you really mean it?"

"Let's go to bed so I can prove to you that I mean it most sincerely." He then asked, "How about having a shower together?"

For an instant Pamela just stared at Andrew. When she still said nothing, he added teasingly, "It would save some water for Udaipur!"

A chuckle escaped her. "I have never thought of that. Yes, why not?"

The hotel provided wonderfully fragrant sandalwood soap, lotion, and cream. It didn't take long for Pamela to respond to Andrew teasingly applying soap to himself first, then on her, beginning with her arms. In no time they played like children enjoying each other. The whole suite was filled with the scent of sandalwood when they tumbled into bed.

After a short while, Andrew got up and withdrew something from his slacks's pocket before returning to bed. "Pamela, my love, I have here a token of my love to you." He opened the little purple leather box to show Pamela the glowing amethyst pendant.

"Oh, Andrew!" she cried out in astonishment. "How did you get it?"

He laughed. "While you and Mr. Patel admired the bridal jewelry."

"I had no idea!" She removed the pendant with gentle fingers. "It is most beautiful! Thank you! Thank you, my darling Andrew! Can I wear it?"

"Yes, why not?" He helped her put it on.

Pamela turned thoughtful. "I have still not given you anything!"

"I have you! You are my gift for life!"

"I will try to be the best possible wife to you," Pamela promised solemnly and kissed him. She got out of bed and stood naked with only the pendant on in front of the full-length mirror.

Andrew joined her. "I am glad you like it."

"I think it is the most exquisite piece of all the jewelry. I love it!"

"How about going back to bed to celebrate?"

On the following morning, Mr. Patel picked them up early for the drive up to the Maharana Palace, a mighty fortress palace. It crowned the entire plateau ridge. Even after leaving the car, it seemed that they were climbing for a long time to reach the gate. Standing close to the foundation of the giant fortress' walls was overwhelming. Both Pamela and Andrew were surprised by how thick the walls were! No wonder it had never been destroyed by conquerors!

In the first building were narrow hallways with doors on the left and right sides. The rooms were small. Those quarters had been for the military officers. Going to the next building, the rooms were larger and had more windows. The architecture was mixed. It appeared that buildings had been added whenever needed.

Finally, they reached the main palace where they were greeted by a handsome peacock. The entrance was through a beautifully arched opening. They found themselves in the first audience hall, which was richly decorated with colorful tiles. Sturdy pillars supported carved wooden ceilings. The view from the windows allowed an almost bird's-eye view over this proud city of Udaipur! Most houses were painted with pretty colors. They appeared like an eccentric mosaic.

A guide who insisted on following them informed them of the tragedies dictated by the code of honor. Whenever the Rajput princes realized that there was no way for them to conquer the invading enemies, they gathered their women, locked them up in rooms, and burned them alive! Then the princes with their soldiers would go out to face the enemies in lost battles. They died at the sword of their enemies to satisfy honor! It was quite similar to the Japanese kamikaze pilots' suicides for honor!

The reception halls and throne rooms were richly decorated with marble inlaid with Rajput motifs. The throne, which looked more like an additional dais on an elevated platform, was covered with rich brocades. It looked very uncomfortable. They were surrounded by ornamental walls and ceilings supported by robust pillars with decorative carvings. Countless rooms had balconies. Some had been sleeping quarters of princes and dignitaries, but they seemed small and modest. Often they had to exit one building to find a door to the next.

The royal harem, the *zenana*, was particularly pretty. The walls were either painted or decorated with flower motifs in colored marble. The ladies must have loved peacocks because it was the most repeated object of decoration. A large courtyard with a shallow pool had been a place where the women met and refreshed themselves. There were even low uncomfortable sofa chairs. Each window had a carved stone filigree screen of different designs to prevent visitors from seeing the royal ladies.

However, the women were able to see the processions, which must have been spectacular! Princes in glorious brocades wearing sparkling diamonds and pearls with imposing headdresses or turbans on horseback or elephants. These dignitaries were always surrounded by their own bodyguards who were often clothed in equally fine attires with elaborate turbans indicating their ranks. Other important visitors, also beautifully and richly gowned and riding as proud as any prince on splendid horses or elephants with their entourages, must have passed below these windows. They knew to avoid looking up at the filigreed windows and balconies where the most beautiful women were hidden. Perhaps they were looking forward to and hoping that they would be honored with an exotic performance of sparsely veiled beauties entertaining them later!

In one of the courtyards sat an old man, crowned with a mandarin-orange-colored turban with a magnificently groomed moustache connected to an imposing beard framing his wonderfully chiseled face with deeply carved lines into his dark skin and enjoying puffs from his hookah while ignoring the inquisitive and staring people taking photographs.

Continuing the exploration was a constant surprise as the buildings changed in architecture. Some buildings had carved wooden balconies that seemed too fragile. Some windows framed views of forested hills and ridges and countryside dotted with smaller and larger lakes and palaces.

Not very far below the Maharana Palace Fortress was a charming small palace in impeccable white marble. It also had delicate flower-inlaid motifs. The palace enjoyed an unobstructed view of the fortress above.

It was well after noon when they returned to the city.

"There is a small hotel with a restaurant across from the City Palace with a terrace shaded by trees. You may enjoy seeing your palace from the opposite side," Mr. Patel suggested.

It was a modest but clean place, and the food was good.

"You mentioned," Andrew addressed Mr. Patel, "that there are studios where artists paint miniatures. I think that would be an interesting place to see, don't you agree, darling?"

Pamela smiled. "I am glad you remembered. Yes, I'd love to go there."

It was true! The artists were sitting at tables copying Persian and Moghul miniatures. With acquired skill, they recreated these ancient works of art! Some peered through magnifying glasses to capture the minutest details! The reproductions were always in the same format as the original.

"Andrew, may I buy a miniature for you?"

"Oh ..."

"Which one do you like?"

They both studied with renewed interest to select one.

"This one! I like the charming little pavilion surrounded by a flower garden where the two lovers are meeting in secret while a faithful lady-in-waiting is keeping watch by the window to alert them if anyone dares to approach. How do you like it, Pamela?"

"I agree. It is exquisite and delicately copied on silk. I'll buy it for you."

Mr. Patel showed her where to give her credit card.

Later on that evening Andrew suggested that Mr. Patel and Mr. Khan take a day off. He assured him that Pamela and he could manage well since they were planning on seeing only the City Palace Museum, which was attached to the hotel, and the Jagdish Temple next door. He also told Mr. Patel that they wanted to sleep late.

The breakfast was served on their private terrace from where Pamela and Andrew enjoyed the panoramic view. The Lake Palace appeared to be floating on the gleaming surface of the lake. On the opposite shore from their hotel was a stone staircase leading down into the lake. Two women were washing laundry while a toddler was exercising by climbing and descending the steep steps. Pamela watched, worried he might fall, but he was amazingly agile!

Andrew was interested in the Jagdish Temple, which was built in Indo-Aryan style and was part of the huge City Palace complex. By now they were used to buying jasmine flower garlands and leaving their shoes with a custodian who was always happy to receive a coin.

The interior was huge! The visitors, mostly women, children, and tourists, were admiring the many statues and mosaic inlays. When Pamela and Andrew reached the main altar, they were astonished by its size! As everywhere, the priests were happy to receive additional coins for the flower garlands. The statues were lovingly decorated with ropes of pearls, some sparkling, and some flower garlands. Also, the usual bowl offerings with food for the monks were put at the bottom of the statues. The atmosphere was hushed and serene.

The City Palace Museum was filled with beautiful sculptures. Most of them were of voluptuous females. Both Pamela and Andrew preferred the hall where serene statues of Buddha and Buddhist monks sat or stood in eternal silence. Pamela was tempted to touch the incredibly smooth surface of some granite and marble sculptures with the long cloths that looked draped over their bodies in an amazingly realistic way!

"Pamela, where would you like to have lunch?"

"Our hotel restaurant is pleasant, and the food is safe."

A nice window table was offered to them, and then they were given the menu.

"The *parch seekhi* sounds tempting," Andrew said.

Pamela laughed. "What is it in English?"

"Gigot of lamb on a spit. It's about the only Indian dish I can pronounce!"

After perusing the menu choices, Pamela decided, "I'd like the lake fish in the coconut gravy we had the other day."

"There is also the chickpeas dish we both liked. How about beer to help us with a nap afterward?"

While they enjoyed their lunch, Pamela asked, "Andrew, I have been thinking about what we could give to our two families as a special thank-you for making this, our honeymoon, possible and so special. I was thinking that we could select two miniature paintings, one for the Prescott family and one for the Payne family. What do you think?"

Andrew chuckled. "It is amazing that you thought of this possibility because I, too, have had the same idea! Would you like to go back to select two?"

The doorman at the studio remembered them and smiled. "Good afternoon, sir, madam."

"Ah, you remember us," Andrew praised.

"Yes, sir. You look happy."

Pamela laughed. "We'll tell you the secret. We are on our honeymoon!"

The doorman's face turned into a wide grin. "I not tell! Happy life!"

"Thank you."

Both found it hard to select from all the miniatures because they were exquisite in execution! After a long search, they found and decided on several. They selected one romantic scene for Lilly. For Tony and Scotti, they chose hunting scenes with rajas on elephants. Then for the Prescott parents, they selected an exquisite Persian miniature and, finally, for Pamela's relatives, a scene with ladies with a deer bathing in a pond, surrounded by flowers. Each miniature was carefully inserted between two cardboards, then wrapped in a plastic sheet and, finally, slipped into a padded envelope.

On the way out, they discovered in another section tiny, medium, and large sandalwood boxes with a thin marble plaque attached on top. They had very lovely semiprecious stones inlaid with Indian and Persian designs.

"Oh. these would be nice little gifts for your mother, Lilly, Elly, and Liz! Then I know Aunt Hillary would love to have one."

Andrew purchased six of the boxes.

"Now we have to find things for our men."

"I think all of them would like a nice silk tie," Andrew said.

There was a material store on their way back to the hotel.

"Andrew, this is what you need … nice shirts, yes, and a handsome jacket."

"Where would I wear them?"

"Here and in England, of course!"

At that moment a salesperson approached. "May I be of help, ma'am, sir?"

"Yes, please," Pamela responded immediately. "My husband is considering having shirts made."

"Pamela!"

"Very good, sir. For what occasions?"

"Not formal. I like the shirts that always look very handsome on Indians, like Ravi Shankar wears," Andrew explained.

Pamela elaborated. "Shirts with high collars that are worn without a tie."

The tailor showed them several bolts of very fine cotton fabric. By the time they left the store, there was an order for three shirts, seven beautiful silk ties, one medium-weight raw-silk jacket, and two pairs of slacks to be sent to the Rambaugh Palace Hotel in Jaipur, their next stop.

CHAPTER 23

A Message from a Stranger

*T*here was a message waiting for Pamela and Andrew. It appeared that Mr. Patel had managed to receive permission for them to visit the Lake Palace Hotel for a drink!

"Would you like to go, darling?"

She smiled. "Yes, it might be interesting. Will Mr. Patel take us?"

"No, apparently, we'll be picked up by a water taxi from the Lake Palace, which will bring us back later on."

After a phone call with Mr. Patel, Andrew explained, "Mr. Patel will only take us to the private landing dock. From there the water taxi will take us to the hotel. Then we'll be guided to the visitors' lounge for a drink. Mr. Patel will meet us later when the water taxi brings us back to the landing to make certain that we end up safely in our hotel. What do you say?"

"How soon do we meet Mr. Patel?"

"At seven o'clock in the lobby."

Pamela was already entering the bathroom to take a shower and get ready. She decided to inaugurate her cobalt-blue sari with the turquoise and silver borders. Andrew looked very handsome in a white raw-silk jacket, light-gray slacks, and pale-pink shirt with an open collar.

When they met Mr. Patel, he handed them a small envelope, which Andrew opened. It contained a business card. On the front the name *Anthony Wood* and below *Baron of Tremston* were embossed, and on the reverse side was a personal note: "May I request the pleasure of your company for drinks around seven o'clock at the Lake Palace?"

The gliding over the mirrorlike Lake Pichola seemed unreal as there was no sound except the soft murmur of the boat engine. They were greeted by a young man in uniform with a fanlike turban and well-groomed beard. He led them to the visitors' lounge. He headed straight toward a low coffee table where a gentleman of about fifty years sat on a sofa facing them.

CHAPTER 24

Lord Anthony Wood's Tale

*T*he English-looking gentleman stood up. He was as tall as Andrew. His slightly tanned face with even features was framed by dark auburn hair that was a bit longer than it was fashionable and some silver hair at the sideburns. He was impeccably dressed in white trousers and white shirt with an open collar under a lightweight polo sweater.

Pamela looked into his hazel-brown eyes. For an instant her mind hesitated, then wondered, *He looks familiar. Do I know him?*

He smiled at her. "What a most delightful surprise to meet you! May I call you Pamela?" He kissed her on the cheek. He took both of her hands in his and studied her for a moment, then said, "I apologize for staring at you. You look so very much like your dear mother!"

Pamela felt startled while her heartbeat increased! She felt mysteriously drawn to this stranger, and yet she had never met him before. Still there was something …

Andrew was watching Pamela's somewhat surprised reaction and wondered who this gentleman was and how he recognized Pamela's resemblance to her late mother.

Still puzzled about who this stranger was, Pamela reached out to Andrew to introduce him. "My lord, please meet my husband, Andrew Prescott."

"I am Anthony Wood," he replied while shaking hands with Andrew. "This must be a surprise to you, Lord Andrew." He smiled while explaining. "Your father called me this afternoon to inform me that you two honeymooners are staying here in Udaipur. He asked if I would care to meet you both." Lord Anthony paused. "Please have a seat."

"May I ask, my lord, how you know my father?"

"Michael Prescott, your father, and I worked for many years at the Home Office. We are old friends." He chuckled. "I am your brother Tony's godfather and live in Udaipur. As a matter of fact, Lord Andrew, I have met you a couple of times before at Tarrington Abbey when you were much younger. It is a pleasure to meet you again!"

"Thank you, my lord. As a friend of my father, you must call me Andrew. I am embarrassed to admit that I do not recall our having met. I apologize. Of course, I have seen Tony's wonderful collection of precious and semiprecious stones you send him for his birthdays. He treasures them very much!"

Lord Anthony seemed pleased. "I am glad to know Tony likes his collection. There is no need for apologies, Andrew, for not remembering me." He turned toward Pamela. "Please allow me to tell you how I know, or more accurately, *knew* Elizabeth Mary Rose Scott … Payne, your beautiful mother." He paused while folding his hands so firmly that the knuckles turned white. Finally, he began with "Elizabeth chose Adrian Payne over me … which left me heartbroken."

Pamela looked shocked, then said solemnly, "I am so very sorry, my lord."

"Thank you, Pamela." There was an awkward pause until he continued. "I must tell you that Elizabeth and I grew up together. Our parents' estates were next door to each other. We were fast friends. Our two families assumed that we would marry, especially after I returned from Oxford and she had blossomed into an extraordinarily beautiful woman. We fell in love until she met, at a ball, a dashingly handsome colonel in his scarlet uniform. She told me that they danced three times and that during the third dance, he had proposed to her!" Again Lord Anthony paused to collect himself, then continued. "Elizabeth was thrilled, and her mind was in a cloud. No one could talk sense into her. She would not listen to her parents or me. She accused me of neglecting to propose to her. So without thoughts of consequences, she accepted the rash offer of this handsome stranger." Again, Lord Anthony paused before addressing Pamela directly. "I am going to be very honest and … blunt. I hope you will forgive me?"

Pamela didn't know what to expect but nodded.

He resumed. "Elizabeth's father, the earl, was particularly upset and angry and had this Adrian Payne investigated. He found out more about this colonel who was working at the War Office and did not have a very good reputation. His nickname was Rash-and-Dash. He had apparently been involved with other young ladies but left them all after he had met Elizabeth. Perhaps he had expectations by marrying an earl's daughter. Our families and I myself tried unsuccessfully to persuade her to wait and give their relationship more time. One day she had disappeared! We found out later that they had eloped to Gretna Green! Her father was absolutely furious and refused to acknowledge this marriage or the husband of his daughter. In his initial anger, the earl disinherited her and refused to see his daughter ever again!" Lord Anthony paused for a brief moment. "As for myself, like a wounded animal, I withdrew with my great pain and deep sorrow. I went to Scotland for one month and walked the wilderness trying to understand and accept the loss of Elizabeth and her love. Even though our families remained friends, the event had affected the close relationship."

After a long silence, Pamela asked shyly, "Were they happy?"

Lord Anthony turned thoughtful. "At first, yes, I believe so. Elizabeth's parents insisted they have a proper church wedding in Chislehurst to prevent any kind of social stigma or condemnation.

But her father stubbornly refused to attend! At one time the colonel was attached to the British embassy in Delhi. That is when your mother fell in love with India. She recognized the lack of access to schools in rural areas. While the colonel was back and forth between Delhi and London, Elizabeth studied secretly with an Indian tutor to become a teacher."

"Did you ever meet my mother again?" Pamela asked hesitantly.

Again, it took a moment for Lord Anthony to answer. "Yes. Elizabeth returned sometimes to England, to Chislehurst where her husband had inherited a large mansion from his father. She would stay there at times for weeks alone while her husband remained in Delhi. During one of those times, she asked me to visit her. I realized then how unhappy she was. I stayed for six weeks with the illusion of making her happy. It was a bad mistake for both of us as it opened wounds that could never be healed. Divorce was unthinkable! It would have been such a scandal that could have terminated her husband's career. Shortly before Elizabeth's father was dying, he reinstated her as his sole heiress but sadly refused to see his daughter."

"How very sad," both Andrew and Pamela said simultaneously.

"The colonel left the War Office when Elizabeth's father died. She decided then to sell the entire Swendown estate and bought land in an Indian village to start a school. My mother, who had remained friends with Elizabeth's mother, told me that against all expectations, the colonel turned out to be a very good teacher! I was glad for your mother's sake!" He paused then, remembering. "Pamela, you asked if I ever saw your mother again. As I told you, I did during one of her stays alone in Chislehurst. But later I realized that seeing Elizabeth was a very bad idea. I refused when she invited me on future occasions. Meanwhile, my parents died. I sold Tremton Hall, my inherited estate, and moved to Jaipur. I thought it would help with my grieving. Then, a few years later, I ran most unexpectedly into Elizabeth and her husband at the British embassy function in Delhi to celebrate the Queen's birthday. From then onward, I never attended any social functions where I might meet them again!"

Pamela shook her head in dismay. "I am so terribly sorry, my lord. I don't know how I can make it up to you to soften your pain."

Lord Anthony stepped over to Pamela. "You are very kind, thank you. I should apologize for burdening you with my sorrow." He went to the terrace door and looked out for a long moment, then turned around and said, as if amazed by himself, "I do not know why I have told you all this. I have never told anyone before!" He sighed, then smiled bravely. "This is a happy occasion! I am very pleased to meet you both, Pamela and Andrew! Welcome to India!"

"It is our honor and pleasure to meet you, Lord Anthony!" Andrew replied while Pamela nodded with a smile.

"How long are you staying here in Udaipur?"

"We are leaving tomorrow for Jaipur. We will be staying at the Rambaugh Palace Hotel," Pamela told him.

A smile lit up Lord Anthony's face. "Ah, now I think I understand why Michael, your father, Andrew, called me because he knows that I own an apartment at the Rambaugh Palace. He seemed rather keen on my meeting you both!"

"How amazing!" Pamela smiled.

"I must say I am most grateful to your father, Andrew, for alerting me of your coming to Jaipur. I would have been very sad to miss this occasion to meet you both! However, I am quite aware that you are on your honeymoon and may not wish to have the company of a stranger on your explorations."

Andrew, having sensed Pamela's sensitive reaction to Lord Anthony, said, "I think I can speak for Pamela and myself that we both would enjoy spending some time with you."

Lord Anthony smiled. "Thank you, I am delighted and look forward to showing you around Jaipur. But you must promise to tell me whenever you prefer to be on your own."

And so it was agreed that Mr. Patel would return to Bombay for a few days and then join Pamela and Andrew later on in Delhi.

CHAPTER 25

Rambaugh Palace, Jaipur

When the three arrived at the Jaipur airport, a stately Rolls-Royce awaited them, which belonged to the residents/owners of the condominiums at the Palace.

Lord Anthony made sure that the suite given to Pamela and Andrew was comfortable. It was! The architecture of these old palaces, like Rambaugh Palace, was elegant and generous in space. Inside, many of the ceilings had been painted with romantic motifs by Italian artists. All windows and doors were arched in the graceful multiarch style typical of Moghul architecture that Pamela remembered having seen in mosques. There were many charming small pavilions at the top of the various terraces with the same Moghul arches that framed views of the surrounding countryside and hills while supporting the charming rooftops.

In the honeymooners' suite, a cobalt-blue crystal vase held glowing white and pink bougainvillea on the dining room table. Their bedroom had one large platform bed with a deep-teal-colored spread matching the heavy drapes. The bathroom had a marble tub and a newer separate glass-enclosed shower in a large room with double sinks and one wall was entirely covered with mirrors! There was a separate toilet room with a sink. A broad balcony that connected the two rooms with comfortable-looking garden furniture under wide bright-red umbrellas looked tempting.

Lord Anthony invited Pamela and Andrew to a late lunch at his apartment. After having unpacked, they were welcomed with a wonderfully chilled glass of champagne. He explained, "This apartment belonged to the last maharani. She was a lady who knew exactly what she wanted and demanded it from her husband. In return, she bore him five fine sons. I think it is the most elegant apartment in the whole palace. I love it here, and if you are interested, I would be happy to give you a tour."

"Oh, we would love to see it!" Pamela replied.

"I can show you while you enjoy the champagne."

The living room was spacious with attractive arched openings leading to a huge terrace with one of the private little pavilions overlooking the well-tended garden, countryside, and hill ranges meeting the horizon at a distance.

A low coffee table of French marquetry design was set on an ancient Persian carpet. A pretty arrangement of pink roses was placed in the center. Several attractive antique consoles of French marquetry were set along the walls with beautiful original oil paintings hanging above them. On one wall were old portraits of Lord Anthony's family members. On the opposite wall over the soft leather sofa was only one painting of the late maharaja and maharani, both wearing their fine jewelry of pearls and diamonds draped around their necks, chests, arms, and fingers. While the maharaja wore a carefully wrapped pale-blue turban with one large sapphire brooch framed with diamonds, the maharani had a gold chain placed over the parting on the middle of her jet-black hair with an emerald pendant surrounded by diamonds reaching down to her forehead. A ring with a pearl was attached to her right nostril. Both were clothed in rich brocades.

"This painting was here when I first saw the apartment, I liked it and thought it should remain here."

In the bedroom were more paintings of Lord Anthony's more recent family members, all in matching gold frames. Here, too, the furniture was antique and elegant. The wide bed was covered with a rich silk damask comforter in gold and purple with matching pillows against the headrest. Pamela was about to pass the dresser to walk over to the terrace door when she discovered a small photograph in a strikingly beautiful platinum frame. She bent closer and was stunned to immediately recognize her mother wearing a deep-purple sari! She looked at Lord Anthony.

He said, simply, "Elizabeth, your mother, was the only woman I ever loved!"

Andrew joined them to look at the photograph. "She was a very beautiful lady! I wish I had known her."

"In a way, you can still meet her in Pamela, who bears a remarkable resemblance to her mother."

How very sad! He must have loved her very much that he kept her photograph here during all these years! *Pamela thought.*

Adjacent was a room with a glass dome over a shallow marble pool. Along one wall were two reclining chairs with a small table between. The walls were painted with life-size Moghul figures copied from miniatures. In one corner was a glass-enclosed shower and next to it a deep marble tub. There was a small passage to the toilet facilities.

Lord Anthony led them back to the living room into the dining room and through another archway to his library with built-in mahogany bookcases. They were filled with handsome leather-bound volume sets. Near the door to the terrace stood a large desk. "This is where I spend most of my time … in the endless world of books whenever I am not at the mines or traveling!"

When they returned to the dining room, a waiter in a handsome uniform and elaborate turban was placing silver dishes on the side console, ready to be served. Even though there was bright sunlight outside, two tall silver candelabras with purple candles were lit.

"I hope," their host said, "you will forgive me for taking the liberty of ordering dishes I hope you will enjoy?" He sat at the head of the table with Pamela on his right and Andrew on his left side.

"What exquisite china!" Pamela observed.

"You like it?" Lord Anthony was pleased. "I will arrange that the set will be given to you after I am gone as a souvenir of your visit with me."

"Oh, I didn't mean ..." Pamela felt embarrassed. "Oh, thank you, Lord Anthony! But I hope that it will be in the very distant future!"

The food was delicious! The first course was chilled cucumbers stuffed with prawns accompanied with lime sorbet; a beautifully decorated lamb pilaf with pecans, ginger, and saffron; eggplants with mushrooms; chicken curry; and finally, okra with caramelized onions. To change the taste, a refreshing lemon sorbet and a sweet carrot halvah and a rice pudding flavored with rosewater were served.

To accompany this feast, Pamela and Andrew had a choice of Indian beer, chilled pinot blanc or claret before the coffee and tea was offered.

"This is like our wedding feast!" Pamela praised. "I don't think I'll need dinner tonight!"

Lord Anthony laughed. It was the first time he had laughed since they had met. "Perhaps you wish to rest a while as it is too hot to go outside. If you wish, we could do some sightseeing later?"

"Ah, my lord, you guessed correctly," Andrew agreed. "A nap sounds irresistible. But we would be delighted to go out with you later, don't you agree, darling?"

The bed in their suite was comfortably wide and cool with smooth sheets. After having tried unsuccessfully to fall asleep, Pamela and Andrew remembered their conversation during lunch.

"It is so sad that Lord Anthony had fallen hopelessly in love with my mother, then lost her!"

"Yes. He said that their parents had been very good friends and it had been assumed that Elizabeth, your mother, and he would marry."

"I feel so badly for him!" Pamela continued. "He mentioned—and one could feel—that he was still hurting to have lost her to my father."

"Do you think she was happy?" Andrew wondered.

"I really don't know. I never saw them in any affectionate way."

"Maybe Lord Anthony will tell us more when we go out with him later. Pamela darling, let's try to have a nap."

The moon was already shining when Andrew woke up. "Pamela, wake up, we overslept!"

She opened her eyes. "Is it morning already?"

"No, it's evening! We were supposed to go out with Lord Anthony!"

Now wide awake Pamela said, "I'll call and apologize."

Lord Anthony laughed and understood. "You must have been very tired from your previous excursions. If you like, we can leave the time to meet open for tomorrow. You call me when you feel relaxed and ready. Please covey my greetings to your fine husband."

A glorious sun greeted the new day!

While enjoying breakfast in their room, Pamela said, "I could get used to this!"

"I am very sorry, your ladyship. Unfortunately, I have not the means to offer you such indulgencies. At the most, I will be able to bring you breakfast in bed on your birthday!"

"That sounds lovely. Once a year will be wonderful!"

Pamela put on her new orange-red-pink Rajasthani skirt with one of the new white blouses.

When Andrew saw her, he laughed delightedly. "You look like a little girl!"

A shiny Rolls-Royce was waiting in front of the Rambaugh Palace entrance. Lord Anthony greeted them and asked if they felt rested. Once they were comfortably seated in the passenger section, Lord Anthony said, "I thought you might enjoy a drive through the city first. Jaipur is a busy and important city because it is here the caravans are formed to traverse or return from the desert."

Most building were built of pink sandstone. Pamela and Andrew observed the bustling and busyness of the people and overloaded trucks using their horns in vain at the cows, camels, even some stray dogs, goats, and the totally oblivious elephants with their masters proceeding unhurriedly while next to them men pushing carts with produce from the fields nearby along the dusty roads were advancing slowly. They were on their way to bring their wares to local grocers and restaurants. Even the pedestrians were completely unimpressed by the impatient horns from trucks and buses while, it seemed, daring fate and God to cross the streets right in front of the heavily swaying overloaded trucks!

And then there was suddenly the Hawa Mahal—the Wind Palace!

"It is called so," Lord Anthony explained, "because the wind plays and teases with timeless songs through the intricate filigreed window screens cut from sandstone. It used to be the royal ladies' *zenana*. This beautiful pink palace was for those inside a lonely prison because of the tradition to keep the exotic beauties hidden behind screens."

"Do you think there were rivalries among the women?" Pamela asked.

Lord Anthony responded, "It is said that there was one lady, a foreigner of exquisite and immaculate beauty, of whom the maharaja was fiercely possessive. She was not allowed to remove her head veil even in front of the other ladies in the *zenana*. Her face, it was said, was so perfect that only the maharaja was allowed to see her. Even when she danced for his special guests, she never removed or let the veil slip from her face. People said that when she danced, one could believe that there was not a single bone in her body. She moved like sunbeams—silent and fluid! She was housed in a separate section of the Hawa Mahal to prevent jealousy or harm from other ladies!"

"She must have been lonely," Andrew sympathized.

"Yes, certainly." Lord Anthony nodded. "But there was also a rumor that she had a lover! One of the three eunuchs guarding her. When the rumor and suspicion reached the maharaja's ear, he, himself, killed her with his jewel-bedecked sword while the guilty eunuch had to watch before he, too, was executed. Her body was then burned before anyone ever saw her beautiful face."

"Brutal justice!" Andrew commented.

"Lord Anthony, could we walk a bit to browse the stores?" Pamela asked.

"Yes, of course. Only I must caution you that there are very skilled thieves, grown-ups and little ones, who can reach into your pockets without you noticing it. Best is to keep your passport, money, and credit cards in front of you, along with your camera. Even removing watches from unsuspecting tourists offers an irresistible challenge to them!"

While they were mingling with other pedestrians, they enjoyed part of the life this unique city had to offer.

"I feel an affinity with these people," Pamela said at one point.

Lord Anthony looked at her with a distant gaze, remembering, *Elizabeth said the very same words!*

They walked as closely together as was possible with the sometimes-rushing people who would push ahead regardless of who stood in the way! Both Pamela and Andrew felt the restless pulse of the city. It was wonderfully busy and yet, in some ways, a happy scene with the unintended concert of hawkers' and shopkeepers' shouts, the camels' throaty complaining to their owners, and the funny trumpeting of elephants competing with the traffic horns. In spite of this nonstop concert, people went their way pursuing their goals.

They continued their stroll until Pamela discovered lovely bedspreads sewn together from old sari borders and then mounted on a heavier material. "Andrew, look! Do you think we could buy one for our bed at home?"

Lord Anthony told them, "I know of a store a few buildings from here where you can buy very good quality bedspreads like these."

At the store Pamela and Andrew were astonished at the variety and beauty of these old sari borders sewn into all kinds of covers for pillows, tables, dressers, and beds. It was true that these covers were of superior quality and the correct sizes for king-size beds. There was one in particular that Pamela liked. The sari borders were in purple, gold, turquoise, and a little bit of ivory. The spread came with five matching pillow cases. "It's absolutely the most regal bedspread I have ever seen!"

Andrew nodded. "I agree." He asked the salesperson for the price. It was very expensive! Andrew felt badly but thought it was too much money. "Please, Pamela, remember our humble cottage. This bedspread is meant for a palace."

Pamela blushed, then hesitated for an instant. "Yes, of course, darling, you are right, it wouldn't suit in our cottage." She tried to hide her disappointment. "For a minute I got carried away, I am sorry!"

Lord Anthony pretended not to overhear their conversation.

They did select and buy three pillow cases with painted miniatures on silk.

"Thank you, darling," Pamela smiled. "They will look lovely in our living room!"

By the time they left the store, it had turned much warmer outside.

"If you don't feel like the temperature is too warm, may I suggest we have some lunch?" Lord Anthony asked. "I know a small stand near here that serves very good food. It is very modest but clean. You might enjoy experiencing a roadside stand."

It was modest—just a few plastic chairs in orange and green colors, like the colors of the Indian flag! Collapsible bridge tables covered with bright orange plastic cloths under green umbrellas stood waiting to accommodate diners. Behind the counter was a blackboard that noted the day's choices, like chicken curry with potatoes, lamb coconut curry, okra and onions, yoghurt with cucumbers, mango chutney, and peas and lentils for the basmati rice. A big advertisement assured that there was plenty of Coca-Cola, ginger ale, tea, and coffee.

"May I order for you?"

"Yes, please, everything looks good," Andrew said.

They shared all the main dishes with naan, dahl for the rice, and ginger ale. Each dish was surprisingly delicious. Then to crown their tasty meal, they ordered the round cake balls soaked in syrup called gulab jamun with vanilla ice cream and coffee. For a roadside stand, the food was not cheap.

"Can most people afford food like this?" Andrew asked.

"No, it is mostly professionals and businessmen who have no one to cook for them do come here. Usually, business and professional people receive their lunch canteens with dishes cooked and delivered from their home. Perhaps you may have seen in Bombay, for instance, men carrying ladderlike trays on their heads with lots of canteens arranged on top. Those are meals they pick up at the homes of workers and deliver them by lunchtime to the various offices. It requires an incredible organization to manage thousands of deliveries every day!"

"I guess there comes the mathematical genius of an Indian brain into play." Andrew nodded with admiration.

"There are two more places I would like to show you. We'll go by car."

As if by magic, the Rolls-Royce had been following them and was ready to take them to the famous Birla Mandir.

"The Birla family is one of the most generous philanthropists in India," Lord Anthony explained while they were approaching the Birla Mandir temple. It was a complex building with several stupas that gave it the appearance of a palace. The wide-open square in front was a convenient place for hawkers offering their ware to devotees and tourists on their way to the impressive temple presiding at the top of the stairs. Close to the entrance were the usual flower vendors.

Lord Anthony bought three jasmine garlands and, at another stand, some candy and other sweets. Again, they entrusted their shoes to the warden who put them close to his person after seeing the generous tip.

The interior of the temple was huge and overwhelming with the enormous statues of gods and goddesses in their gold-painted garments and sparkling jewels! Pamela, Lord Anthony, and Andrew offered their garlands to an ancient-looking priest who smiled when he noticed the candy and sweets Lord Anthony had given to Pamela to present them to him.

It was welcoming cool inside.

At the exit sat two dust-covered beggars in dreadfully shabby clothes. Pamela gave ten rupees to each. In return she received smiles and blessings.

"How are you doing?" Lord Anthony asked. "Do you feel like seeing the famous observatory called Jantar Mantar?"

"Is it far from here?" Pamela asked.

"No. We will go by car."

Andrew knew about the observatory but had not expected it to be so large. It was mind-boggling to think that during the eighteenth century these astronomical calculations had been made by the famous mathematician and brilliant astronomer, Sawai Jai Singh! He was also the founder of the city named after him, Jaipur. His genius was also reflected in the design of the streets, which had prospered by its industries and agriculture. Like Udaipur, the hills hid precious and semiprecious stones and minerals.

"I am afraid I cannot remember much of the explanation regarding the observatory," Pamela admitted.

"Very few people, other than astrologers, can understand and remember exactly how the various calculations were made," Lord Anthony consoled her.

They studied some charts, which looked very complex and intriguing.

Approaching the hotel, it was the first time both Pamela and Andrew noticed how generous the layout of Rambaugh Palace was. The charming pavilions on many terraces serving various suites and apartments rendered the appearance of a fairy-tale palace.

"I wish my schoolchildren could see this lovely palace."

"Oh, you are a schoolteacher like your mother was?"

"Yes, I am a Montessori teacher, freshly licensed."

"Congratulations! How many children do you teach?"

"Between twenty and twenty-five from ages five to seven." Pamela smiled. "A wonderfully innocent age! They are very impressionable and absorb whatever you do, say, or show them."

Before entering the hotel, Lord Anthony reminded Pamela and Andrew, "Please tell me honestly if you are tired of my company. If so, I'll leave you to your own enjoyment."

"No," Pamela responded spontaneously, then looked at Andrew, who nodded. "I think we both enjoy your kind company."

"In that case, may I suggest we sit on my terrace and have a drink before going downstairs for dinner? I am fortunate that my terrace receives early morning sun, but toward evening, it gets agreeably cool."

"That sounds lovely, thank you," Andrew responded.

"Perhaps we could take a shower to wash away the dust before joining you on your terrace?" Pamela laughed. "We promise not to go to sleep."

"In that case, I am looking forward to your company around six o'clock?"

The terrace was deliciously cool and comfortable with cushioned garden furniture. Pamela enjoyed a gin and tonic while Lord Anthony and Andrew had scotch on the rocks. It felt good to relax!

"Pamela," Lord Anthony began after a few moments of no conversation, "may I ask you a personal question?"

"Yes." She smiled at him. "If I know the answer, I will tell you," she added teasingly.

He hesitated for an instant before asking, "Pamela, when were you born?"

She was surprised. "On March 28, 1959."

For an instant Lord Anthony' face looked shocked, then he nodded slowly. He was silent as a sudden sadness spread over his face, but he said nothing.

After an awkward moment of silence, Andrew picked up the conversation by telling their host about the Elephanta Caves and the leaking boats.

It didn't help. Both Pamela and Andrew noticed that their host's mind seemed somewhere else. They wondered if one of them had inadvertently said something that offended him. Even during the following dinner in his dining room, he was remote.

Finally, Andrew decided to ask, "Lord Anthony, have Pamela or I said anything to offend you? You seem withdrawn?"

He shook his head as if he were awakening. "I am so very sorry if I have not been attentive." He smiled to reassure them. "No, neither of you have said or done anything to offend me in any way."

"Please tell us if you are not feeling well," Pamela asked.

"Oh, no, thank you. There is nothing wrong with me. Perhaps I am just a little tired."

"In that case, we should leave so that you can rest," Pamela offered.

"I think you are right, Pamela. Rest will restore me. Thank you for understanding."

They stood up to leave.

"We wish you a very good night, Lord Anthony," Andrew said.

"Thank you, Andrew. There s only …" Lord Anthony stopped himself.

CHAPTER 26

" *Yes?* "

"*Y*es?" Pamela looked at him, waiting.

Lord Anthony hesitated for an instant before he said, "Pamela, I believe you are my daughter."

She stared at him. "What?" She sat down again. "What did you say?"

"Yes, it is very possible. No, actually, it is almost certain that you are my daughter." He inhaled deeply. "I am afraid I must explain. Andrew, please sit down." He waited until Andrew was again seated. "I know this must come as a shock to you both! You see, I calculated from the time you, Pamela, were born. I counted the years backward. Your mother was alone in Chislehurst during the months from mid-June to end of July in 1958 while her husband was at the British embassy in Delhi. She had written to tell me how unhappy she was. As I told you before, she invited me to visit her and stay with her for a while. I went in mid-June and stayed until middle of July of that year. It was most unwise of me to accept her invitation. In spite of her marriage to Adrian, she still wanted me. We were young and still in love! We thought we could handle the situation. But we both had underestimated our resisting the power of love."

Pamela stared at him, then suddenly she turned away and started sobbing.

Andrew went to her and embraced her. "Darling Pamela, please don't cry."

Finally, she was able to say "This is why Papa never liked me. He knew!"

"To confirm your belief, my lord," Andrew sounded very cautious but firm, "Pamela and you must have a blood-type test done."

"Yes, Andrew, you are correct! I know my blood type, but in order to make absolutely certain regarding parenthood, I am willing to do so if Pamela is also willing."

Pamela seemed dazed.

"What do you think, Pamela?"

"Yes. Yes, of course! But isr't it too late to do this as we are planning to leave for Agra in a couple of days?"

"We can go to the emergency station at the local hospital. They can take our blood samples and analyze them. I am confident that we will receive the results almost immediately as they have the laboratory open twenty-four hours."

Suddenly, Pamela seemed eager. She stood up. "In that case, let's go!"

During the drive to the hospital, none spoke.

At the emergency station, Lord Anthony was gently scolded by the nurse in charge about their urgency. "You ought to know, Lord Anthony, that we are here for real emergencies, not for cases that can wait until the next day!"

"It is a kind of emergency, my dear nurse," he responded. "These two visitors will leave in a couple of days. We need to know the result of the young lady's blood type to see if it matches mine. It is very important."

"All right then, you can sit here while I send a technician to attend to you, my lords, ma'am," the nurse said with some reservation.

"Thank you so very much for your understanding!" Lord Anthony praised.

Two hours later Lord Anthony and Pamela received the results separately in two envelopes.

Both were Rh-negative!

At first, after comparing the results, Pamela felt stunned and yet relieved. Lord Anthony was silent and waited for her reaction. He observed her gazing at him before a brilliant smile blossomed on her face as she went to him extending both hands. "Then you are truly my father!" Tears were sliding down her cheeks. She turned to Andrew. "Darling Andrew, I have a living father!"

He rushed to her and embraced her. "I am truly happy for you and you, Lord Anthony!"

"This must be why I immediately liked you!" Pamela told her father.

"My radiant daughter! What a heavenly gift!" He kissed Pamela on both cheeks. "Now we have a very important correction to make!" He smiled. "You cannot continue calling me Lord Anthony! What would you like to call me, Pamela?"

"Definitely not *Papa!*" She responded spontaneously. "May I call you *Father*?

"I would be most honored and proud to receive this precious title from you, my dearest Pamela! Thank you!"

It was almost midnight when they returned to the Rambaugh Palace.

"If you are not too tired, I would like to invite you to share a toast to this totally unexpected family reunion, if you will. I have a very old French cognac that has been sitting in my liquor cabinet waiting for years to baptize a special occasion. I believe we will never have a more joyous reason to celebrate!"

"You are very kind, Father!" Pamela smiled at him. "But you were very tired earlier. Even before we went to the hospital."

"You see, Pamela, I was not really tired. I felt profoundly shaken when you told me your date of birth and, with it, the possible revelation. Now that I know for certain, I feel greatly relieved and am wide awake! I have received the most beautiful consolation gift from my beloved Elizabeth—you, Pamela, our daughter!" Even though he was smiling, tears rolled down his cheeks.

The cognac in the crystal glasses had a rich amber color and a seductive perfume.

"I cannot adequately express my utmost gratitude to you, dear Andrew, for having brought, unwittingly, my daughter to me!" He paused. "I didn't even know I had a daughter! Elizabeth never told me! It is, for me, in a way, a touching consolation for having lost my Elizabeth. The only reason I can think of for her not telling me is her fear that, if the truth were to come out, it would create a big scandal!"

Both Pamela and Andrew waited for him to continue.

"Pamela, you have given me a far greater joy than you can ever understand or appreciate. I have always loved your mother very deeply in my soul. Thank you for coming into my lonely life!" He raised his glass. "May you, dearest Pamela, and your beautifully sensitive Andrew enjoy and treasure each other for the rest of your lives!"

The first sip was smooth like velvet.

"May I also offer a toast?" Pamela asked.

"Of course."

"I have lived a little longer than twenty-one years on this earth, but I have experienced only two enormously soul-enchanting days! My wedding day when Andrew promised to love me and keep me! And today!" She turned toward her father. "I cannot possibly express how profoundly happy I am to have found you, my father! Thank you!" She went to him and kissed him.

A comfortable silence lasted for a few moments until Pamela's father asked, "What are your plans for tomorrow?"

"We thought," Andrew replied, "we might visit the City Palace Museum or the Albert Hall Museum."

"Perhaps we could keep the museums for your next visit."

"For our next visit?" Pamela asked.

Her father chuckled. "Yes, why not? Now you know the way to Jaipur!"

"What were you going to suggest for tomorrow?" Andrew asked.

"Well, yes ... it is a bit late, but I would like to suggest that you come over here for a hearty breakfast around eight o'clock so that we will be ready around nine to drive to Jaisalmer, a small town with a lively population of traders. It is across the Aravalli Mountain Range. The climate is hot but blissfully dry. You will get to see a bit of the desert and her people. I think you will enjoy it."

"Oh, that sounds more fun than museums. We didn't have this suggestion on our list," Pamela said.

"This is very kind of you, thank you ..." Andrew hesitated a moment, then, with a smile, said, "Pamela's father."

"So for now, I bid you good night."

"Good night, Father." Pamela embraced him and kissed him on the cheek.

"Sweet dreams, my daughter and my son, Andrew." They shook hands.

Back in their suite, both Pamela and Andrew were silent for a long while.

It was Pamela who spoke first. "Darling, how is it possible? I felt so very strange when I first saw Lord Anthony ... as if I already knew him! I sensed immediately that I liked him and felt drawn to him."

"You must have felt an affinity between you. I noticed during the last few days how he observed you whenever you were not aware. There is an invisible bond between you, a connection."

For a while they both followed their own thoughts until Andrew observed, "I wouldn't be surprised if my father had suspected something. He knows your birth date, and he must have also remembered when Lord Anthony, your father, stayed in England for several weeks during 1958. They probably met several times. Your father must have told him about Elizabeth. His love for her ..."

"Do you realize, Andrew, I never was a Payne—I am a Wood! Now I know why my mother's husband never talked to me! He must have known! Probably even hated me!"

"I think this is why my father called Lord Anthony in Jaipur and traced him to Udaipur while we were there so that we could meet!"

Pamela shook her head in dismay. "I cannot imagine my mother keeping this secret ..."

"Think, my love, if she had openly acknowledged her affair, quite possibly, it would have ruined your father's, I mean, her husband's career and her standing in society. It might have even affected her school in India. They had to keep your paternity a secret!"

Pamela nodded. "Still, I wish ..."

"It just occurs to me! Pamela, do you have your mother's letter with you?"

"Yes, because there are many details she mentioned about the school. I thought it might come in handy. Why do you ask?"

"When you showed me your mother's letter, I felt that there was something strange. I couldn't explain it then. Please, show me her letter again."

Pamela went to her travel bag and retrieved the letter. They both read it again.

Andrew nodded. "Do you realize that she refers always to 'her husband'? Here, in the third paragraph, she writes, 'I want you to remember always that your father—even though he doesn't know you—and I love you very, very much!' Here is the clue! 'Your father, even though he doesn't know you'!"

Pamela nodded. "You are absolutely correct, Andrew! In a way, my mother admits that I am not her husband's, meaning Adrian Christopher Nigel Payne's, daughter! But she omits, most probably intentionally, to mention Lord Anthony Wood by name as my biological father."

"Yes, I am afraid so."

"Oh, Andrew, I cannot tell you how very grateful I am to your father to have called my father so that we could, finally, meet each other!"

Pamela and Andrew woke up early with anticipation to see Jaisalmer. They met with Pamela's father at eight o'clock and enjoyed eggs, bacon, French cheese, a tasty potatoes-and-onion dish, toast, croissants, orange juice, and very strong coffee. Pamela wore her blue Rajasthani skirt with a white blouse.

"You look very young and charming, Pamela," her father praised. "Do you have a sun hat?"

"No, I thought of buying one."

"Good. There is a boutique in the basement here where you will find hats, umbrellas, sunscreen lotions, and sunglasses." To Andrew, he said, "I happen to have a brand-new panama hat for you if you like."

The boutique had a wide choice of articles for protection against the sun. Pamela found a lightweight hat with a wide rim.

The drive from Jaipur to Jaisalmer was toward the northwest direction across some hills. When they reached the summit, they could see the vast desert stretching out below. Sheep and goat herds roamed some fields near villages. It was amazing how quickly the landscape changed from scattered vegetation to desert sand. It was lunchtime by the time they reached Jaisalmer, where they found a small open-front shop that offered some food.

"Would you like to stop here and eat what the local people eat, or would you prefer to go a bit farther to a restaurant that offers some European dishes?"

"Wouldn't it be more fun to eat here, Andrew?"

"Yes, something smells very tasty."

They were about to sit at a small counter on high stools when the owner rushed over to wipe the countertop and seats. He looked very pleased. Before sitting down, Pamela's father went to his driver and invited him to join.

The dishes were written on a small blackboard, but they were in Hindi!

After receiving translation, Pamela asked for the cauliflower curry while Andrew selected an eggplant dish. A lamb biryani and chickpeas with onions curry dish completed the main selection. Andrew invited the driver to join them at their table. He sat quietly next to Andrew. He answered shyly the translated question from Andrew if he had family. Yes, he said, a wife since five weeks!

"Congratulations!" Andrew offered spontaneously.

"May you both be very happy!" Pamela and her father added.

They toasted the new husband with ginger beer while Pamela's father and the driver preferred the sweet Indian tea.

"These dishes taste different from the dishes by the same names in Bombay or Udaipur. They have more chilies."

Lord Anthony smiled. "You will find as many different dishes as there are cooks." He asked for a large bottle of sealed-top bottled water and glasses. The water tasted wonderfully cool and seemed to sooth the impact of the chilies!

Pamela whispered to her father, "Look at these wonderfully expressive and interesting faces!"

He chuckled. "Yes, Pamela, you are definitely my daughter because I, too, enjoy observing faces. I used to paint some. Unfortunately, my talent is sadly insufficient to do any justice to the originals."

Before going back to the car, Pamela insisted they stop at a sweets shop. They selected a box with mixed sweets for their driver and his new wife.

After lunch they drove a bit farther out of town to a caravan stop. The moment they exited the car, Pamela, her father, and Andrew found themselves surrounded by a lively group of traders offering carpets for sale. They were thick woolen dyed in deep-red, dark navy-blue, and ivory colors. The designs were plain but pretty. Nearby was a cluster of tents where women sat on small rugs offering woven wool scarves, vests, and leather handicrafts.

To please them, Andrew bargained for a colorful vest with the help of translation by Pamela's father. "Come to think of it, I'll also buy also vests for my father and brothers." He bargained and got four vests for five-hundred rupees.

"Well-done, Andrew! Both seller and buyer made out well," his father-in-law praised. "Where did you learn to bargain?"

They told him about the skirt and blouses bargains in Udaipur.

The camels were resting in a small group chewing. They seemed ill-tempered and noisy. Pamela kept away from them. A large herd of sheep were driven by several barking dogs and three shepherds on horseback. The faces of the men were thin with marked cheekbones and eyes set deep in their sockets. Their hair was partly covered with some draped-around and twisted cloth but were gray with dust while their skin was almost black with deep wrinkles.

Fascinating faces! Pamela thought again and again.

One of the shepherds asked Pamela something, which, of course, she couldn't understand. When the shepherd repeated his question, her father laughed and translated for her, "He is offering you ten sheep if you marry him!"

She was amused and smiled. "Tell him, please, that I received a far more generous offer and that I am already married."

During the trip back to Jaipur, Pamela told her father about the school in Dhalarnabad.

"I wanted to ask you about Elizabeth's school. No, it must be your school now, Pamela, isn't it? What are your plans for the future of the school?"

"I would very much like the school to go on. Mrs. Chowdry, a board member—only two are left—has expressed the importance for the students presently enrolled to continue. But I do not like the headmistress, a Ms. Bannerji. I absolutely don't trust her!"

"Remember, Pamela, she lied to us about Mrs. Chowdry's taking a nap," Andrew said.

"Yes. She may have lied to us about other things as well. Do you know of someone trustworthy who could look into the financial difficulties the school seems to be having in spite of a generous monthly financial support?" Pamela asked her father.

Her father thought for a long moment, then shook his head. "Unfortunately, I don't know anyone in that area who could look into the financial affairs."

"Andrew and I were thinking that perhaps a financial consultant could look into the way Ms. Bannerji is running the school."

After a moment of hesitation, her father offered, "Perhaps I could help?"

"Would you really?"

"It just so happens that I have a friend in Lonavla. He is Lord Edward Sommers. During the hottest summer months, we usually meet and stay in Lonavla. He has a lovely bungalow in the hills where we spend several weeks each year reminiscing on our lives and the world ... the way it used to be,"

"Dhalarnabad is less than one hour's drive from Lonavla via Khandala."

"I think I know where Dhalarnabad is, but I didn't know Elizabeth had her school there. I only knew that she had founded a school somewhere in India with the proceeds from the sale of her father's estate."

"It is absolutely amazing how fate works," observed Andrew. "You received your daughter, and then you may be helping to rescue the dream-school project of Pamela's mother!"

Pamela explained to her father, "I had asked the headmistress to forward to me the financial records from over the last five years. They were supposed to be given to me before we left Lonavla. Then I asked for them to be sent to Udaipur. We haven't received anything yet! I left instructions to forward them here to Jaipur."

"I hope you will receive them soon," her father responded. "You study them, and if there are problems that need looking into, let me know. I'll find a reliable financial consultant if necessary. I'll be happy to do this for you ... and Elizabeth."

Pamela addressed her husband, "Andrew, you are so correct by pointing out how amazingly fate works!"

A little later, they enjoyed a light dinner in the ornate dining room before going early to bed.

On the following day, all three visited the City Palace Museum and the Albert Museum.

Later that evening Pamela's father suggested that he would be delighted to go with them by car to Agra. On the way, they would stop at a lovely resort to have lunch. "We should leave by ten o'clock so that we arrive in Agra early. I estimate around five o'clock. We would be in time to check-in at the Royal Taj Mahal Hotel, have dinner, and watch the sunset at the Taj Mahal mausoleum!"

Pamela was wearing her Rajasthani black skirt with the tiny mirrors and a white blouse. After leaving Jaipur, they stopped at another caravan stop. This one was crowded with tourists. The camels seemed to be in foul mood, loudly complaining while workers removed their heavy burden.

"Would the young lady like to ride a camel?" one of the men from the caravan asked.

Pamela shook her head. "No, thank you."

"Whyever not?" Andrew asked.

"They look dirty and smell … rather unpleasantly," she whispered.

CHAPTER 27

On the Way to Agra

*T*he drive to Agra was interesting because Pamela's father asked the driver to choose small roads so that she and Andrew got to see how villagers lived and worked hard for their meager rewards. Human functions knew no privacy. It was easy to see where wells from the hills sustained life to humans, animals, and vegetation. They were interdependent.

At one point the Rolls-Royce started smoking under the hood. They were forced to stop at the nearest hamlet. Almost immediately, the car was surrounded by curious onlookers. Pamela was the first to get out of the car and was greeted in a gracious way "namaste," which she returned. She was wearing her red-orange Rajasthani skirt, which the children seemed to like. They were very shy. Some smiled uncertainly and half hid behind their mothers, whereas the men and boys were mostly fascinated by the big car. Most likely, they had never seen a Rolls-Royce before. As soon as the steam in the radiator stopped sputtering, the driver opened the lid very carefully. Then Pamela's father bought water from an old woman who was carrying a copper vessel on her head. She was thrilled to receive money and didn't mind to return to the cistern to get some more water for herself. Finally, the radiator seemed satisfied.

While waiting Pamela sat on a tree stump and was almost immediately surrounded by children. She knew that there was no point in telling them a story, but she showed them how to count up to ten in English with her fingers. Very soon the older ones started repeating the numbers and were thrilled when she clapped her hands in praise. All too soon the car was ready to resume the journey to Agra. The English visitors waved goodbye while the children responded likewise.

For lunch they stopped at a resort that was in an oasis. Lush palm trees provided shade not only for visitors but also for gentler plants. Ten small straw-thatched circular buildings offered comfortable private suites with the latest appliances. The windows of each were directed to assure privacy. There was an open-air dining area with a large BBQ in the center. In spite of the shade, Pamela's father suggested they eat in the indoor dining room, which was welcomingly cool! There were a few other guests, but they kept to themselves.

The choice of menu was large, but today's specials were roasted chickens, tandoori baked chicken, and tandoori prawns, and of course, biryani rice. In addition there were lamb and boneless goat dishes, which they didn't order. Ginger and mango chutneys were served. The rest of the menu were European dishes, which they didn't order. Ginger beer and raita buffered the effect from the abundant hot spices in the tandoori dishes. They all chose ice cream with coffee.

When Pamela approached the car, she noticed immediately that the driver had washed and polished it. "Mr. Khan, your Rolls-Royce looks like new!" The praise brought a big smile to his face. Then she asked, "Did you have some lunch?"

He nodded eagerly. "Yes, yes my lady. Good lunch!"

Driving through so many rural areas and villages brought some new understanding to Pamela and Andrew as to how hard the people had to work to survive and their complete dependence on the weather, the rains, and the harvests.

At one village, the car had to stop as a cow had been killed by a truck. The road was completely blocked by the overturned vehicle.

A woman approached the car and asked in Hindi, "My sister has just given birth to a baby girl. Can she name the baby after the ma'am-sahib for good luck?"

Pamela's father translated. Since they had to wait for the road to be cleared, Pamela got out, and Andrew followed to see the young mother. They were led to an adobelike hut with a woven palm roof. The young mother was sitting up on the primitive stretcher and was nursing the baby. She smiled when she saw Pamela. "How you?" she asked in heavily accented English.

"I wish you every happiness with your baby girl." Pamela admired the tiny wrinkly face of the baby who kept her eyes tightly shut.

Another woman who had followed inside repeatedly called out, "Name! Name!"

"I am Pamela. P-a-m-e-l-a."

The mother nodded eagerly, pointing to her baby and repeating slowly, "Pamela."

A clever child wiggled through the few women and offered a slate and chalk to write the name down. Pamela thanked her and wrote her name in block letters and showed it to the mother, who smiled. Luckily, Pamela had some money with her to give to the older woman, probably the new grandmother, and said, "Food."

She was amused when she found Andrew outside feeling quite a bit insulted, explaining that he had been barred entry to the hut!

CHAPTER 28

Agra—the "Taj Mahal"

*I*n Agra the Royal Taj Mahal Hotel was in the center of a well-tended garden with bougainvillea of brilliant purple, orange, pink, and white colors. The entrance was welcoming with sitting areas near the reception counter. Pamela was looking around the lobby. The architecture was an interesting mix of modern and Moghul styles.

While Andrew and Pamela's father waited in line to check-in, it occurred to Andrew that they had not decided what he should call him.

"Pamela has decided to call me father. How do you feel about it?"

"Well, I call my father that. Come to think of it, so does she."

"In that case, we'll have to find another title."

Pamela joined them. "It just occurred to me that we have a two-bedroom suite here! Couldn't Father stay in the second bedroom in our suite?"

"A very sensible suggestion." Andrew immediately accepted. "Let's see how the accommodations are, then decide."

"Pamela, Andrew, I don't want to interfere in your privacy. After all, you are on your honeymoon!"

The suite was spacious and very well laid out—the living room in the center separating the two bedrooms with bathrooms.

"This is perfect! What do you think, Andrew, Father?"

"I think it is excellent!" the two men agreed.

Shortly before sunset Pamela, her father, and Andrew reached the Taj Mahal mausoleum! The apparition in white marble was lovingly bathed in pink by the good-night kiss of the sinking sun. The minarets stood like proud guardians at the four corners of the wide terrace. The magnificent precious stones inlaid with delicate flowers and notations from the Koran were stunningly beautiful. What artistry!

A guard approached them. "You must leave. We are closing."

Pamela greeted him with "Namaste" and then said, "Sir, we drove all the way from Jaipur to see the most beautiful Taj Mahal in this world! Can we not very, very quickly see it from the inside? Please?"

The guard frowned while contemplating for a long moment, then he swayed his head and waved them inside. "Very, very quickly!"

A happy thank-you smile and a generous tip were his rewards!

It was quite dark inside. They descended the stairs carefully to find the solemn sarcophagi of Begum Mumtaz and her husband, Shah Jahan, in their silent slumber.

"We will come back tomorrow at sunrise!" Pamela promised.

Before going to bed early, Pamela, Andrew, and her father had a bite to eat in the hotel restaurant.

When both Pamela and Andrew were in bed, she observed, "How extraordinary that Lord Anthony Wood felt that I was his daughter, and the man I never cared for was not my father!"

"When you first saw your real father, when he embraced you, were you surprised?"

"Yes! Perhaps for a split-second, but I liked him immediately. There was something ... I cannot explain. I felt a connection."

"Now that you know why you both felt drawn to one another it makes absolute sense." Andrew nodded.

"You know, Andrew, I always felt uncomfortable with Papa. He never talked to me. I knew instinctively that he didn't like me. There was a mutual dislike between us. The only time he would smile at me was when my parents were entertaining and he wore his scarlet dress uniform with stripes and medals. He knew that he was dangerously handsome and relished the attention he received."

"Do you think your parents were in love?"

"I really cannot say. I was too small to know what love was."

"Do you think your mother's husband knew that you were not his child?"

For a long moment Pamela didn't respond, but then she said, "He must have known by the date of my birth! Because he was not with my mother at the time she conceived me. I imagine they didn't divorce because it would have created a scandal and could have possibly terminated his career," Pamela explained.

"It must have been miserable for both of them to be chained to a loveless marriage." Andrew sympathized with both.

"Do you think I can ask my father why he chose to live in India? Did he, too, inherit an estate?"

"Perhaps you ought to wait until our conversation turns to that topic."

"Yes," Pamela agreed, "you are right. Let's try to go to sleep. Remember, we have to get up at four o'clock to see the sunrise at the Taj Mahal mausoleum."

Andrew yawned in response. "Getting up early is the cruel price for gathering memories."

It was predawn when Pamela, who was wearing her turquoise sari, her father, and Andrew left their hotel. There was a chill of the night in the air. The "tears of the night" were still clinging to the flowers and plants like transparent crystal drops. The roads were almost deserted. Only here and there one could see men driving oxen carts with harvested produce to sell at the market in the hope to earn enough money to buy the necessities to live and survive. Pamela observed motor scooters on which women passengers in saris sat dangerously sideways on the back seats. They didn't have a pommel of a sidesaddle to hook a leg over. She worried that the saris might get caught in the wheel.

The sky turned into a tender pink when the sun—a rose-orange ball—ascended serenely from behind a hill, painting the majestic white marble monument in pink!

When Pamela, her father, and Andrew approached the entrance, there were lots of people waiting for the doors to open. The same guard of the previous night asked them to follow him. He led them through a small, almost-hidden door inside the mausoleum compound. Pamela felt guilty for receiving preferential treatment. The guard continued leading them along the reflecting pool toward the breathtaking vision of this sacred resting place. He explained some of the inscriptions from the Quran and pointed out many precious inlaid stones that had been inserted with amazing skill and precision! Will those artists ever know how much their creations are admired by people from all corners of the world?

Again, they descended the stairs into the actual tomb chamber.

A moment later another guard in uniform joined them with a European woman. She wore a white sari for mourning. She didn't seem to notice the three visitors who watched her discreetly. For a long moment she stood as if in transcendental meditation. Then she began to sing in an extraordinarily beautiful alto voice. She began with Beethoven's "*Kyrie Eleison*" and ended with "*Agnus Dei*," both arias from his *Missa Solemnis*. The woman's rich voice embraced and filled the crypt with the heavenly sound of mourning and joy!

For Pamela, it was the most soul-touching experience. She felt transfixed.

The magic, however, evaporated quickly when the voices from outside announced that the general public was allowed to enter to view and admire this magnificent work of art and homage to love!

After lunch they drove to the deserted city of Qutub Minar. It had once been a vibrant and important city until repeated droughts caused the wells to completely dry out, thus rendering the city uninhabitable. The ancient partially crumbled brick walls and carved stone gates bore silent witness to lives lost. How tragic it must have been for the people to leave everything behind in search for a new place.

Not far from there was Fateh Burj Sikri (Fatehpur Sikri), which had also been abandoned for the same reason. The remaining minaret had been built with bricks to it's amazing height of 120 meters!

Walking between these ancient ruins of cities built and lived in by people, Pamela found weeds and small plants as well as some bushes struggling forth between tumbled marble blocks and bricks. She felt sad for the fate of the inhabitants of times long passed!

Pamela's father invited her and Andrew for dinner at a very elegant restaurant. For this occasion, she chose to wear her purple sari with the golden threads border design. When her father saw her, he smiled in approval. Andrew wore one Indian-style shirt, which had been made for him in Udaipur. To their amusement, Pamela's father also wore a similar shirt with a matching vest.

"We are all adapting to India," he praised.

"Yes, Father." Pamela chuckled. "I wish I could wear saris to my school in Farmington. They are amazingly comfortable."

"Perhaps we ought to start a touch of Indian fashion in Farmington?" Andrew suggested.

The restaurant, Indira Mahal, was an unusual palace-like restaurant. The architecture was in elegant Moghul style with typical arches separating dining areas to render an intimate atmosphere. The tablecloths were pink with white napkins elaborately folded to look like a peacock. The waiters wore white slacks and light-gray tunics with raspberry-red sashes matching their turbans. There were small oil lamps in silver bowls on each table and attached to the walls.

It appeared to be very popular with English people and diplomats.

At one point, after they had ordered their menu selections, a stranger approached the table. "Anthony? What a jolly surprise to see you here!"

Lord Anthony recognized the intruder's voice immediately. He shook hands and asked, "How are you, Randolph?"

"Gosh, how long has it been since we last met?"

"It was the Queen's birthday celebration at the British embassy in Delhi, about eighteen years ago."

"Well, there you are, far too long!" The man had an embarrassingly loud voice. He looked at Pamela and Andrew. "How about introducing me to these charming young people? I envy you!"

"Please meet my daughter, Lady Andrew, and her husband Lord Andrew Prescott. They are on their honeymoon. Mr. Randolph Brighton, a former colleague."

"Then congratulations are in order! What the devil, are you chaperoning them?" He asked half teasingly. "They look grown-up enough to know what to do."

"We are enjoying a family reunion," Pamela explained to the stranger.

"I'll be … I can't say it with a lady present." He turned toward Pamela. "You look familiar. Have we met before?"

"No. I assure you we have never met," she responded politely.

Randolph frowned, then turned to Andrew. "You are a Prescott? Not Michael Prescott's son?"

Andrew laughed. "Well, yes, as a matter of fact, I am his eldest son." He stood up and shook hands.

"Delighted to meet you, Lord Andrew."

"Likewise, Mr. Brighton," he responded politely.

Against good judgement but feeling forced to be polite, Lord Anthony offered, "Would you like to join us?"

"I would very much, but I am with a very rich elderly lady who doesn't like to share me … if you know what I mean."

During this awkward conversation, Pamela folded her hands under the table in silent prayer that this Randolph person would go away! "Thank God!" she whispered to her father and Andrew after the intruder returned to his table.

"Who is he?" Andrew asked.

"An unstable fellow, I am afraid. I tried not to introduce you, but when he asked, I had to. He is the sort of fellow who will boast that he met Viscount Andrew Prescott and his new bride. It will be all over London."

"How do you know him?" Pamela asked.

"For a short time, he also worked at the Home Office but, somehow, disappeared suddenly. The next time I met him was here in Delhi at a function. I cannot say he is a friend of mine."

"I am glad," Pamela sighed in relief.

This sincere remark caused Andrew and her father to laugh.

CHAPTER 29

A Confession

After they were comfortably seated in their hotel suite, Pamela decided to ask her father when he moved to India.

He contemplated for a few moments, then sighed deeply before he began. "I think I told you about Elizabeth's and my growing up together as neighbors and having fallen in love. But then she met and married the colonel who had worked for a while at the Home Office, then changed his career. He bought a commission in the Royal Regiment. He was a smart fellow and rose in rank to colonel, which is quite an achievement! He was very popular and in demand with ladies. He was a very new colonel when he met Elizabeth at a ball. She fell head over heels in love with him. Elizabeth's parents, I, and other friends tried to advise her to wait a while to get to know this man better. But she wouldn't listen or heed any advice. Even the threat from her father to be disinherited if she were to marry that fellow did not stop her! One day she had disappeared! Only later we all found out that she married this colonel in Gretna Green. To avoid a scandal, he was transferred to the British embassy in Delhi.

"To make a long story short, about two years later, I received a very unhappy letter from Elizabeth, your mother. Her husband stayed in India at that time while she returned home for a couple of months. I was very surprised when I received an invitation to come to stay with her. At first I didn't know what to do as I still felt devastated and heartbroken. The worst was that I was still in love with her. We were young, and n spite of her marriage, Elizabeth confessed that she had made a terrible mistake in marrying Adrian. This confession, if you will, stirred new hope in me, and I went to stay with her from mid-June to the middle of July in 1958. We both thought that we could restrain ourselves. But we were both weak and irresponsible. We didn't think of possible consequences.

"As months went by, I felt more and more guilty for having been with your mother. It was morally wrong, and I felt miserable and shameful. I often wondered how Elizabeth felt about our having been together. I decided to avoid seeing her at all cost! Her father had reinstated her as his sole heiress. I also told you earlier that she had sold her parents' estate. But I had no idea what she planned to do with the money.

"About one year later my father passed away, and I inherited his estate, which included a couple of mines near Jaipur. I resigned from the government and went to India to inspect the mines and decided to invest in additional mines in the same area. It made sense to settle down in India. I had also hoped that in creating a distance between Elizabeth and the painful memories of our love, it would help me to forget. But all too soon I realized that one cannot move away from certain memories because they are deeply engraved in your heart!"

"Did you know that my mother was pregnant?"

"No, she never told me. It was several years later when I heard someone mention that she had a daughter. I didn't ask how old she was.

"Then, one day, I met Elizabeth and her husband at a reception at the British embassy in Delhi for the celebration of Queen Elizabeth II's birthday! She carried on as if there had never been anything between us. In a way, I was glad but it did hurt! It was then I learned that your mother had returned to India with her husband to open a school for rural children. Her husband turned out to be an excellent teacher. They received and enjoyed great admiration from the

Indian government and the British community for their dedication to offer free education to children who otherwise would not receive good enough education to improve their lives."

"After that unexpected encounter did you see my mother again?"

"No. I avoided going to diplomatic functions. I hid like a coward, not trusting myself. Until I heard of the horrible accident ..." Pamela's father withdrew a handkerchief from his pocket and dried tears that overflowed his eyes.

For a while, they were silent.

Finally, Andrew asked, "What did you do then?"

"I had to make a choice between returning to England or to remain in India. I chose the latter."

"We are asking so many questions. I am very sorry," Pamela apologized. "You have been very honest and patient. Thank you, Father! You see, you are the only person who knows what happened. If only I had known of you then!"

"Yes, if only we had known of one another." Her father paused, then asked, "Pamela, after your mother's and her husband's death, what happened to you?"

It was a long story. Pamela told him about her early childhood, school and college years, and then finding Andrew through the late Mrs. Hood.

"Andrew, it was your father who called me first in Jaipur, then traced me to Udaipur to inform me about you and Pamela being here in India. In hindsight, I truly wonder if he might have suspected something about the timing of your birth, Pamela. After all, he and I were working at the Home Office at the time when the dashing colonel conquered the heart of the very vulnerable young Elizabeth. Your father, Andrew, was very keen on my meeting you both. It just so happened that I was in Udaipur on business when your father called." Pamela's father smiled. "And then I found my beautiful daughter and a handsome son-in-law!"

CHAPTER 30

Worries and Responsibilities

uring the following night, Pamela couldn't sleep. She finally got up and sat on the terrace to listen to the gentle noises of the night.

Andrew must have noticed her absence because he found her sitting very quietly. "Darling, it's too cold out here. You'll catch cold. Come back to bed."

They returned to their bedroom. "I couldn't sleep because I wondered if I should return to Dhalarnabad with my father to introduce him to Ms. Bannerji and the school. What do you think?"

"You haven't told him about the headmistress yet."

"Not in details. But he offered to help. I think it is important that Ms. Bannerji realizes that her 'unchallenged rule,' as Mrs. Chowdry described it, has ended."

"It's not a bad idea. Of course, it all depends if your father agrees. He may not have time to go with you to Dhalarnabad. And of course, it would alter our scheduled trip. Why don't you ask him at breakfast?"

As planned, Pamela asked her father at breakfast if he could go with her to her mother's school at Dhalarnabad.

"I think, Pamela, this is an excellent idea to introduce me to this Ms. Bannerji, the faculty, and the students. If we can drive tomorrow to Delhi, we then can, hopefully, catch a nonstop flight to Bombay and take the train to Lonavla." He turned to Andrew. "Will you join us, or will you stay in Delhi and then follow your itinerary to Calcutta and Cochin?"

"It is completely up to Pamela," Andrew replied.

"I know you are on your honeymoon, but if all goes well at the school, Pamela could rejoin you later in Calcutta or Cochin so that you can enjoy the last few days together."

Pamela suggested, "Darling, why don't you go and meet Mr. Patel as arranged in Delhi and follow the itinerary? I'll rejoin you as soon as possible. Please understand that I feel that it is very important to continue my mother's school in the best way she had intended."

"I think it is incredibly kind of you ... father of Pamela, that you are willing to help with this problem! Thank you very much!"

Anthony Wood nodded. "In that case, we mustn't lose time! It may be good for this headmistress to know that there is a man in India who can check what is happening at the school."

"Mr. Patel should be in Delhi now, so he can get the tickets to Bombay and Lonavla for you." Andrew picked up the phone to call Mr. Patel.

"I promise to take very good care of our Pamela," Lord Anthony said.

After Andrew talked to Mr. Patel, he learned that all flights from Delhi to Bombay were booked for the following day, but Mr. Patel was able to reserve and buy two seats on an early seven o'clock flight the day after. There would be enough time to reach the train to Lonavla.

"What do you prefer, Pamela and Andrew?" Pamela's father asked. "To stay here in Agra where I know some wonderful stores or go sightseeing in Delhi? You can always do the other thing on your next trip to India."

"I'd love to shop. What do you think. Andrew?" Pamela asked.

"Fine." Andrew asked Pamela's father, "Do you have something in mind?"

"I would like to buy a nice piece of jewelry for Pamela."

Pamela shook her head. "Father, you have no idea! I have already inherited far too much jewelry, from my mother and from Mrs. Hood. If I were to live one hundred years, I couldn't wear all of them!" She smiled. "I wouldn't mind getting another sari. I like to wear them!"

"In that case, we'll stop at Shamirs. I think they have a better selection than in Delhi."

It seemed true! The walls at Shamirs, a labyrinth-like store, were covered with shelves and piles of saris and materials. There were more colors than the most perfect rainbow could ever produce!

"Good morning, ma'am, sirs. How may I help you?" a salesperson asked politely.

"We are looking for a festive sari," Pamela's father answered. "Pamela, in what color would you like?"

Her eyes scanned the shelves until she found saris in pale lilac to rich plum colors. She pointed to a dark-lavender sari. "May I see this one, please?"

With practiced efficiency, the salesman pulled out a whole stack of rolled-up saris in similar colors with rich embroideries or woven gold or silver borders.

He spread out one after the other across the counter. They were all magnificent! It was very hard to decide. The salesman explained the pattern on one sari, "This one has exact copies of the precious stones inlaid at the Taj Mahal. This silk is heavier because the weight of the silver threads needs stronger material."

Pamela gazed at these gorgeous works of art by artisans who, probably, received low wages. She turned toward her father. "Are these not too elaborate for me? I thought of buying a sari for weekends. These are for weddings or receptions, perhaps even to go to an opera or theatre."

"How about this one?" Andrew pointed to a dark-navy sari with silver borders out of which flowers seemed to flow.

"It is magnificent, Andrew! Come to think of it, where would I wear it? Perhaps I should rather buy material to make a gown that I can wear more often?"

"We have the same color materials in silk, cotton, raw silk, and polyester in the adjacent room. Please follow me."

Her final selection was a fine raw silk material in a deep-lavender color. "I would like this material."

"We have tailors who can advise you what kind of gown you may want and measure you if you like, ma'am."

"That is a very good idea. Let them make the gown. Do you have a style in mind?" Andrew suggested.

"We are spending much too much time and money on me! I could just buy the material and take it home. What about you both?" Pamela's eyes discovered amazingly beautiful silk ties with matching accent kerchiefs. "I would like you both to choose a couple each, please!"

Both Andrew and her father selected lovely ties and seemed very pleased. Then Andrew and Pamela selected additional ties for his father and brothers.

A couple of stores farther was a carpet dealer. The selection, quality, and workmanship of the finest silk to wool carpets surprised them! Both Pamela and Andrew liked one particular carpet, but it was horrendously expensive.

After an hour of exploration, an exquisitely beautiful blue Tabriz was going to be sent to Farmington for the living room. It was to be a surprise wedding gift from Pamela's father.

At restaurants both Pamela and Andrew were reasonably familiar with what dishes they enjoyed. After dinner they sat on the terrace, which connected both bedrooms from the living room, and chatted while sipping Port.

At the end of the evening, they changed their minds and decided to go to Delhi on the following day.

CHAPTER 31

Old and New Delhi

*U*pon arrival at the Empress Mumtaz Hotel, Pamela watched Mr. Khan, the driver, directing porters to withdraw the by-now two suitcases carefully from the car to take them up to their suite. Unfortunately, the hotel had made a mistake and had only one two-bedroom suite reserved for Mr. and Mrs. Prescott. Otherwise, it was fully booked.

"You are most welcome to stay in our suite," Andrew offered to Lord Anthony.

"Since meeting you both, you haven't had much time to yourselves alone. I feel like I am intruding and depriving you of your enjoyment of your honeymoon!"

"We'll make up!" Pamela smiled. "We feel very comfortable with you and enjoy being with you. Please say yes. We don't want you to stay at another hotel!"

Reluctantly, her father agreed to stay.

On the following day, Mr. Patel came to meet them at the hotel in Delhi. When Pamela introduced her father to him, he said, "Ah, yes. I have heard of you, my lord." Mr. Patel explained to Pamela, "Your father owns several mines in Rajasthan. I have heard that men like to work for him because he takes great care in securing the mine shafts and tunnels. He also pays well and on time. The workers enjoy decent housing and health care for their families."

Pamela was very pleased to hear of her father's good reputation.

To facilitate sightseeing in Delhi, they drove by car to the Red Fort, then continued passing the various government buildings, admiring the wide-open space and avenues. The Chawri Bazaar near the fort was lively, and it was fun to watch people bargaining with shopkeepers while gesturing excitedly. Some people were walking with purpose while others moved more leisurely, stopping here and there to examine the displays.

The faces! Pamela thought repeatedly and enjoyed looking as discretely as possible at the diversity of features and clothing. *If only I could paint them!* She very quietly took photographs of them.

After lunch Pamela's father insisted, "And now you must experience the Meena Bazaar in Old Delhi!"

What a difference! It almost seemed that they had gone back in time! The roads were dusty and crowded with every imaginable thing offered by vendors. The stands spilled into the narrow streets and alleys. The buildings looked so deteriorated that one was amazed that they were still standing. The electric and telephone wires were bunched together, crossing back and forth low overhead. Some wooden balconies looked dangerously fragile. Laundry was hanging from spanned ropes helter-skelter across the streets, almost interfering with the chaotic cables attached to crumbling walls. Rickshaws were being pulled by men who seemed only of skin and bones! What a hard life! The entire area was covered with crusted ancient dust. It was mind-boggling to Pamela that here and there a person offered a shy smile in faces that had been cruelly carved with signs of premature aging due to the incredibly hard living conditions!

And yet what surprised both Andrew and Pamela were the expensive gold jewelry stores next door to spice merchants and produce and clothes vendors. The scents and smells changed as they strolled along the roads—spices, fruits, and perfume among others. The jewelers seemed unconcerned about the possibility of thieves taking something from their displays, which were unprotected and lay temptingly on display!

"Oh, look at this beautiful silver jewelry!" Pamela exclaimed.

"Select what you like, my dear!" her father encouraged. "Wouldn't you rather have gold?"

"No, Father, with some of my new saris with silver threads, a silver brooch would be much nicer. I prefer silver to gold. It is less intrusive, I think." She perused the display, then pointed to a brooch with an exquisite sapphire framed with a filigreed border. "This one would be perfect for many of my saris with silver borders."

"Then you must have it!" her father promised and instructed the owner of the store to arrange it in a box with antitarnish lining.

CHAPTER 32

Return to Dhalarnabad

*I*t was five o'clock on the following morning when Pamela found it hard to say goodbye to Andrew. She had insisted that he not come to the airport. She had a hard time controlling her tears. "I'll join you either in Calcutta or Cochin!"

The flight to Bombay was, luckily, uneventful. From there they took the train to Lonavla. On their arrival, Pamela was introduced to Lord Edward Sommers, who had invited them to stay at his bungalow close to Lonavla. It was positioned to take maximum advantage of the panoramic view of the lush canyons.

Lord Edward was a friend of her father's and a gentleman with fine features that were framed with long white hair.

"I am delighted to meet you, my lord." Pamela smiled while shaking hands with him. She immediately liked him.

"The pleasure is entirely mine. May I call you Pamela?

"Yes, by all means."

Over dinner Pamela told Lord Edward about her mother's school and the problems.

"I have heard of the Lady Elizabeth Mary Rose School in Dhalarnabad. It is a prestigious school. And you, Pamela, are the daughter of the founder?"

"Yes. I inherited the school."

Her father explained, "There seems to be a bit of a problem, but I am optimistic that it can be resolved."

Pamela smiled at him. "It is amazing how things work together … like a Swiss watch!"

"With your permission, Pamela, may I tell my friend about your mother and us?"

"Yes, of course."

After her father finished telling the whole story, Lord Edward remained silent for a long moment. "It is amazing in what wonderous ways fate mends human mistakes with consolations least expected!" He stood up and embraced a surprised Pamela. "I am extremely pleased for you to have found your father! He is a man of noble character, and I am honored to call him my friend."

"He is, for me, a most unexpected and precious gift!"

"We have to celebrate!" Lord Edward went to a cabinet and withdrew a bottle of very old port. He filled three crystal glasses. "I wish you both, father and daughter, many creative and enriching years ahead."

On the following morning, during breakfast, Lord Edward offered, "Would you like me to come with you, or shall I just give you my driver?"

"What do you think, Father?"

"Perhaps we ought to go first, just Pamela and I, to see what kind of reception we'll receive."

The moment Lord Edward's driver, Mr. Tennant, approached the school gate with the Bentley, the guard became immediately alert. He saluted smartly while the driver lowered the window. "Whom do you wish to see?"

Pamela lowered her window and greeted him with "Namaste."

The guard recognized her and immediately returned her greeting with his own "Namaste," then rushed to open the gate.

Mrs. Chowdry came outside to welcome them. "What a nice surprise!"

Pamela smiled. "Good morning, Mrs. Chowdry. May I introduce my father, Lord Anthony Wood? Father, this is Mrs. Chowdry."

"Good morning, my lord. Welcome to our school."

"Thank you, Mrs. Chowdry. Pamela has told me of you, and I am delighted to meet you. She has also informed me about her last visit here. Pamela invited me to see for myself as to how we might be able to assist."

"Is Ms. Bannerji free to meet us?" Pamela asked.

"Speaking of the devil … here I am!" Ms. Bannerji approached. "Again, you have not let us know in advance of your visit, Mrs. Prescott."

Pamela was amused that the headmistress had once again dropped her title. "Good morning, Ms. Bannerji. I would like to introduce to you my father, Lord Anthony Wood. I am afraid this visit came about quite unexpectedly. It is important for you and the school to meet him. It is rather warm. Perhaps we could go to your office, Ms. Bannerji?"

"Well, yes …" she agreed reluctantly.

"I would like Mrs. Chowdry, as a board member, to be present at this discussion," Pamela said firmly.

Once they were seated in Ms. Bannerji's office and the headmistress was sitting nicely protected behind her desk, Pamela began, "During my last visit you, Ms. Bannerji, mentioned financial difficulties the school is experiencing presently. Has anything changed since then?"

"Not really. We are still in need of withdrawing money from the expansion trust fund."

"Perhaps you remember, Ms. Bannerji, that I had requested that the financial reports for the last five years—from 1976 through 1979—be forwarded to me first to Lonavla, then to Udaipur, then Jaipur. But I did not receive any reports!"

"I am afraid I cannot find any of them."

"How is this possible?" Pamela asked while suppressing her frustration. "You mentioned during our last meeting—and I am certain that Mrs. Chowdry remembers this as well—that you said you were doing the accounts yourself!"

"Yes." the headmistress was trying to control her anger at being challenged. "And I told you then that this is a small school and we do not require an accountant or treasurer."

"Where do you keep your financial records, bills, and documents? Here in this office or at your residence?"

"They ought to be here … somewhere," Ms. Bannerji replied evasively.

"Do you lock up your file closets and office every time you leave each evening?"

"Yes, of course!" Ms. Bannerji grew angry. "You, Mrs. Prescott, are insulting me!"

"It is not my intention to insult you or anyone else for that matter. My demanding to see the financial records is natural. I can assure you that it does not give me pleasure to remind you that I am the owner of this school. I have the authority to stop all funding immediately!"

Mrs. Chowdry inhaled sharply. "Oh no, please!"

"The reason why I brought my father with me today is to inform you, Ms. Bannerji, that I have appointed my father, Lord Anthony, as the new headmaster, administrator, and personal representative of mine for this school. For the time being, you are temporary assistant manager and report to him until we have been able to study and sort out the financial records."

"But I was appointed headmistress of this school," Ms. Bannerji protested.

"Yes, I understand that this happened at the time of Mr. Chowdry's sudden demise." Pamela turned to Mrs. Chowdry. "I am very sorry to have to mention this sad event."

The woman nodded. "Yes, I understand."

"May I ask who appointed you headmistress at that time?"

"I cannot remember which one of the deceased board members appointed me."

"May I see your résumé, please?" Pamela asked.

"Résumé? I never needed a résumé!"

Pamela could not hide her surprise. "What did you do before you received this position?"

"How does this have any relevance to the financial records?"

"Your résumé, if there is one, would show whether you were qualified for this position. Have you had any previous experience with education or organizations as manager or treasurer?" Pamela explained patiently.

Ms. Bannerji stood up in bursting anger. "I want to remind you, Mrs. Prescott, that I was obviously qualified for this job!"

Lord Anthony had heard enough. He reminded the headmistress in a quiet but firm voice, "It is a common curtesy to address people with their titles. My daughter is to be addressed as *my lady* or *Lady Andrew*."

The headmistress turned to him. "How are you going to be headmaster and administrator for this school as her *ladyship's* personal representative from UK?"

"Ah …" Pamela's father nodded. "I do not live in the UK. I live here in India."

For a split-second Ms. Bannerji made a face but said nothing more.

"As of today, Ms. Bannerji, you are temporary assistant manager of my school. There will be no more withdrawals of money for the school or otherwise without my father's approval. If this does not please you, you are welcome to leave," Pamela said.

There was an awkward moment of silence.

Suddenly, Ms. Bannerji smiled. "Lady Andrew, I thought your father died here years ago?"

For an instant Pamela was shocked at the woman's impertinence. She recovered quickly. "As it turns out, it was a serious mix-up and misunderstanding," Pamela responded calmly. "It is a private matter that does not concern you or the school."

"Is it possible to meet the faculty and students?" Lord Anthony asked to change the topic.

"You can wait for lunchtime at one o'clock in the main hall," Ms. Bannerji informed him ungraciously.

"I hope, Ms. Bannerji, that we will be able to work well together," Lord Anthony offered.

"Only time will tell, Mr. Wood."

Pamela was about to correct her, but her father took her arm and led her to the door. "Thank you, Ms. Bannerji. We will wait until lunch."

After they left the headmistress behind in her office, Pamela asked Mrs. Chowdry about Ashok's parents. She briefly explained to her father of the tragic incident of the boy having been killed by a panther and that, with him, the parents' hope had also died.

"It is very kind of you, my lady, to remember the Bhindis. They are still enjoying your gift of food and said that they pray each day for your happiness."

While waiting for lunchtime, Pamela, her father, and Mrs. Chowdry walked in the garden. Pamela explained to Mrs. Chowdry, "My father grew up together with my mother. They were always very close to one another. It is for this reason he is very keen in keeping the school in the spirit she had intended."

"I am so very glad and grateful, my lord."

At lunchtime Ms. Bannerji, still occupying the center chair at the head table, stood up to inform all present, "We have a slight change here at the school. The new head and personal representative of the owner is Mr. Wood."

Pamela immediately stood up and corrected her. "I am afraid Ms. Bannerji is somewhat mistaken. The new headmaster, administrator, and my personal representative at this, my school, is my father, Lord Anthony Wood. He is to be addressed as either *Lord Anthony* or *my lord* and offered respect due to him and his position. Ms. Bannerji is, as of this morning, temporary assistant manager. Lord Anthony has expressed the wish to meet briefly with the faculty after lunch. Thank you."

"So I have already been replaced," grumbled Ms. Bannerji.

The two visitors chose to ignore her remark. It was a very tense atmosphere at the head table during lunch.

When the faculty was assembled in a small room after lunch, Mrs. Chowdry asked if she could introduce both properly. "You will remember having met Lady Andrew, the daughter of the late Lady Elizabeth, the founder and benefactor of this school. Lady Andrew is the present owner. She has appointed her father, Lord Anthony Wood, headmaster, administrator, and personal representative for her ladyship. He resides here in India."

It was interesting to observe the response from individual faculty members. Except for one person, it seemed that they welcomed a change.

One middle-aged man stood up. "Lady Andrew, Lord Anthony, my name is Adrian Whoolsley. I think I speak for most of us here in bidding you a heartfelt welcome! I have been at this school for eighteen years and remember well how it used to be when Lady

Elizabeth supervised the school. Her husband, we called him Mr. Adrian, was a great teacher and well-liked by faculty and students! I am very sad to inform you that I have witnessed, with deep regret, the gradual deterioration of the spirit among faculty and students. By this, I do not mean that academically, the high standards slipped. To the contrary! The tests and exams are conducted like mean races. Our students are petrified even before the time of the exams. There is, in my humble opinion, too much pressure put on them to perform better than ever, regardless of the mental stress it creates. The emphasis to excel and succeed over all the other schools in our state is at the cost of spirit and friendship between students as well as teachers."

Pamela nodded. "Thank you very much, Mr. Whoolsley, for your honest observation. May I ask the other members of the faculty if they agree with this assessment?"

"Yes." A young Indian teacher stood up. "Yes, Lady Andrew. My name is Sanjid Ray. Adrian Whoolsley spoke for all of us. I am afraid I have to tell you that each one of our seven-member faculty is presently forced to look for another teaching position."

"May I ask for the reason?" Pamela was surprised.

"It is for personal reasons. We have not received our salaries for the last three months. Unfortunately, we are unable to continue here as we have no other sources of income."

Pamela frowned. "I am absolutely shocked to learn of this!" She looked at her father, who nodded. "I would like my father to address this important matter. He is now, as new headmaster and administrator, supervising present and future expenses by and for the school and all related matters."

Lord Anthony began by saying, "My daughter and I are deeply shocked and saddened to learn of this serious and inexcusable neglect of the school's responsibility toward faculty and students. I am going to begin this afternoon to look into this unacceptable situation. I am promising to each and every one of you that you will receive your salaries due to you by, hopefully, tomorrow or, latest, the day after tomorrow."

"Are there any other urgent matters you wish for us to know?" Pamela asked.

The teacher who had led the children in singing the school hymn, a young Indian, stood up. "My name is Kumar Singh, I am the music teacher. First, may I convey to you, Lady Andrew, and to you, Lord Anthony, our gratitude for your sincere interest in the school. You will never know that we feel you are godsent! We love our students and spare no effort to nurture their needs—be they emotional, academic, social, or physical. The children are very gifted and eager to learn. It would be a disaster for them to have to leave if the school were to discontinue. Their parents would never be able to come up with the required monies to allow their children to continue their education."

Pamela nodded. "Yes, I agree. It was my mother's wish to assure the continuation of this school and to increase the grades up to college levels by adding a new building and additional teachers. It is my father's and my own wish to follow in this direction. We will meet this afternoon with the bank manager at Lonavla to orient ourselves with the financial situation of this school. Meanwhile, we want to reassure you that each and every one of you will receive all monies due to you. I wish to thank you for your patience and understanding."

CHAPTER 33

Troubles

*I*mmediately after their meeting, Pamela and her father went to meet with the bank manager in Lonavla. At first the manager, a Mr. Gordiji, informed them that Ms. Bannerji had called to inform him not to give out any information regarding the school accounts. It required quite a bit of explaining and convincing the bank manager that Pamela was the late Lady Elizabeth's daughter and that she had inherited the Lady Elizabeth Mary Rose School. Pamela introduced her father as the new headmaster, administrator, and personal representative of Pamela for the school. Only then did they receive ledgers from over the last five years.

Pamela explained, "You will understand that we will have to take these ledgers with us to study carefully the activities of the regular account. You see, Ms. Bannerji, the previous headmistress, either did not keep financial records or she didn't want to show them to us. This is the reason for our coming to you, Mr. Godriji. We understand that the separate expansion trust fund, which was not to be used for regular school expenses, has been used to pay expenses. We will study them carefully tonight and will return the ledgers to the bank tomorrow morning."

The bank manager did not like to give out the ledgers and asked an employee to copy them but was informed that the copying machine was broken. The manager had no other choice but to give the ledgers to Pamela. Just before leaving the bank, it occurred to Lord Anthony to ask the manager to check if there had been any withdrawals made earlier in the day.

A few minutes later a clerk came to show them that a cash withdrawal of one-hundred-thousand Rupees from the expansion trust fund had been made at half-past two o'clock in person by Ms. Bannerji. He said, "I saw her. She seemed in a hurry."

"Thank you," Pamela said while looking at her father. "She must have come right after lunch while we met with the faculty members." She addressed the bank manager again, "I understood that there was a strict clause attached to this expansion trust fund account that no one was to touch or withdraw any money from it. Can you explain why this clause was not being observed and honored?"

Mr. Gordiji grew nervous. "I had no knowledge of this condition. It must have been lost or misplaced. I vaguely remember that when the regular account for the school was exhausted, Ms. Bannerji came to me and asked that the expansion trust fund be made available to pay the bills for the school. I saw no reason not to oblige."

"Do you remember when that was?" Lord Anthony asked.

"Oh, about two to three years ago," Mr. Gordiji replied, then went to a shelf at the back of his office to search for a file. "This is the converted expansion trust fund into the current regular account for the school." He offered the file to Lord Anthony.

Inside the cover was a note attached that identified the account as Expansion Trust Fund for the Elizabeth Mary Rose School located in Dhalarnabad to be used exclusively by the written permission from the founder and owner of the school—Lady Elizabeth Mary Rose Payne—and her heiress/daughter, Pamela Desirée Payne!"

"Who has signed the transfer from the expansion trust fund to the regular school account?" Lord Anthony asked.

When the bank manager looked at the first page in the file, there was a note:

I, Ms. Desi L. Bannerji, headmistress of the Elizabeth Mary Rose School in Dhalarnabad, give permission and assume authority, myself only, to attach the expansion trust fund to the regular school account.

January 1978

Ms. Desi L. Bannerji

Headmistress of the Lady Elizabeth Mary Rose School

"Who accepted this note?" Pamela asked.

Mr. Gordiji grew more nervous. "I am sorry. I cannot recall."

"She had no authority to do this. The bank violated the trust as custodian of the deposited expansion trust fund. Whoever allowed this violation is guilty of serious neglect, if not a crime!" Lord Anthony said gravely.

"Father, I think we ought to return to the school to check the office."

"First, we have to calculate all the salaries due to the employees. Meanwhile, Mr. Gordiji, freeze the account so that there will be no additional withdrawals by any unauthorized persons. Do not destroy anything in this file. My daughter, the present owner of the school, will sign all necessary documents for transfer of legal authority over both the school and the expansion trust fund accounts by tomorrow morning."

They left a very nervous bank manager behind.

Pamela and her father spent a very long evening and late night studying the ledgers from over four years to compare withdrawals. It was a challenge to calculate the salaries owed not only to the faculty but other employees as well! By two o'clock in the morning, they had rough estimated amounts figured out for overdue salaries and other regular expenses.

New ownership and authorities documents were ready to be signed and registered for legal transactions at the bank and anywhere else. Pamela had her mother's letter with her. She was glad that her mother had written the letter on her official Lady Elizabeth Mary Rose School stationary with the Swendown arms printed on it.

A sleepy Mr. Godriji received both Pamela and her father first thing when the bank opened so that they could withdraw the required monies owed to the employees of the school.

The moment the car drove through the school gate, Mrs. Chowdry came running. "I have bad news. Ms. Bannerji seems to have left!"

Pamela and her father exchanged knowing glances.

"I am not surprised. We need to search the office first," Lord Anthony said.

In the file closet were a couple of shoeboxes with unpaid bills but no financial records. In a desk drawer they found several money withdrawal slips from the bank and a few coins.

"Where is Ms. Bannerji's apartment?" Pamela asked.

"She lived in the headmistress' residence, the building of your parents," Mrs. Chowdry explained.

In the master bedroom, the closets were open, and some clothes were still hanging or folded on shelves. Some clothes were thrown on the bed that, apparently, hadn't fit in the suitcases Ms. Bannerji had packed in a hurry.

"Mrs. Chowdry, can you tell if anything is missing from the house?"

"Oh, I can't say at first glance. It has been three years since I was asked to move out, after my husband had died and Ms. Bannerji moved in. As far as I know, nobody had ever been invited into the house during her occupancy."

"We need the police inspector to come here," Lord Anthony decided and picked up the phone to request the inspector to come immediately to the school. They locked up the house and went back to the office to wait for the inspector.

One hour later Police Inspector Murthi and his deputy arrived. After having been briefed, the two men searched the office thoroughly, pulling out fully file drawers to check below, where they found sale slips and bills for clothes and building materials.

"Building materials?" Mrs. Chowdry puzzled. "There was nothing built here in several years."

The door to an adjacent room to the office was locked, but it was no problem for the police. They broke it open. There were additional bills. Some paid, others not. Lots of them were for personal items and purchase of land in Utabaugh. The puzzle was solved when the inspector found on one piece of bill that the building materials were to be delivered to Utabaugh—a small town about 120 kilometers away from Dhalarnabad. In addition, there were torn up bank withdrawal receipts and some cash left at the bottom of a desk drawer. They had been signed by Ms. Bannerji. Inspector Murthi showed them to Pamela and Lord Anthony.

Inspector Murthi alerted by phone his colleague in Utabaugh to look out for a Ms. Bannerji and follow her secretly wherever she went to find out where she was building a house and then to arrest her.

The inspector and his deputy took photos and fingerprints, collected bank documents, bills, and other items of interest, and packed them in boxes. Inspector Murty also searched thoroughly through the house Ms. Bannerji had occupied to collect whatever could serve as evidence in a court case. It was already afternoon when the police left to write a report.

With Mrs. Chowdry's help, Pamela wrote down the names of each school employee with the salary amount due and paid to him or her. For each person, Pamela's father, as new headmaster, inserted the correct amount into an envelope with a note for the receiver to sign as having received the entire overdue salaries. During the whole afternoon, the employees filed into the office to receive their pay. Both Pamela and her father thanked each employee for their loyalty and patience. In return, they promised to stay and continue in their positions at the school.

Pamela agreed that her father should turn over the immediate managing of the school to Mrs. Chowdry for some time. They agreed that as little as possible should be told about Ms. Bannerji to the faculty, other employees, and the students.

Mentally and physically exhausted, Pamela and her father returned later that afternoon to Lord Edward Sommer's bungalow to study the ledgers once more.

The ledgers from 1975 to 1977 had regular amounts withdrawn toward the end of each months for salaries, then some reasonable withdrawals for food and running the school.

"Mr. Chowdry died at the end of 1977," Pamela calculated. "Ms. Bannerji took over, and look, Father, right from the beginning, the withdrawals increased rapidly! No wonder the regular account for the school became exhausted."

"It was then she took the liberty to authorize herself to withdraw from the expansion trust fund," her father commented. "Here, look, Pamela, the number of withdrawals are weekly with increasing amounts."

"How shrewd she was to dupe the bank manager!"

"The bank manager neglected his fiduciary duties by ignoring the strict directives of the expansion trust fund and allowing that woman to withdraw money at will! He is also guilty!"

"Are we going to sue?" Pamela asked her father.

"We have to think about this very carefully because you are in the UK and I won't be able to stay too long at a time here. Perhaps Edward can recommend a competent barrister here in Lonavla or Pune."

"Father, do you think Lord Edward would be willing to join the school board? He could be a great help to us!"

"Before we ask him, we need to brief him of the delicate situation of the school at present. If he is willing to accept, I would be most delighted!"

"Oh, I hope we can persuade him!" Remembering the bills they had found in Ms. Bannerji's desk drawers, Pamela said, "We need to find out if some grocery suppliers and other merchants have outstanding bills. What a mess!"

"Don't worry, Pamela, we'll resolve this. Inspector Murthi has all the bills for building materials and personal items Ms. Bannerji so freely purchased from the expansion trust fund."

"If she goes to jail, perhaps we can put a lien against her house?"

"Very possibly, yes," her father agreed. "Meanwhile, you have to authorize Mrs. Chowdry and me to withdraw money for the continued running of the school."

It was a relief to know that each member of the faculty and employee of the entire school had been paid all their salaries due to them and that they had promised to stay on.

And so while the police compiled evidence for criminal cases against the former headmistress and the bank manager, Lord Anthony, as new headmaster of the Lady Elizabeth Mary Rose School, started to resolve the financial woes of the school.

On the last evening in Lonavla, Lord Edward, Pamela, and her father were relaxing on the terrace overlooking the beautiful canyons with the lush forests. They had shared their discoveries at her school with Lord Edward. He had recommended a well-respected barrister in Pune for Anthony, as new headmaster, to approach in the hope to engage him for the planned lawsuits.

After a long moment of silence between Lord Edward and his guests, Pamela decided to inform her father and her host that she would be able to replace much of the stolen money from the expansion trust fund. "Andrew and I found gold coins in the garden of our cottage I have inherited. Initially, we had decided to finance this honeymoon trip from some of the gold coins. But then our families gave us this trip as our wedding present. I am willing to use some of the coins to replace the missing money in the expansion trust fund and reestablish a regular account for the normal running of the school. This will ensure that my mother's dream will continue!"

Her father responded, "My dear, don't rush things! First, we have to see how things develop here. Also, you mentioned that you both found the gold coins and feel that Andrew has some claim to them. I can help out and create a new account for the immediate running of the school with strict authorization for temporary withdrawal permissions for Mrs. Chowdry, you, and myself, and if you like, Andrew."

They called Andrew in Calcutta, who agreed to his father-in-law's suggestion of temporarily loaning the money to the school and awaiting the outcome of the lawsuit.

"Lord Edward," Pamela began, "I would like to ask you if I may request a tremendous favor of you."

"My dear, you may ask, and I shall respond according to my abilities."

"Thank you, my lord." She paused an instant. "As you know, my school is in trouble with the management. My father has already most generously agreed to help out with the management along with the only remaining board member, Mrs. Chowdry. However, she will have to resign as a board member in order to take over the temporary running of the school. Father has very kindly agreed to manage the immediate problems. Mrs. Chowdry knew my mother personally. During my last two visits, I have had various opportunities to talk to her privately and observe her. I am confident that Mrs. Chowdry will make certain that the continuation of this school will be in the spirit my mother had intended. The school was founded to enable rural children to enjoy free first-class education to offer them the opportunity to improve their lives and, hopefully, improve the lives of their communities. I was talking earlier with my father and wondered if I might ask you to become the first board member of a new board?"

Lord Edward nodded thoughtfully before he responded. "First of all, my dear Pamela, thank you for your confidence and offer. May I ask what the duties and responsibilities of each board member will be?"

"I am afraid I am not very experienced in this matter. I would expect the board to supervise independently the management of the school and to ensure and foster the enrichment of the children's education and their emotional, social, and physical well-being as well as ensuring that the faculty is qualified and inspiring for the students and that all employees are treated with respect and receive adequate salaries and living quarters."

"Quite a task, I would say. But very important!" Lord Edward paused before continuing. "Pamela, I am willing to join your school as your first new board member."

Pamela was so relieved and delighted that she got up and gave him a big hug. "Thank you so very much, Lord Edward!"

Anthony shook hands with him. "Thank you, Edward. It is awfully kind of you!"

Lord Edward felt pleased. "You both are very welcome. I look forward to this challenge! In addition, I have a friend here in Lonavla, Dr. Vinod Sharma, a physician, who might be willing to join the board. And then there is another dear friend, Lady Grace, who used the be a dean at a college in Chesterfield who just might be interested to join the board."

"Oh, if they both agree, we would have three board members!"

"A good beginning, I would say!" Lord Edward smiled.

"I promise, I will return as often as possible to assist in whatever way I can," Pamela said.

"Pamela," Lord Edward began, "quite selfishly, I feel regret that you cannot stay longer here and bring sunshine into your father's and my life." He smiled while looking at her. "It is amazing how much you resemble your dear mother! She was very well-liked and admired and received treatment as if she were royalty."

"You are very kind, my lord." Pamela smiled at him.

"I will be happy to assist your father and Mrs. Chowdry to find a suitable new headmaster or headmistress. By the way, are you keeping the name of the school?" Lord Edward asked.

"Yes, absolutely! And the Swendown arms will remain over the gate and on the labels of the students' jackets and as the logo on the official school stationary."

"Good! The Lady Elizabeth Mary Rose School has an excellent reputation! I am honored to become part of it!"

"Thank you, Lord Edward. I am confident that between you and my father, you will find a vibrant person to revive our school!"

"I am very pleased to hear this. Hopefully, it will bring Anthony here more often!"

Before leaving Lonavla, Pamela went once more to the school with her father and Lord Edward to introduce him to Mrs. Chowdry, the faculty, and students.

Pamela's father asked her if she wanted him to accompany her to Bombay and see her off safely on a flight to Cochin, but she told him, "Thank you so very much, my dear father! No, Andrew told me on the phone that Mr. Patel has arranged his assistant, a Mr. Haldi, with the driver, Mr. Dalal, to meet me at the train station in Bombay and take me to the airport. He will have the airplane ticket to Cochin for me." She kissed her father on the cheek.

"I cannot tell you what an enormous gift and support you have been and are from now on to my mother's … my school, Andrew, and me! I would be most grateful if you could stay on a couple of days to make certain that everything is taken care of. In a way, I feel badly for leaving with all the pending problems, but I know you to be the best possible person to reassure everyone at the school that a better future for the children is the mission of the school," she said while drying tears with her handkerchief. "It is so terribly inadequate to just say 'Thank you for everything.' You have done so much for me! I will never be able to reciprocate adequately your gift of love!"

"When I come to England in five months, you will have plenty of ways to thank me."

She smiled. "I am so very glad that we have these five months to look forward to your coming! You will have to stay with us as long as possible! We have still so much to catch up on!"

The last announcement was made to board the airplane. Pamela tried unsuccessfully to blink away her tears, lamenting, "Father, we had so little time together."

Once more, her father embraced her tightly. "Now that we have found one another, we'll make up!" he called after her.

She found her reserved seat and was able to wave goodbye but felt so terribly sad to see her father standing alone on the platform. She waved until she was blinded by tears.

CHAPTER 34

Andrew Explores Kolkata (Calcutta)

*D*uring the days Pamela and her father were meeting the challenges in Dhalarnabad, Andrew and Mr. Patel flew from Delhi to Calcutta. They reached Calcutta in the late afternoon and checked-in at the Imperial Victoria Hotel.

"For this evening, I have only one suggestion, Lord Andrew— that you see the famous Hooghly Bridge, which is lit at night and looks very pretty."

Andrew agreed that it was very impressive. He and Mr. Patel enjoyed a late dinner at a small restaurant with a view of the Hooghly River from where they could watch the boats with their lights reflected in the flowing water.

Even at a late hour there was a lot of traffic in the streets— trams, trolleys, cars, trucks, scooters, carts (some pulled by oxen), and a never-ending stream of pedestrians navigating dangerously between the moving vehicles.

The suite at the hotel was very pleasant and comfortable. Since it had two bedrooms, Andrew invited Mr. Patel to take one.

"Oh, my lord, I do not know that I should."

"Nonsense!" Andrew replied, "Pamela isn't here, therefore, I see no reason why we cannot share these accommodations." He still sensed some hesitation in Mr. Patel. "We have spent so much time together, I think it would be nice for me to have your company."

"If you are quite certain, my lord?"

"Absolutely."

The large living room window overlooked the maidan, a wide-open space in middle of important government buildings and museums.

"Please tell me, Mr. Patel, what have you planned for tomorrow?"

"You should see the Badri Das, a Jain temple. It is a particularly beautiful building. One is allowed inside to see and admire the richly carved interior. Then there is the Nakhoda Masjid, a very large and stunning mosque! Of course, you must visit St. Paul's Cathedral, which was built in Indo-Gothic style architecture. Some say it was made to make the British feel less removed from their Anglican churches in Great Britain."

"Interesting," Andrew observed. "You have three monuments of three major religions! I am interested in seeing them all."

They breakfasted in the hotel dining room, which was elegant with chandeliers, crisp white tablecloths, sparkling crystals, and china. A nice window table was offered to them so they could watch the lively traffic on the Hooghly River and Bridge.

Andrew felt partly guilty for not having gone back to Dhalarnabad with Pamela but reasoned that her father, who was more familiar with Indian affairs, was of greater help and support than he could have offered. He took lots of photographs of the temple, mosque, and St. Paul's. At each place, the devotion and love for these holy sights rendered the visitors serene and peaceful.

At lunchtime Mr. Patel took Andrew to a tiny hole-in-the-wall eating place and asked permission to order dishes for both of them. Several seafood dishes were served with naan. Each one was very different from the others, but each dish was very tasty and enjoyable. They shared a large bottle of beer and felt too lazy in the afternoon to continue their sightseeing. Instead each succumbed to the temptation for a long nap.

Refreshed, they ventured out in the evening to mingle with other pedestrians.

"Tomorrow I would like to visit some museums."

"Very good, my lord. I was hoping to take you to the Victoria Memorial gallery and the museum, which is very well worth visiting. Another museum of interest to you might be the East India Company, which documented and explained their amazing success ... often achieved by dubious means, if I may say so," Mr. Patel added hesitatingly.

Andrew nodded. "I am afraid so. The company maneuvered some deals in less than honorable ways with quite unreasonable demands while forcing and influencing changes not always in the interest of the rulers or their peoples." After the visit Andrew concluded that the East India Company was not a bright and shiny star for the British in Indian history.

It was good to end the day's excursion with the pleasant picture gallery!

There was still one morning to explore. Mr. Patel took Andrew to back alleys where the workshops of artisans who created sculptures of clay and papier-mâché were busily forming some rather voluptuous Kali goddesses. Even the revered god Ganesha, with the elephant head, was widely reproduced with affection. After the sculptures were dry, they were painted with bright colors and decorated with countless beads and garlands, flowers, laces, and cheap pearls, then mounted onto carts. At the time of the parade, the many gods and goddesses were carried in a swaying procession toward the sea, surrounded at the shore by chanting and happy crowds who watched eagerly as the sculptures first wobbled on the water, then slowly sank, and finally, melted away.

Day and night, the traffic was constant and noisy. It still surprised Andrew how trusting or daring some pedestrians were as they wound their way between the honking cars, trams, and other intimidating vehicles!

Andrew was ready to leave for Cochin in Kerala. While he was dressing and adding final items to his suitcase, he realized how much he missed Pamela. She had called him and promised to meet him in Cochin on the following day!

CHAPTER 35

Reunion in Cochin

For each flight Pamela always asked for a window seat so that she could see the earth below. At first, flying over Bombay in daylight amazed her at how spread out the city and suburbs were. She could easily differentiate the wealthier, industrial, and poor districts.

The flight seemed endless! For some time the land was covered with layers of clouds. Coming closer to Kerala on the Malabar Coast, she saw fertile vegetation and beaches. Before landing in Cochin, she could easily see lakes and canals flanked by lush palm trees separating paddies.

At Cochin International Airport she felt very much relieved and very delighted to see Andrew, who enfolded her into a bear hug to welcome her enthusiastically. "Welcome to the backwaters, my darling! You will love the houseboat!"

For another moment she remained in Andrew's embrace as she didn't want to let go of him. "Oh, Andrew, I missed you so much in spite of being terribly busy! I can tell you that my father was truly godsent! I, nor you, could have never done it alone! He knows the ways Indians think and deal." She paused. "Father sends you his love." She was out of breath.

"First of all, my love, you must relax. Just leave all thoughts of problems and worries to others and let me take care of you. We have a very nice dinner waiting for you. The *boatwalla* and his servants are anxious to meet you. I showed them our wedding pictures, and they said that I am fortunate to have such a beautiful wife. I agree with all my heart! I missed you too!"

"Mr. Patel, how are you?" Pamela greeted their guide.

"Thank you, my lady, I am fine." He chuckled and added, "Your husband is fine, too, now that you are reunited."

The car stopped at a small wooden pier where a houseboat was moored. Pamela had never seen a houseboat like it. The exterior was woven by canes and appeared wrapped up.

The boatwalla and his servants were lined up and waiting to greet Pamela.

She smiled at them while joining her hands in greeting. "Namaste!"

They returned her greeting with the same gestures. "We are happy you have come, my lady," Mr. Ferez, the boatwalla, offered.

"Thank you for your welcome. I am happy to be here and back with my husband. He said that you have been spoiling him. Thank you!" She shook hands with Mr. Ferez first and then the other servants, who seemed very shy.

"Here is your 'palace on silver water'!" Andrew helped her to climb on board.

When she saw the comfortable sitting arrangement on deck, she smiled. "I like it already. It looks very inviting. Please show me the whole boat!"

"Would you not prefer a glass of nice cool champagne to relax and then look around?"

"Yes, that sounds tempting and invigorating, thank you." She sat down on one of the woven cane chairs with soft pillows.

Andrew sat next to her. "What would you..." He stopped abruptly when he noticed that she was crying. "Oh, darling, why are you crying?" Andrew felt helpless.

Pamela swallowed. "I am utterly exhausted. I have never before felt so totally burned out. I am sorry. I don't wish to cry because I am so happy to be with you!"

Andrew reproached himself. "I should have stayed with you."

"No, no!" Pamela hastened to assure him. "Father was absolutely fantastic! You couldn't have done more than he did! He was truly amazing!"

Mr. Ferez came with a servant who carried a tray with two champagne glasses, a bottle, and a plate filled with salty snacks and nuts. He popped open the bottle and poured, then offered the glasses to Pamela and Andrew.

"These are different kinds of samosas," Andrew explained. "Some have lamb, some vegetables, and others have crabmeat fillings. Here is mint chutney. As you know, it enhances their flavors."

She took a bite of the crab samosa and was surprised how wonderful it tasted. She turned toward the boatwalla. "Did you make these?"

"No, my lady, it was my cook. He will be very happy to know that you like the samosas."

"Wait until supper!" Andrew laughed, "The cook is a magician!"

Smiling, Mr. Ferez and his servant withdrew.

They sipped the champagne and enjoyed the tasty samosas while gazing at the lush tropical trees and blooming bushes along the shores. The water was like a mirror, clearly reflecting the surrounding landscape.

After a while Pamela requested, "Andrew, please show me the houseboat."

"I'll be happy to. You can take your glass with you."

Mr. Ferez appeared like a genie. "May I show the lady my houseboat, my lord?"

Andrew laughed. "By all means, Mr. Ferez. You know more about it than I do."

It was a clever living arrangement. The living area with the comfortable cane chairs was on a deck that had a removable ceiling. The dining table with chairs was under a permanent roof that was an extension of the roof terrace.

A narrow hallway led to the first well-furnished bedroom with its own shower and toilet facilities. Farther down the corridor was a second bedroom with an adjacent bathroom. A spiral staircase led to the partly covered sun terrace where two water tanks were located—one for cold and one for hot water. At the rear of the houseboat were two additional small boats attached. One housed the kitchen and servants' modest quarter, and the second was for Mr. Ferez, the boatwalla. Mr. Patel remained in a small house on land nearby.

Pamela told Mr. Ferez how impressed she was, which pleased him enormously.

"Darling," she asked Andrew, "do you think I could take a shower before dinner?"

"Yes, of course. We'll have to tell Mr. Ferez to make certain that there is enough hot water."

Again, the boatwalla appeared and assured them that there was plenty of hot water.

Half an hour later, a feeling-refreshed Pamela joined Andrew on the deck wearing the comfortable long lounge dress with the elephant prints she had bought in Ajanta. Her hair was still damp.

She joined him and sighed with pleasure. "How wonderful it is to relax and to be back with you!"

"I feel the same way!" Andrew agreed. "How many times have we said 'This is the beginning of our honeymoon'?"

Pamela chuckled.

The dining table was very elegantly set with a silver five-candles stand, pretty china and crystal glasses, and good quality silverware neatly arranged on a pale-yellow linen tablecloth.

The dinner turned out to be quite amazing! The cook sent first a cool cucumber and yoghurt mousse with a touch of nutmeg surrounded by tiny mango petals. Then this was followed by lobster in a saffron-butter sauce; a lamb pilaf with cardamom, raisins, and almonds, decorated with shaved toasted coconut flakes; and sauteed okra with tomatoes spiced with cumin as well as spinach with candied orange peels and naan. For dessert he offered meringues with lemon custard and fresh sweet raspberries!

Pamela insisted after the dinner to go to the rear of the houseboat to congratulate the cook for the fantastic menu. She teased him, "If you ever want to come to England to work for me, please let me know. I would love to have you!"

The cook smiled from ear to ear. "I come, lady."

"May I know your name please?"

"Ali Achmedi."

"I'll give you our address," she promised. "Thank you again!"

When dusk silently descended, the boatwalla, with the help of a servant, lit small lanterns next to Pamela's and Andrew's chairs so that they could read.

It was incredibly peaceful. Only once in a while could the sound of a jumping fish plopping back into the still water or a call of a lonely bird be heard.

"I could stay here forever," Pamela whispered.

"Me too! It was an excellent idea of Mr. Gupta in London to add this time of relaxation at the end of our trip."

After a while Pamela tried unsuccessfully to suppress a yawn. "I am afraid I am not very good company tonight. I am already half asleep."

"Then you should go to bed, darling. I'll join you in a little while."

Andrew joined her a few minutes later. "I missed you so during the last days. I was awfully worried about you! The only thing that kept me from following you back to Dhalarnabad was that I knew you were with your father. Knowing the ways of Indians, he was of better assistance with the school's problems and situation than I could have ever been. I hope you know that."

When he didn't receive a response, he realized that Pamela was already fast asleep. She didn't even wake up when he showered before joining her in the bed. When he gently drew her into his arms, she mumbled something while cuddling up to him and continued sleeping peacefully.

A glorious sunrise greeted Pamela when she walked onto the deck in her dressing gown. The sky was painted orange, pink, and purple then turned into a gentle blue. She sat down in one of the lounge chairs while absorbing the peaceful surrounding. Her thoughts went back to her father. Finding him was still the most unbelievable event in her life, and yet she felt an affinity with him. She smiled, remembering how he had said that she looked amazingly like her mother. But Pamela felt that in character, she was more like him! *My mother must have felt desperately lonely to ask my father to return to her while her husband was in India.* She realized that if Andrew's father had not telephoned his friend, Anthony Wood, in Jaipur, she would have never met her father! The knowledge that she had a living father—her real father—still filled her with awe, a profound contentment, and reassurance! It seemed to her as if she had been given a support on which she could lean on and trust. Thinking of how he was willing to take over her mother's school with all the existing problems filled her with gratitude and great relief.

What would I have done without my father? It would have been very difficult to make this feisty Ms. Bannerji leave! Andrew would have had to return to Dhalarnabad to kick her out and sue her! Now, thank God, Father and Lord Edward are taking over and are hiring a barrister from nearby Pune.

"Good morning, my love! How are you on this beautiful morning?" Andrew bent down to kiss Pamela.

She smiled at Andrew. He looked so young with his hair tousled and wearing only his dressing gown and pajama bottoms. "I am very well, thank you. I am sorry I fell asleep before you came."

"You needed to sleep and relax. I am glad I didn't wake you up when I joined you." He stretched his arms as high and wide as they could, then decided, "Let's ring for breakfast. The bellpull is here."

But before Andrew reached it, the boatwalla greeted them, "Namaste! Good morning, my lady, my lord. I hope you slept well?"

"Namaste! Yes, Mr. Ferez, thank you, we slept well. The bed is very comfortable."

"I am pleased you slept well. What would you like for breakfast?"

"Do you have coffee?" Pamela asked.

"Of course, my lady. Coffee, tea, chocolate, and milk! For cool drinks, we have orange, mango, grapefruit, coconut, pineapple, and kiwi juices."

"We like strong coffee in the morning. Lots of it, please. What would you like, Andrew?"

"I would like orange juice, two scrambled eggs on two toasts, and one toast with some jam." He turned to Pamela. "Besides coffee, what would you like?"

"I'd like just orange juice, a couple of toasts, and orange marmalade, please."

"Very good. Lady Andrew, do you prefer bitter or sweet marmalade?"

Pamela smiled. "You have Scottish bitter marmalade?"

"Yes, of course," Mr. Ferez assured with pride. "The eggs, my lord, have been freshly laid. There is a fish, a local fish, which is very delicate! Perhaps you both wish to taste it?"

Andrew hesitated an instant, then asked, "How do you prepare it?"

"With a touch of turmeric and ginger in butter. It is very light."

Pamela chuckled. "If it is as good as yesterday's feast, I'd like to taste it too."

"Would you like music with your breakfast?" the boatwalla asked.

"Oh no! It's so wonderfully peaceful here, we enjoy the calm," Pamela responded.

The fish, a fresh fish from the lake, was delicious!

Mr. Patel joined them after they had their showers and felt ready to explore the backwaters. The three of them climbed into a smaller boat with a man who rowed. "I thought you might prefer to have a quiet boat instead of a motorboat since we are not in a hurry."

Both Pamela and Andrew agreed.

The canal was flanked by long and narrow strips of land separating the rice paddies and other vegetable fields. The slender boat glided silently through the mirrorlike waters along the tropical banks and a few other houseboats. They saw very few people. Some women were washing clothes while others attended to the rice and vegetables. A couple of birds protested the intrusion but settled down after the boat had passed their habitat.

They reached a small island where they left the boat. Mr. Patel suggested they have a picnic lunch on the island.

A ruin of ancient stones attracted Andrew's interest. Mr. Patel was happy to relate its history. "Apparently, several hundred years ago, a Portugese count, who had lots of money, had this small towerlike fortress built for his Goan lady lover. The story had passed on from one generation to the next and so on. The count had met the girl when he lived in a small village along the Goan Coast. It is said that she was of extraordinary beauty but very proud! The Portugese was already married and, being Catholic, could not divorce his wife! But he didn't want to lose this girl. She was only thirteen but quite grown-up. He lost his mind and heart to this girl and fled with her to this island, far away from where his wife lived. The count, it was said, had the tower built in secret by slaves and killed the men who had built it so that they would not disclose his secret. The story must have been enriched by passing from one storyteller to the next. It is said that the count's wife did manage to find out her husband's secret and had him killed. In revenge, she left the girl alone in the tower to die abandoned."

"What a sad story," Pamela sympathized.

"I know a nice clearing where we can have our picnic," Mr. Patel suggested.

Suddenly they heard shouts and saw two men approaching in a small motorboat. They called, "Mr. Patel! Mr. Patel!"

Andrew joined Mr. Patel at the landing pier. Mr. Patel asked the men, "What's so urgent?"

CHAPTER 36

A Shocking Telephone Call

*T*he older man called, "I received a telephone call for Lord Andrew! I have a number he must call back as soon as possible. We can take him back."

"Do you know who called?" Andrew asked, thinking that it might have been Pamela's father.

"Prescott ... or something like that," the man replied.

"Show me the telephone number."

It was his parents' home number at Tarrington Abbey.

Andrew realized that it must be something important. "Wait here. I will get my wife. We'll return with you so I can call back."

Pamela saw the worried face of Andrew when he approached the picnic place. "What is it?"

"I don't know. They called from home. It must be urgent! We have to return to the houseboat and call home from there."

They sped in the motorboat to the houseboat as fast as possible to reach the telephone.

Initially. it was difficult to get the international connection. Finally, Andrew succeeded.

Andrew's mother answered the phone. "Andrew," she sobbed into the phone, "your father died of a heart attack. Please come home as quickly as possible."

For an instant he was too stunned to respond, then he gathered himself. "Mama, what did you say? Father? Oh my god! We'll come as fast as it is possible! Where are Tony and Scotty? How is Lilly taking it?"

"They are all here."

Tony took the receiver. "We are all shocked. Please, Andrew, come as quickly as you can. I cannot tell you how deeply sorry we are. We are staying here with Mama."

"Thanks, Tony. Yes, I'll call the airlines to get the first flight out. We are presently outside Cochin. I don't think there are nonstop flights to London from here. We may have to fly via Delhi or Bombay. I'll keep you informed. Meanwhile, please take care of Mama."

Pamela had overheard and understood the tragedy. She embraced Andrew in a silent reassurance that he was not alone. Then she said, "We must also call my father! He will want to come!"

She was able to reach him at the school. He promised to come to meet them in Bombay to fly back to London together.

Mr. Patel's experience with the airlines helped them to board the first flight from Cochin to Bombay and from there to London on the next flight at one o'clock in the morning on the following day.

There was no time to pack anything. Pamela and Andrew took their passports, money, and the most necessary items and rushed by car with Mr. Patel for the Cochin airport. On the way to the airport, Mr. Patel promised to take care of the packing and cancellations. They were fortunate to catch the first flight out for Bombay.

Everything had happened so fast that there was no time to even talk or think of what it really meant to lose Andrew's father!

Pamela's father met them in Bombay. Mr. Patel had been able to obtain a seat for him on the same flight to London.

The hours spent on the flight from Bombay to London seemed endless. Pamela sat next to Andrew, who leaned back in his seat with his eyes closed. He had been almost completely silent since the telephone call. He barely acknowledged Pamela's father joining them in Bombay. She held his hand in both of hers in a protective and silent communication of being there for him. Her father sat across the aisle. He sensed Andrew's need to first absorb the shock of this unexpected tragedy and what it meant!

CHAPTER 37

A Painful Goodbye

It was a dreadfully sad homecoming! The whole family and several friends had gathered, but the house was almost silent.

Andrew went straight up to his mother's room and embraced her. "I am here now, Mama. There is no need for you to entertain or meet anyone if you prefer to stay in your rooms."

"Andrew." His mother burst into tears. "It was not meant to be like this, not so soon!"

"I know, Mama, I know. I want you to rest. I am going to take care of what needs to be done. Tony and Scotty will help me. Would you like to have a tray sent up to you? Pamela is also here with her father. Would you like her to be with you?"

"I am so very glad that you are home, my son! No, Andrew, I must be with my family and the friends who have come to pay respect. Lilly, little Lilly, has been absolutely splendid! But she needs to rest now. Did you say Anthony Wood came also?"

"Yes. Did you know that he is Pamela's father?" Andrew asked.

She smiled. "Michael had suspected it! That's why he wanted you all to meet. Isn't it astonishing? I am so glad for both of them!" Then she turned somber. "We have other matters to do."

"Where is Father?"

"On his bed. He looks peaceful."

On the way to his father's bedroom Andrew met Pamela in the hall. She waited for him to say something. He just took her by the hand and led her to his father's bedroom. He never let go of her hand as he approached the bed. It had been made up, and his father lay in a black suit on top of the brocade covers. It appeared as if he were sleeping very peaceful.

Two tall candles were burning at each side of the head end of the bed.

They both stood in silent prayer for a long while. Finally, Andrew led Pamela out of the room, saying, "He didn't suffer. He is at peace."

"Yes."

Lilly told them later that when their mother had found her husband slumped over his desk, she had not spoken to anyone for one hour until she was able to talk with Andrew. She also said afterward that their mother was remarkably strong.

Even though both Pamela and Andrew were exhausted, there was so much that had to be done immediately. Luckily, Andrew's brothers, Tony and Scotty, and Pamela's father were very helpful in making telephone calls informing people who needed to know. Andrew drafted announcements for newspapers. Details for the funeral decisions had to be made before they could even think of retiring to catch a few hours of sleep.

Esquire Abbott, the family solicitor, arrived in the late afternoon. He had prepared all necessary documents. They decided that the reading of the testament would take place the following week.

It was extremely painful when a beautiful mahogany coffin was delivered and Andrew's mother insisted in helping to lay out her husband. She wanted him in his dress uniform of his naval rank with all the medals attached to it. When this was done, the coffin was transferred to a bier, which was draped with black velvet cloth. It was set up in the large entry hall to remain there so that all the servants and friends could pay their last respect. Four tall candles were set at each corner of the coffin. A large vase with white carnation and holly was put on a small table at the foot end of the coffin.

The late Michael Anthony Donald Prescott, the fifth Earl of Tarrington, appeared to be at peace!

During the afternoon, the new dowager countess was sitting silently near the window in her bedroom when Pamela was invited to see her. At first they embraced without speaking, then her mother-in-law said, "Pamela, my dear, Michael liked you very much." She paused and reached for Pamela's hand before continuing, "He was so very pleased that you found your father. You see, Michael always had suspected a closer connection between Elizabeth, your mother, and Anthony, your father! Did you know that our son, Tony, was named after Anthony, who is his godfather?"

"Yes, my father told us." After a pause, Pamela continued, "I will always be most grateful to your husband, my Prescott father, for having taken the initiative and arranging for my father and me to meet! I only wish I had known your husband, my Prescott father, better! There was so little time."

"We all would have wished him to be with us for so much longer!"

There was a knock on the door. "May I come in, Priscilla?"

It was Pamela's father.

"Anthony, my dear, it is so good to see you! Thank you for coming! I only wish it was for a far more joyful occasion."

He enclosed her in a gentle embrace. "Dear Priscilla, my heart goes out to you and all your loved ones."

"Thank you, dear Anthony." A tear escaped her eye, which she wiped away quickly. "You should have seen Michael when you told him that Pamela was indeed your daughter. He made us all sit down in the library and sip champagne to celebrate your revelation!"

"You know, Priscilla," Anthony explained, "it was only after Michael's telephone call—when he told me that Andrew and his bride, Elizabeth's daughter, were on their honeymoon in Udaipur—and when he mentioned Pamela's birth date that I realized the strong possibility of her being my daughter!"

"Yes, isn't it amazing?" Priscilla smiled, then remembered the present situation. "Where is Andrew?"

"He is with Esquire Abbott taking care of some formalities," Pamela said. "I promised him I would help in whatever way I can. Will you please excuse me?"

"Yes. I am so grateful that Andrew is back and is with Esquire Abbott taking care of what needs to be done."

"Perhaps I ought to leave you as well, Priscilla, to allow you to rest?" Anthony asked.

"No, Anthony, I would enjoy reminiscing with you about our happy times together with Michael and Elizabeth when we were so very young!"

Pamela found Andrew and Esquire Abbot in the library. The solicitor had brought with him all the required documents that needed to be signed and transferred to the name of the new earl.

It was only then, when Andrew was asked to sign on the line under which the title "The Sixth Earl of Tarrington" was typed that he realized in earnest his new position! He, Andrew Edward Michael Prescott, was now the new earl! He didn't sign immediately. He inhaled deeply and walked over to the window overlooking the wide lawn with the mature oak trees, the dormant flower beds, and the small path leading toward a gazebo across a man-made pond with the ever-weeping willows. He glanced up at the gray sky, which promised rain. His mind spoke to his father. *Father, I am not yet ready to accept this burden! There are so many people—employees, tenants and family members—who depended on you … and now must depend on me. I am so very scared that I may not do as good a job of protecting and caring for them like you did. Please guide me to do the right things. I have so much to learn and so very little time!* Andrew remained standing at the window for a while longer. Only then did he return to the desk to sign the documents. When he had finished, he discovered that Pamela had come to the library. He nodded while thinking, *I am not alone. I have Pamela to help me!*

She closed the door and waited for Andrew to say something.

"Darling, I want you to meet Esquire Abbott, our family barrister." He turned toward him. "Please meet my wife, Pamela."

Pamela went over to where the barrister stood near the desk and extended her hand. "I am pleased to meet you, Esquire Abbott. I only wish it were for a happier reason."

He inclined his head. "Countess," he said and noticed that she almost withdrew her hand in surprise. "I am pleased to meet you also. And I share your wish."

Andrew informed her, "I spoke with the vicar. We'll have a modest church ceremony tomorrow for just the family, our few friends, and those employees who wish to attend. My father will be laid to rest after the church service. We'll have a memorial service sometime later as well as the reading of my father's will. After the funeral, we'll offer a modest luncheon buffet."

It was a long sleepless night for both Andrew and Pamela. Finally, after two o'clock, they decided to get up and go down to the library. Andrew started to draft a short eulogy to be read during the luncheon after the church service. Pamela started a fire to warm the room, then sat down in one of the chairs next to the fireplace and kept silent company.

It was almost a relief when the sounds of family and servants were beginning their day. The breakfast in the family dining room was eaten quietly.

At ten o'clock the family, friends, and employees gathered while Andrew, with the help of his brothers, closed their father's coffin. As the new earl, Andrew draped the silk flag with the earls of Tarrington's coat of arms over it. The coffin was then carried to the hearse by the late earl's three sons, his valet, and two other employees who had volunteered for the honor. It was transferred and taken to the local church. While all men followed the hearse on foot, Priscilla Prescott—the new dowager countess, wearing a transparent black veil over her head—and Pamela and Lilly, both wearing black coats, shared one limousine. The other friends followed in additional cars. On the way, many tenants and residents from Tarrington lined the streets. Some threw flowers toward the black hearse.

At the church, the coffin was placed on a draped bier in front of the altar. There was only one bouquet of white roses and carnations placed on it. The service was short. The vicar remembered the kindness of the late earl. He especially mentioned how the late earl had provided the means to enforce the crumbling foundation of the church and provided funds to have the leaking roof replaced. In the short sermon, the vicar reminded the grieving family and friends of the consolation and hope for resurrection Christians embrace for a reunion with the departed loved one.

After the service, the same men transferred the coffin to the hearse and later carried the coffin back to Tarrington Abbey. It was laid down in the family crypt in a parklike setting on the estate. The small crypt was almost hidden by countless beautiful wreaths with banners.

During the following luncheon, Andrew addressed the gathering only briefly, "My late father, Lord Michael Anthony Donald Prescott, the fifth Earl of Tarrington, had thought of each and every member of the Prescott family, his dear friends, and his loyal employees in addition to a sum he has designated to be distributed among all his tenants' families." He paused a moment then continued with a choked voice, "With the help of God, I will continue in my father's footsteps and do my utmost to care for you all."

During the following week, the last will and testament of the late Earl of Tarrington was presented by Esquire Abbott. Andrew was amazed as to the extent his father had provided for each family member, his friends, his employees, and his tenants. Andrew's mother, the new dowager countess, Priscilla Mary Prescott received the dowager cottage on the estate with a handsome income. Then Lilly, Tony, and Scotty received each more-than-adequate sums for settling down anywhere they pleased. Some older employees received generous pensions and permission to remain in various cottages on the estate while others received good sums of monies. To the great surprise, Anthony Wood, Pamela's father, even received a sizable sum of money to enable him to visit his daughter often at Tarrington Abbey! Even Esquire Abbott received a sum of money for his loyal services over the years.

Before leaving, Esquire Abbott informed Andrew that in order to come up with the monies awarded to the individuals mentioned in his father's will, he had sold a sizable piece of land. Luckily, it was at the outer rims of the estate where developers were keen on building a large development. The income of the sale was sufficient to honor all the gifts.

It was very late when Andrew and Pamela said goodbye to the last family members and friends. Exhausted, they collapsed into the comfortable chairs close to the fireplace in the library.

Pamela's father intended also to withdraw so that Pamela and Andrew could be alone, but Andrew insisted that he join them. Lord Anthony began to explain, "As you know, I will have to make arrangements to return to India. I have an open ticket. I plan to go to Dhalarnabad first, to check on the progress of the school and the lawsuit. I'll keep you informed. Then I'll have to attend to my affairs in Jaipur. But I'll keep you posted with all developments. Pamela and Andrew, you both need not worry about the school or me. You have enough projects and challenges ahead in the next weeks or so."

"Oh, Father!" Pamela was near tears. "Do you have to leave already?"

"Yes, you know I have to. But remember, I'll return in five months!"

"Oh, Andrew," Pamela remembered suddenly, "this reminds me, I haven't even told Ms. Thrifoot that I won't be back teaching!"

"And I haven't informed Farmington Administration and Police that I won't be able to continue as mayor or barrister!" Andrew realized.

Pamela shook her head. "Everything changed so unexpectedly." she asked, "What about the cottage?"

After considering the question for a moment, Andrew replied, "For the moment, darling, I hope you won't mind if we cannot do anything about it."

"I will have to ask the town gardener to keep the lawn mowed and the flowers watered. Then I'll have the utilities cut off except the water. The post office and bank need to be informed of address change."

"Do you have any lawsuits pending, Andrew?" his father-in-law asked.

"No, luckily, all my cases were resolved in court before we left. So there is no problem. But I need to resign as mayor."

"Will they find out who you are?" Pamela's father asked.

"I imagine that after the newspapers published our wedding, most people know by now who we are. And especially now, with the announcements in the various newspapers of Father's passing."

In spite of Pamela and Andrew trying to convince his mother that there was no rush, Lady Priscilla was eager to move to the dowager cottage on the estate. Lilly and Pamela helped her decorate the rooms to her liking. While she was looking for a cook/housekeeper, she came for all the meals to the abbey or received them at the cottage.

CHAPTER 38

Anguishing Silence and Doubts

*W*eeks turned into months. While Andrew and Pamela attended diligently to their new duties during daytime, she observed that during the evenings, Andrew was withdrawing more and more into silence. It hurt her deeply to the extent that one day, during a telephone conversation with her father who had returned to India, Pamela asked him for advice.

"Each person has his or her own way of mourning the passing of a loved one. You have to be patient."

Each evening, after the day's work was done, Pamela joined Andrew in the library. They would sit for hours without talking. She remained by his side to let him know that she was there for him to help in whatever way possible. But she sensed that Andrew's problem was not the overwhelming work—it was the pain of the sudden loss of his father that haunted him. Evening after evening, after the staff was dismissed, Andrew sat silently next to Pamela. What amazed her the most was that during daytime, he was alert, in total control, and active while addressing and responding to all the duties expected of him relating to his family and estate matters. It was only when they were alone that he withdrew.

It had been almost three months since the sudden death of Andrew's father, and still, he kept his silent evening hours. Pamela began to wonder if he felt he had made a mistake in marrying her. It hurt her deeply! She wondered if she should leave for Farmington.

She stayed awake long hours during the nights, wondering what to do. During one of those sleepless nights, Pamela went downstairs to the library to read when the door opened and Andrew appeared. "What are you doing here, Pamela?"

"I couldn't sleep."

He sat down next to her but said nothing more. She reached for his hand and held it between her two hands. It was during this fragile moment of silent reassurance that Andrew leaned back on the sofa while, for the first time, tears began rolling down his cheeks. He turned toward her and collapsed in grief. Finally, the dam that had held back his grief burst. He wept bitterly and desperately for a very long time while being held in Pamela's arms. She understood that all the tormenting and unbearable grief was flowing out of him. When there were no more tears left, he fell into an exhausted sleep. She held him in this loving cocoon during the rest of the night.

He woke up at four o'clock and was surprised that he was in Pamela's arms and that they were in their nightclothes but sitting in the library. "Didn't we go to bed last night?"

Pamela felt incredible relief. "Well, we started out in bed, but then you followed me here. Why don't we go up and try to get a couple of hours sleep?"

Andrew smiled.

This smile went straight to Pamela's heart! It was the first since they had returned from India!

They slept for a couple of hours in each other's arms until Pamela felt sick and tried to get up carefully to go to the bathroom where she was really sick.

"What happened?" Andrew asked when she returned looking white and exhausted.

"I feel sick."

"Oh, you must have caught a cold during the night. It's my fault!" Andrew looked at his watch. "It's time for me to get up, but I want you to stay in bed."

Pamela tried to smile, explaining, "I am not really sick. It's definitely not a cold!"

"Still, you look far too pale. I want you to rest today."

"Thank you, darling. I'll be fine in a little while."

Just as Andrew was about to leave the bedroom, Pamela felt sick again and rushed to the bathroom.

"I am going to call our family doctor to check you," Andrew decided.

"Darling, please believe me, I'll be fine in a short while."

"I don't want you to do any work today, Pamela, promise?"

"I promise for this morning."

"You are a stubborn woman," Andrew grumbled while enfolding her in his arms.

"I will see you at lunch," she promised.

CHAPTER 39

A Silver Lining and Hope

*D*uring the same day, in the evening, after the staff had retired, Andrew drew Pamela next to him to nestle in his arms. "You seem completely recovered from your cold of this morning."

She smiled. "Andrew, my darling, you'll have to expect me to be a bit sick each morning for a while."

"No, that is not acceptable! I want you to see our family doctor. He is very sensitive, and my mother always liked him."

"My darling, how long have we been married?"

He reflected an instant. "More than four months. Why?"

She sat down on the bed and smiled at him. "We are going to have a baby." She watched him.

Andrew's face reflected first surprise, disbelief, doubt, then hope, and finally, joy. "You mean ... you really are going to have a baby? A son! The future heir to the earldom of Tarrington!"

Pamela laughed at his enthusiasm. "Yes, but I have to caution you that it could turn out to be a girl!"

"A baby girl! Yes, that, too, would be nice!" He was quiet for a moment then ordered, "Pamela, I want you to stay in bed!"

"Absolutely not!" she protested. "I am healthy!"

"Darling Pamela"—he knelt in front of her—"don't you understand you have to take care of my baby?"

Pamela laughed. "Our baby, darling!"

"Well, yes. But you ought to stay in bed! I'll send for Mother in the morning. She'll know what is best."

"Yes, you may call your mother tomorrow. Meanwhile, I can assure you that our baby is well cared for and safe with me. Ask your mother if she was sick at certain stages of her pregnancies."

Priscilla Prescott, the dowager countess, after receiving Andrew's telephone call on the following morning, came immediately to the abbey to see Pamela. "How are you feeling, my dear girl?" she asked.

"Thank you, Mother. I am fine now. It's just in the early mornings that I feel quite wretched for a while."

The future grandmother-to-be beamed. "Wonderful, darling Pamela! Andrew is right, you must see our doctor. He may be old, but he is very good. He delivered all my babies with gentle hands!"

Pamela promised to see him.

After the family doctor confirmed the pregnancy, Pamela witnessed an amazing change in Andrew. To her great relief and joy, he smiled again! He was like he had been before!

During that first evening when they were sitting alone on the sofa, Pamela told Andrew, "Do you know that in many countries pregnant women work up to the time of delivery, and in some places, they are expected to return to work a few hours after giving birth!"

"Thank God we are not in those countries!"

Later, when they were preparing to go to bed, Andrew asked, "Am I still allowed to touch you? I don't want to hurt you!"

Pamela smiled. "Of course! Being pregnant is not a disease. It is natural!" She was amused by his ignorance in this particular field. "Come, we'll tell him or her that the new father knows now."

"Father ..." Andrew covered his eyes for a moment. "Oh god, Pamela, I am not sure I am ready yet."

She smiled. "We have at least five to six more months to prepare for being parents!"

Andrew touched, very gently, Pamela's stomach. "Does it hurt when I touch you here?"

She giggled. "What on earth do they teach you at Cambridge or Oxford or other prestigious universities?"

"In my case, it was law, my lady."

"Well, yes, law can be helpful, but ..." she teased.

"What shall we name the baby if it's a boy?" Andrew asked.

Pamela thought for a moment. "It would be nice if we named him Michael Anthony!"

"Yes." Andrew smiled. "And if it is a girl?"

"I think your mother would be delighted if we named her Priscilla ... and perhaps, Elizabeth—Priscilla Elizabeth?"

Andrew kissed Pamela's stomach. "Welcome, Michael Anthony or Priscilla Elizabeth!"

With this joyful anticipation, not only the young parents but also the entire family embraced the future with hope!

Author Biography

Anita Sumariwalla was born in the French-speaking part of Switzerland. Later she studied in France, Italy, England and the USA. She met her future husband, Russy Sumariwalla, in 1959 fleetingly only, who was on his way to the United States to continue his studies. They corresponded until in 1961, Anita followed him to the USA. She soon received a job teaching French to Peace Corps volunteers. She continued teaching French and German in Massachusetts. Russy was transferred to Washington, D.C. area which provided Anita to study painting. Her favorite artists were Paul Gauguin and Pablo Picasso.

Anita published three additional books: 'Alexa-Alessandra - A Story of Love'; 'Memories and Impressions of Switzerland' and 'The Discovery of an Unknown Tomb of an EGYPTIAN PRINCESS'.

She lives now in Oregon with her husband.